D1291790

Things That Give Me The Redass

Bob Melka

Things That Give Me The Redass

Copyright © 2009 R. H. Melka Associates, Inc.

All rights reserved. No part of this book may be used or reproduced by any means, graphic, electronic, or mechanical, including photocopying, recording, taping, or by any information storage retrieval system without the written permission of the publisher except in the case of brief quotations embodied in critical articles and reviews.

ISBN: 1-4392-6239-X

Printed in the United States of America

Redass Press rev date: 11-30-09

To Barbara, Katie, and Chris
for putting up with me

ACKNOWLEDGMENTS

To Mel Schwartz for planting the seed. To Colleen Faris for getting me started. To Pete Brennan, Denny Waldron, and Mike Feagans, for contribution and encouragement. To Santo Laquatra, Jeff Kline, Scott Foernsler, and Susan Deeney for the road adventures. To Melina Burke for in-progress reviews. To Don Rigby for his advice and enthusiasm. To Chris Wilson for his talent. To Darl D. Dingman, John Eaton, Mike Gearheart, Jerry Wilson, and Tom Speed for the beers and the laughs, and to Father John Miday, S.J., for making writing fun.

Things That Give Me the Redass

CONTENTS

INTRODUCTION

the redass (*thə 're-das*) **n.** **1.** a metaphorical affliction one suffers when subjected to frustrating or annoying circumstances, conditions, or behavior for which there can be no legitimate or logical excuse **2.** one's state of mind resulting from any encounter considered to "fry my butt," "chap my buns," or "burn my arse"

Mel Schwartz, an architect buddy of mine and wise beyond his years, told me I needed to write this book. Each summer when our sons were in high school, we'd take them fishing in Canada. Mel and I shared a boat, as did the boys; and we'd head out in different directions after an early lumberjack breakfast, communicating via walkie-talkie to arrange a meeting spot for lunch and share advice on "where they were biting." Other than lunch and occasional radio contact with the boys, Mel and I were utterly alone all day in a fourteen-foot boat. Two guys, especially good friends, can be in the secluded company of one another for hours without a lot of conversation. But when one of them has something to say, it's usually worth listening. One day, between casts, Mel and I were swapping stories of the challenges each of us encountered in our professions. Most of mine centered on my personal Canterbury

1

Tales involving planes, trains, and automobiles, having long been in a profession that required forty weeks of travel each year. Mel recounted his experiences with silly government regulations, mandated minority participation in civil projects, and the experiences of blatant discrimination he has encountered as a white, male-owned business. I empathized in the most supportive way I knew, noting, "That really gives me the redass."

"Bob, you need to write a book about all the things that give you the redass, and you can put this in it," Mel suggested.

That discussion was the genesis of this book, which is probably going to offend some people. I could say that I don't care about offending people, but that is not the case. I care because I would hope that the logic and clarity of my premise would compel all readers to respond with nodding heads and pumping fists. Some who are offended might think I am a jerk, but acknowledge that I am right nonetheless. I'm OK with them. The rest who are offended will disagree because I oppose their agenda. I care about these the most, because I may, after all, be wrong. I am not infallible, and where I am wrong, I want to know about it. So to anyone of the latter persuasion: email me at bob@IGotTheRedass.com. I want to be shown the light. I only ask that you base your argument on facts, sound reasoning, and logic rather than emotion. Good luck.

If I were simply a malcontent, I wouldn't go to all the trouble of writing a book. It wouldn't sell, because most people don't care how whiners and crybabies feel about anything. But getting the redass is different. Everybody can relate to it, because, whether you know it or not, everybody gets the redass from time to time. I would imagine that even Mother Theresa, given the right conditions, got an occasional case of the redass in her day.

The purpose of this book isn't to whine about what's wrong. Rather, this book is intended to instill confidence and provide counsel to other rational people who are unwilling to tolerate shabby treatment but who might not know how to navigate the system and get results. This book is a kind of survival manual, acknowledging that you're not alone out there, and perhaps even sharing some tips in how to stand up for what's right rather than accepting what's obviously wrong.

Maybe I get the redass more frequently than most, and if I do, I may be driven to more extreme corrective measures than the average person. I'm hopeful that this might change, and that more of us will become willing to take on the errant establishment. All that's needed is recognition of the symptoms and a gut check to reconfirm the validity of your discontent. Whenever something gives you the redass, ask yourself, "Am I the only one this bothers? Am I nuts and the rest of the world sane, or is this really stupid and something that needs to be changed?"

For example, there is no reason all of us should be forced to wait in the ubiquitous line at Starbucks. Let's say all you want is black coffee. Wham, bam, thank you, ma'am. The six people ahead of you order things with enough complexity to require their unique formulas be hand-scribed on the cups, which are then passed over the wall to the chemistry major in the creation chamber. Their average transaction is longer than yours by a factor of fifteen. When you finally get to the head of the line, your order is brutally succinct. "Coffee. Big."

The guy fills a big cup, shoves it at you, swipes your card (no signature required), and you're gone. How do you feel? Victimized I hope, because if you're like me, you give a disproportionate share of your coffee money to a company that regularly and unapologetically wastes your time. If you're like me, you get the redass each time you're put through the encounter. But I can't let it be. I'm driven to convey my sentiments to the counter clerk. "Tell your boss that you guys need an express lane for black coffee." I've also let Starbucks' COO Martin Coles know how I feel--not that anything will ever get done about it. But at least I let it out rather than develop some stress-related condition like shingles or irritable bowel syndrome.

Express lanes have been rationally applied and have proven their value in supermarkets, toll plazas, airports, and freeways. How difficult would it be for Starbucks to equip a small station with cups, a self-dispensing urn, and a credit card swipe with three buttons: tall, grande, venti? Any retailer with the brains to pour pee out of a boot knows that the faster and more easily you satisfy the greatest number of customers, the higher the likelihood of repeat business, the lower the operating costs, and the higher the margins. Why hasn't Starbucks, a pretty smart company, figured this out?

Same with the bagel shop. The finicky people ahead of me want their bagels sliced, toasted, spread with cream cheese or mango marmalade or macadamia butter or whatever. All I want is an onion bagel, straight from the bin: no slicing, no toasting, no spreading, no wrapping, and no bag. Just hand it over the counter, because I'm going to eat it on the hoof as I stomp out of Einstein Bros.'s inefficient, un-customer-focused store where I just spent eight minutes to conduct a twelve-second transaction. But before I stomp, I am again compelled to make a pitch in behalf of common sense, "Tell your boss you guys need an express lane for people who just want a bagel out of the bin." I think I'm entitled to have the redass.

Maybe I'm quicker to find fault than most, but I'm also abundantly tolerant of forgivable screw-ups. People who know me think I'm the easiest going guy in the world, largely because they aren't around when I get the redass. Fortunately, my family and friends know me well enough to understand and accept my idiosyncratic fixation with life's petty annoyances. They understand that it's not the annoyance *per se* that ignites my intolerance and drives me to action. It's the underlying cause, several layers beneath the annoyance, that I find intolerable. I can accept and live with stupid behavior. What I have difficulty tolerating is the irrationality of otherwise rational people that spawns, mandates, and perpetuates the stupid behavior. To me, designing and deploying a system that forces the express customer to endure the same, but wholly unnecessary, inconvenience that the custom-solution customer willingly chooses is stupid business. Am I wrong?

When I am the custom-solution customer, I expect to be moderately inconvenienced, and it would be reasonable, in some instances, to pay a bit more. But I would not expect the mass-market customer to suffer or pay along with me. There is an excellent burger chain with over 300 locations called Five Guys Burgers and Fries. Their growth has been phenomenal, undoubtedly due to the quality of their offering: burgers, hotdogs, and fries. Like In-N-Out Burger in the West, they keep it simple and do it right. Better than anybody else. When they open a location, most other burger establishments nearby give up and shutter the doors within a matter of months. I have a lot of respect for their management practices, their execution, and their approach to excellence—with one glaring exception.

I like my burger medium rare. Five Guys posts a conspicuous sign over their counter, announcing "We cook all our burgers well-done and juicy," an oxymoron if there ever was one. I requested of the order guy that they take mine off the grill a little earlier. This simple request was met with unwavering denial. I escalated my sentiments to the manager. No deal. He cited fear of disease, lawsuits, losing his job, and other untoward calamities.

As much as I like and respect Five Guys, the negative connotation in their message and total lack of customer-centricity in product restriction gives me such a case of the redass that I am compelled to deny them my business, about which they couldn't care less, I'm sure. But importantly, their lawyers, if not their customers, are happy.

With me, it's a matter of profound principle. I am the customer, and I prefer that they cook my burger the way I like it, not the way they like it. I believe this is eminently reasonable, insofar as I am the guy paying for it. If any of the other Five Guys want to buy it for me, I'll eat it however they want to cook it.

When I suffer one of these episodes, the transformation can be best likened to a comic book superhero. I become a caped crusader on the single, focused mission of shredding the complacency or indifference or whatever shrouds the problem and exposing the idiocy, hypocrisy, or blatant irrationality of what some individual or group has consciously created and nurtured. I am compelled to confront any source of irritation, some of which are insignificant enough to go unnoticed by many, for which there can be no legitimate excuse. I'm talking about things that any reasonable person would agree are just WRONG! Things like:

- A bar that doesn't know how to make beer cold
- A restaurant that insists on overcooking your swordfish
- A bank that charges you interest at 3500% APR to use three dollars of their money for a few days
- An airline that cancels your flight because they forgot you need pilots to fly the plane
- A hotel that sells the room you reserved and paid for in advance
- A medical school that denies your kid admission solely because of her ethnicity
- A cab driver who won't take you to the airport because of rush-hour traffic
- A state's Department of Revenue that extorts penalties and interest for a week's delay in payment but sits on your refund check for six months
- A retail chain that informs you of its "no refund" policy on your receipt, only after you've bought the item
- An IVR system that makes you press "0" forty-one times before acknowledging that you want to talk to a person rather than a machine

When I encounter situations as inexcusable as these, I'm not content with the simple, immediate remedy to my problem. Rather, I want to drill my way to the core of the screwed-up system and find the person who can fix what's broken, decisively and with finality.

I do not know why I have taken up this mantle. I do know, however, that I didn't choose to ride through life jousting at what some might see as cultural windmills. I was called to it. It is as though the windmills have found and chosen me.

Ω

Many of my skirmishes result from the degeneration of customer service. In most service based industries, the service component has surrendered its rightful supremacy to slick technology, financial pressure, process, systems, apathy, laziness, lawyers, political correctness, and an army of headsets in cubicles, or worse, a corps of well-intentioned third-world polyglots with scripted responses to every anticipated question or situation but yours. In fact, the meaning of service has been obfuscated, if not obliterated, by the need to organize, mobilize, systematize, and deploy considerable resources that, in the end, lack the authority to move off the script and solve the problem, or perhaps even grant a reasonable exception, for loyal customers who want nothing more than that for which they've paid.

In the case of most minor battles, I'll dig in and fight rather than submit, simply because I know I am right. The conflict becomes a matter of principle. I also know that involvement of executive authority will not only address my problem, but more importantly, by having the absurdity of the situation brought to their attention, perhaps set in motion an effort to go to the rudimentary cause and change the way things are done.

An example is the restaurant that overcooks your steak. A well run establishment will have a process defined whereby the manager delivers the second edition, carefully observing while the customer cuts into the center to ensure that it meets expectations. The benefit of this practice goes well beyond simply satisfying the customer or making him feel important and appreciated. The real benefit lies in the fact that, without the manager's firsthand involvement in the problem, action cannot be taken in areas of communication, common understanding, training, attention to detail, or whatever shortfall was the fundamental cause of the screw-up. The manager's involvement results in elimination of a vulnerability, improvement in quality, reduction of waste, heightened customer satisfaction, and importantly, higher revenues, tips, profits, job security, worker satisfaction—you name it. A lot of value accrues to all participants by effectively addressing one simple problem. At the end of the day, it's not hard to take a steak off the grill a few minutes earlier, and, for someone who wants his steak rare, underdone is better than overdone. They can always cook it more.

But higher authority's involvement doesn't always get the job done. Some organizations are so dysfunctional that an attack on multiple fronts is required. My gym is a perfect example. A large, national chain with a dozen locations in Atlanta, I have been on a rant for over five years to help them get the simple stuff right. The light bulb in the men's sauna occasionally burns out, as light bulbs are inclined to do. This is not an unpredictable condition. Each time, I report it to the reception desk on the way out. The programmed reply is "I know. We've called it in." This can, and usually does, go on for days. The first time, after several successive days of naked, sweaty men bumping into each other, I accosted the manager in his office. The content of my message was, in effect, "There's an Ace Hardware across the street, and they sell light bulbs. I can go get one and put it in. I know how they work."

9

He responded that it took a special bulb and that the service that maintains their saunas was responsible for its replacement. I've had saunas in my last two homes, and I have been using standard 60 watt bulbs for twenty-five years. The fact that it's in a sauna doesn't make it any hotter. Have you ever grabbed a burning 60 watt bulb? I don't care if it's on your front porch in January; it's going to be too hot to hold. It makes more heat on its own that it will ever absorb in a 185 degree sauna. In effect, it is constantly giving up heat to the air surrounding it, since heat flows from more hot to less hot, and the bulb is hotter than 185 degrees. This "special bulb" excuse was bogus and the whole situation was nuts. I had to call "tilt" and explain it to him.

The next day, the sauna had a sign on the door, "out of order." It was easier for the manager to tape it shut than take the initiative and fix the problem. Now, it may be that he is precluded by corporate policy from performing maintenance of any sort on any equipment whatsoever. This is probably a good rule when applied to treadmills and spa pump motors and the main circuit panel. It is a stupid rule when applied to replacing a light bulb. The facility manager should have started up his chain of command, if necessary, and gotten the rule changed. If he'd really been on top of his game, he would have done both: changed the bulb because it was the right thing to do, then get the policy modified.

The men's locker room has a rack, upon which there should be a roll of small plastic "wet bags" for swim trunks and sweaty workout gear. Routinely, the rack is empty. I'll stop by the front desk on the way to the machines to advise them of the situation and get, "I know. We've got them on order," as though that solves the problem for the hundreds of members who are now forced to mix wet suits, towels, and sweaty T-shirts and jocks with whatever else they maintain in their gym bags.

"Maybe you should up your order," I suggest.

"We order as much as we're allowed," is the response. So now, I'm forced to go to their storage and supply room when I find the rack empty, and either bring out a roll or, when there are none, bring a case of waste basket liners into the locker room and set it under the rack. I shouldn't have to do that.

When the satellite TV is knocked out in a storm, there have been occasions when the rows of screens in front of the treadmills and stair climbers have been black for a week or more. "We've called them," is the standard response, "them" being the repair service Direct TV has contracted for repair calls in the Atlanta area.

I like to watch CNN or Fox New on the cardio machines, so after a week of waiting, I had to get it fixed myself. I tracked down Direct TV's corporate switchboard number in El Segundo, called the CEO Chase Carey's office, worked my way down to the guy responsible for commercial sales. LA Fitness was a large, strategic customer. His office understood that hundreds of his customer's customers, the members at my location, were unhappy. This is not a good situation for a vendor, when you're pissing off your customer's customers. Direct TV exercised its customer prerogative and demanded immediate response from <u>their</u> vendor, the repair contractor, who was out there the next day. The facility manager could have done the same thing. It only took me fifteen minutes, but I shouldn't have had to do it. The facility manager should have trained his "customer gun" on whatever level in the value chain was necessary to get the job done. You can't simply accept a supplier's indifference when you're the customer and your request is reasonable.

The problem is not that LA Fitness is badly managed or has dull people working at their facilities. The problem rests with us. Quietly and largely unnoticed, a society that has advanced to profound levels of learning, technology, and human kindness - a society of surprisingly intelligent, well-meaning people of influence - is allowing a miniscule corps of managers and bureaucrats to make decisions and set direction that infuses American life with episodic stupidity. I'm not talking about an occasional blunder. I'm talking about a conscious effort to conceive, define, create, implement, and perpetuate organized idiocy. A classic example takes place hundreds of times each day in airports across America. We regularly board and ride the underground transportation between terminal buildings without incident. We grab a pole or strap, swaying and leaning contentedly, countering the forces of inertia as the car bumps along at 25 mph, accelerating and decelerating at each of the terminal stops. Minutes later, we must, by federal regulation, be strapped into our seats before the Captain can signal the tug to push us away from the gate at a speed that never exceeds a slow walk—maybe 2 mph. If a single person stands to retrieve a book from the overhead or, God forbid, walk to the biffy rather than pee in his tweeds, the offense is egregious enough to earn the Captain a stiff fine if he doesn't stop the plane, the tug, and the ground crew walking alongside the wingtips until the offender is belted into his seat.

It's not that I want to get up and wander around during push-back. I'd rather relax with a magazine and a pre-departure cocktail. What gives me the redass is that I am paying for the idiot bureaucrat in the FAA who came up with this dumb regulation, that he's going to get a government pension, and that he's not even subject to full FICA withholding. And it's undeniably a stupid regulation; otherwise surely subways and buses would all have restraint straps. I have concluded that all "zero tolerance" rules are conceived by illogical people with an inflated sense of self-importance who assume we are as stupid as they are. Rather than permitting judgment to prevail, we end up with fines for pilots and first graders being thrown out of school for bringing a one-inch, plastic G.I. Joe pistol onto the school bus.

What ever happened to the concept of putting competent people in positions of responsibility and letting them apply intelligence and reasoning to make smart decisions? "Empowerment," was once the outcome of progressive decentralization of authority. We saw effective application of this notion by smart operators such as SAS Scandinavian Airlines and the Marriott Corporation. It is effectively woven into the culture of FedEx through their "Purple Promise," which is simply a commitment that every FedEx customer experience should be entirely positive. The mantra of these three companies is this: If you believe the customer's request is in any way reasonable or justified, do whatever it takes to satisfy him. An employee is never disciplined for erring on the side of customer satisfaction. At worst, the employee learns a valuable lesson and the customer benefits, even if the benefit may not have been entirely justified. But at the end of the day, the customer was satisfied, and he's probably coming back with more money.

With few exceptions, this culture has virtually ceased to exist. What passes for contemporary empowerment and all its resulting dysfunction is the unintended, if preordained, consequence of the flattening of the managerial pyramid we experienced through the nineties, coupled with the politically correct, if flawed, notion that positions of responsibility are not necessarily bestowed on the most qualified candidate. Unpopular as the reality may have become, when an organization allows ANY consideration other than demonstrated excellence into the resource selection process, something less than excellence is certain to result. It is tantamount to surrender prior to the battle. Probability of success is diminished and opportunity for failure increases proportionately. Do the math.

So we have arrived at a place and time where organizations implement lunacy by policy or by accident or by legislation. It doesn't matter which door you look behind; the prize is going to be the same: dysfunction and frustration. And the pity is, nobody is doing anything about it. There is no organized effort to rein in this mindset run amok and set society back on the rational footing that, for decades, was the foundation of our culture. We've become a herd of lemmings, following one another over the precipice of complacency, apparently distracted by the pursuit of greater needs—like male enhancement pills or a car that can parallel park itself.

Several years ago, I found myself increasingly less willing to participate in the culture of customer passivity. There was a defining moment in the Sheraton Tara in Braintree, Massachusetts, when, in a figurative sense, I threw open the window and announced to the world, like anchorman Howard Beale in Paddy Chayefsky's dark satire "Network," that I was mad as hell and not going to take it any more. I had just checked into a lovely room with an inoperative TV and two burned out light bulbs. Rather than call the front desk, I went off in search of a face-to-face confrontation with the Manager. I was polite, but clear and unrelenting in pursuit of an answer to a simple question: How and why does something like this happen?

The manager upgraded me to a suite, thanked me for bringing it to his attention, and committed to enforce a process whereby the housekeeping staff checked all lights, clock radio, and TV as a final step in the cleaning process. From that point forward, every time I was victimized by a blatant miscarriage of common sense, I strapped on my cape and went to war.

I've found, over the years of my crusade, that when you know you're right and they're wrong, somewhere there is a person with the intelligence, character, and clout to say, "You're right. We really screwed up. This is dumb. We've got to fix this." To say or do anything else would be an open, conscious admission to participating in the stupidity.

Sometimes it's simply a matter of, "Let me talk your boss." In rare cases, the idiocy is so deeply woven into the organization's fabric that you've got to bring out the nuclear weaponry to get the right person's attention. The key is being right, knowing that you're right, and then forcing the appropriate person to look at the situation in the clear, harsh light of reality.

In too many cases, the lunacy has achieved critical mass and is beyond my ability to effect change, examples being Starbucks and Einstein Bros. Nonetheless, I am compelled to let somebody know. Certain technology, particularly speech recognition and Interactive Voice Response (IVR) systems, has bested me, I must confess. I can't fix it. But I find relief in expressing my sentiments a couple steps up the food chain in the Quixotic belief that somebody might pass my observations along at the next meeting they attend. Ideally, others in the meeting will have heard the same reaction, adding their observations and maybe, just maybe, the groundswell of discontent will rise high enough to drive change.

The erosion of service and implementation of lunacy results from the perfect storm that has been quietly brewing under our social radar, seeded by the confluence of technology, Wall Street greed, globalization, political correctness, lawyers, government, and most importantly, our own apathy. We've all stood by and watched as these component influences coalesced into what has become a briar patch so tangled and insidious that it may have outgrown our ability to kill it or even trim it back.

Technology has supplied access to limitless information, instantaneous communication, and poorly designed, inflexible processes that, unless we use extreme measures and a flanking strategy, distance the customer from remedy by limiting or precluding participation in human dialogue and rational thought.

Wall Street, beyond its own unremitted greed and its well-intended but fickle demand for earnings, has forced companies to cut beyond the fat into the muscle of their ability to serve the customer. Through the nineties, we called it downsizing and reengineering, but it was effectively the elimination of middle management. The Army works because of sergeants. Imagine the chaos that would result if the Army eliminated sergeants. Business tried it, and we're stuck with the results.

Globalization has given us cheaper products, generally of acceptable or better quality, but along with them the occasional disaster, like dog food that kills dogs or toys with high concentrations of lead. It's also given us a corps of enthusiastic, eager, third world customer service workers, tasked with rendering service, but lacking authority or empowerment.

Political Correctness and the notion that everyone other than heterosexual, white, Christian males has a fundamental entitlement to not being offended has forced conformance to silly rules and allowed agenda to eclipse performance, excellence, and reason. Multiculturalism has created a world where the ACLU is actually suing companies that require employees who serve customers in America be able to speak English. (You can't make this stuff up)

Lawyers are growing in number faster than they are dying off or retiring. They all have to eat, which is why there is a warning label on your new screwdriver telling you not to stick it in your eye. Everybody lives in fear of being sued, so companies and industries that once provided useful products or services have adopted tortuous practices, raised prices, installed preemptive defenses, or even disappeared altogether. From the birth of aviation up to the early eighties, a middle class earner could buy and fly his own light airplane. That market disappeared in the wake of huge product liability awards, not because of faulty airplanes, but because careless pilots screwed up and flew perfectly good airplanes into the ground. A Georgetown University study found that 43% of medical tests are unnecessary, and as many as 20%-30% of these were found to read false-positive, leading to more unnecessary and costly tests. This CYA shield of "defensive medicine," intended to stave off the flock of hungry lawyers circling overhead, costs the American healthcare system between one-hundred fifty and two-hundred billion dollars annually, according to a 2006 Harvard study. In some markets, it's hard to find an obstetrician because malpractice insurance premiums, e.g. about $200,000 per OB/GYN in Florida, have destroyed the financial incentive of the practice.

Government at the federal level has lost its way. Until recently, Congress and the Senate was a relatively harmless cluster of egomaniacal gasbags who generally acted in their own self interest first, and then considered how to best serve that interest by considering their constituents. With the near-collapse of our economy, we're seeing the genuinely dark side of how damaging their power can be. Until we take back control by drafting Joe the barber and the lady down the street to go to Washington and fix it, the gasbags will continue to give away our money in ways Jefferson couldn't have imagined in his worse nightmares. They shower fifty-three million of our dollars on ACORN to bully and intimidate banks into granting mortgages to the unqualified. Then they force Fannie and Freddie to back all the worthless paper. Naturally, it all blows up, the banks are on the ropes, so they use more of our money to bail them out. They give BofA forty-five billion, who then goes shopping and buys the bankrupt Merrill Lynch, having suffered a fatal meltdown on all the bad loans. Merrill, now suddenly flush with our bail-out cash, doles out three billion of it in performance and retention bonuses to the crooks and morons who drove it off the cliff. The scenario reads like a Monty Python skit. Meanwhile, our honorable elected officials continue to spend money we haven't even earned yet, without conditions, strings, or oversight.

It gets worse. Now, they pass thousand-page, complex legislature costing trillions we don't have without reading the bills or understanding what they're voting on. Who in this absurd scenario is the stupid one? Fool me once, shame on you . . .

Reporting to the gasbags is an ever expanding legion of bureaucrats who, unfettered by intellect or market forces, add incomprehensible mazes of silly regulations simply for the purpose of perpetuating their own existence. At best, we're talking about foolishness. We're paying these people to come up with regulations like the one that requires dairies to label natural, unpasteurized, raw, whole milk—the kind that comes from Bessie's udder and goes straight into the jug--as "artificial milk" because it doesn't contain certain federally mandated chemical additives. At their worst, these legions of cost centers are writing policy that will bankrupt us as a nation. Government has become an endless bad dream.

<u>Our own apathy</u> is evident in our willingness to accept usurpation of our control because we've been desensitized incrementally. If someone were to awaken from a thirty-year-coma, they'd want to go back to sleep. But we don't have to put up with it. With apologies to Edmund Burke, all that is necessary for reason to triumph over stupidity is for rational people to get the redass and do something about it. We did it as recently as the seventies. Seatbelts had an interlock device that wouldn't allow you to start your car until the belt was fastened. American consumers refused to accept them. They simply reached under the seat and snipped the wires. The government, in a rare fit of pragmatic realism, capitulated and replaced the interlock with a buzzer or chime. We later rejected, as a culture, the idiotic government campaign to force the abandonment of our traditional measures and adopt the metric system. Canada, you will recall, succumbed. We rose up and flatly refused. Although spotty vestiges of the crusade are slow to die (Time Magazine, always politically correct, lists all measures in both standard and metric forms), we said Hell No and won. This may have been our last, shining hour, but it doesn't have to be.

I have undertaken this book in hopes that others might share my burden by recognizing that we don't have to endure the frustration and disappointment of simple things, or worse, gone wrong. When an airline or a bank or a restaurant or a retailer or a government agency screws up and you're on the receiving end, there is a proven formula for taking control and getting the situation resolved to your satisfaction. First, you need to get the redass. Next, you need to move up the food chain and gain agreement that somebody messed up. If a step or two up the ladder doesn't work, call in the heavy artillery. Go to the top with a succinctly crafted explanation of your plight and two simple questions:

1. "Am I right, or am I being unreasonable?--because if I am being unreasonable, I need you to explain it to me."
2. "How, as your customer, should I feel about this?"

Senior executives who understand the customer's role in the business model also understand that only one in ten unhappy customers complain, that a very small percentage of these complaining customers ever get brought to their attention, and that every customer who feels victimized by a service provider tells ten other potential customers. When you work out the math, your lonely, solitary voice in the darkness is only one of 250 who are out there telling 2,500 others about the experience. A fair percentage of senior executives will not only solve your problem, but more importantly, they will ensure that the cause of your problem is addressed at its roots. They are driven by the prospect of 2,500 lost sales if they don't find and fix the cause.

An aggressive response works equally well in the public sector, albeit with a different set of players, different motivation on the parts of your targets, and a slight modification in your tactics. When a school board does something stupid, like eliminating the tradition of valedictorian because recognizing and ranking achievement may cause lower achievers to suffer reduced self-esteem, one person can mobilize a small corps of equally incensed parents to have the lunacy exposed and force the delusional board back to reality. TV news directors and papers' city editors are always looking for "filler" to supplement slow news days, and public figures—especially in elected positions--hate to look foolish on television or in the press. Your Congressman or Senator is no different. I have their office numbers on my cell phone, along with the White House. And I'm not the least bit bashful about using them and telling their staffers what they're doing wrong.

Like Yossarian, Joseph Heller's protagonist in *Catch 22*, rational people must ask themselves "Am I nuts, or am I the only sane person around here?" Fortunately, if you make a little noise and have a strategy, you'll find that the majority probably share your perspective. Find the right person among that majority, and you'll be surprised at what you can accomplish with a good case of the redass.

CRAINING CHE DEPARCMENC OF MOCOR VEHICLES

If you are reading this you've undoubtedly had at least one less-than-satisfying experience with that paragon of bewilderment, the DMV. Admittedly, there needs to be an authority that can grant the right to drive to those who have proven worthy of the privilege, and some agency needs to be tasked with assessing that worthiness. Somebody needs to keep track of who owns what vehicle and provide law enforcement with a means of differentiating one beige Honda Odyssey from another. What somebody DOESN'T need to do is make the process as onerous as possible for their captive customer.

Perhaps it's just me, but most of my experiences with the DMV have left me shaking my head in disbelief. And, having suffered through seven corporate moves, I've been privileged to experience regional varieties of this dysfunction. Georgia, my home these past twenty years, is up there with the best of them.

Georgia's version of the DMV is two distinct bureaucracies. The Revenue Department's Motor Vehicle Division controls titles, registration, license plates, and polices the requirement to carry liability insurance. The Georgia Department of Driver Services issues licenses. Both functions, until recently, were under the authority of the Head of Georgia Highway Patrol. Since the split, one function, the DDS, has gotten better. As an example, a reminder of pending expiration is now received in the mail, and one can apply for a replacement license on-line, paying by credit card. Bang—the replacement shows up a couple days later. If a visit is required, say to replace a lost license, their customer service policies, as defined, approach those of an enterprise that actually has to compete. For example, if your wait exceeds 20 minutes, the $20 fee is waived. Pretty cool for a government agency, eh?

Problem is, most of both agencies' policies are often ill-conceived and not fully thought out. Those that are well-conceived and logical are poorly implemented, monitored, or enforced. Departmental leadership, while well intentioned, seems otherwise occupied. Their rank and file people are mostly typical government employees, some well intended, but many with bad attitudes, no clue regarding the meaning of customer service, and all with robotic adherence to regulatory minutia in the face of conflicting but overwhelming reason and logic. Virtually every personal encounter I've had with these people for the past twenty years has been fraught with challenges. Too often, I've had to enlist the input of senior department executives to get their people to perform. I've learned, over time, to expect that a visit to the DMV is preordained to give me the redass.

Before the days of online renewal, Georgia's driver's license department had satellite locations in several Atlanta area Kroger supermarkets. They were set up with a booth, the blue screen, the camera, the little line on the floor tiles to toe for the portrait---the whole megillah. These were solely for renewals or out-of-state transfers. No testing was offered, just license issuance. I went to the Kroger near my office one afternoon, arriving about 3:30 pm. There was a line of about fifteen customers. The line was moving much too slowly. At about 4:15, I asked the guy behind me to hold my place, and I approached the counter location where a uniformed clerk was peering into a monitor as she pecked away at her keyboard.

"Why isn't this line moving faster? What's the holdup?" I inquired.

"They're having computer problems downtown and the other person called in sick," she shot back as though I was partly to blame.

I returned to the line and relayed my findings to the other line victims, all of whom were beginning to form the kindred bond that provides the secondary plot for disaster movies.

"You know, they close down at five," a man behind me offered. "I was here yesterday and just missed it. Hope I don't have to come back again tomorrow."

Clearly, all of us were not going to get through the process by five pm. It was already 4:30, and there were at least a dozen or so in the queue. I asked the Second-Day Victim, "You mean they shut down with people already in line, or you were late getting here?"
"No," he said. "There were five or six of us who'd been waiting at least a half-hour. At five o'clock, she told us they were closed and

to come back tomorrow, but to get here earlier. That's why I came at three today."

No way anybody should be allowed to run a monopoly business like that. Closing off the line to new arrivals, yeah; that I can see. If the staff needs to go home at five, have a 4:30 line cutoff—or even 4:00; but to post hours of operation and not serve customers who show up for service within that timeframe? That's just wrong.

As all had feared, at five o'clock the clerk summarily announced that the office was closed and everyone would need to come back tomorrow. I got the clerk's name from her nametag and departed with a minor case of the redass. I figured I could get this situation fixed, but I shouldn't have to be the one to straighten out the DMV.

It doesn't take a civics scholar to conclude that a good place to start a discussion about dysfunction in state government is the Office of the Governor. The phone number is readily available, the office is adequately staffed with generally competent people, and they actually answer telephones when they ring--a rarity in the world of voicemail and IVR. It took a one-minute call to Governor Barnes's office to get the position, name, and number of "whoever is in charge of the whole driver's license issue and renewal process." A pleasant, articulate lady told me that would be Commissioner Hightower, who also happened to be the top dog at the Georgia State Patrol. I called the number she gave me and was connected with the Commissioner's assistant, who asked if she could tell him what the call was about. I asked her to just tell him that "I also manage a bunch of people, and if I had his job, I'd want to hear my story."

My approach would be this: if he knew and approved of the turnaway policy, I would simply advise The Commish that I would copy him on my strongly worded letter to Governor Barnes. If this was NOT the policy, I wanted to know what he was going to do to rein in his rogue field people, insofar as the lady at Kroger Northridge was obviously out of control.

To my pleasant surprise, he assured me that the clerk was out of order, concurring that anyone in line by five o'clock should be served. "That's why we pay overtime," he explained. He told me he appreciated my call, that he would send out a memorandum to all stations, and that it shouldn't happen again.

I returned to Kroger the following day, arriving at 4:45. I was served at 5:15. The clerk from the previous day was absent. I hoped it was her day off. I didn't want her to get fired, just trained in how to run a service business, monopoly or otherwise.

Ω

The situation may have improved, but not by much. Several years ago, I bought a Harley. To drive a motorcycle in Georgia, a licensed automobile driver applies for and receives, upon successful completion of a written exam, a "motorcycle permit," designated on the driver's license with the letters MP under the heading of classification, and an expiration date six months from the date of issuance. Ostensibly, the rider is judged capable of basic operation in daylight hours; and at some later date, the rider demonstrates two-wheeled competence to a testing officer in a parking lot full of traffic cones and interested bystanders. The rider is then issued the "MC" classification on a newly issued driver's license. I'd been driving motorcycles for thirty years, having owned several while in college and the Navy, but as a good citizen and to keep my insurance company honest, I dutifully presented myself at the DMV testing center one afternoon at about 4:00. I took my number, and when called, approached the window and requested to take the written exam. I was given a form to complete and instructed to have a seat.

I noticed a bank of thirty or forty testing stations with computer keyboards and monitors, occupied by only two or three users who, upon completion of the exam, cycled through a series of windows. I approached the window where the test candidates were dispatched and asked why more of the stations weren't being utilized. A surly woman with a mane of dark, bushy hair and a scowl to match answered, "We're short handed." I advised her that if she would assign me one of the empty stations, I would complete the test and save us all some time. She asked if I'd like to speak to the station manager. Naturally, I said yes.

I returned to my seat and completed the form, waiting until perhaps 4:25, when a morbidly obese black woman bursting from her Georgia State Patrol uniform led me to her office in the rear of the station and asked me what I wanted to see her about. Handing her my application form, I explained the apparent inefficiency of the testing process and suggested that they assign vacant testing stations to those of us waiting to be tested. That way, the clerk could get that requirement out of the way, thus saving all their customers some possibly valuable time. She looked at me like I had six heads and explained that they were short handed today and, as a result, everything took longer. It was clear that she couldn't comprehend the solution I was proposing. There was obviously no contingency plan in place to account for short handedness, insofar as there didn't need to be. The staff didn't get to go home earlier if they worked more efficiently, so what was the incentive? Certainly, it was not the customer's convenience. Concluding that the discussion was going nowhere and that I shouldn't have to help the DMV improve its efficiency in the first place, I chose retreat as the most practical strategy.

I suggested that they ought to review their processes and rose to leave her office and wait my turn. She interrupted my departure with a terse, "We quit testing at 4:30 anyway, so you'll need to come back tomorrow and maybe we'll have more staff." I looked at my watch. It was 4:32. Naturally, I protested. Naturally, I got nowhere. She handed me my form, grinning at me from behind her gray metal desk. I envisioned Jabba the Hutt with pudgy, folded hands.

Now I had the redass. I launched the same attack as the Kroger caper, the difference being that now I had a cell phone. I returned to my seat and called the Governor's office, which transferred me to the Commissioner, who was out in the field. His assistant said she'd call him on his mobile phone and ask him to call me, which he did several minutes later. I relayed my story, he thanked me, and in a few minutes the surly one summoned me to her window and assigned me a testing station.

The test was tougher than I had anticipated. There were several ambiguous questions. I should have read the study guide. A few minutes after I'd completed the test, Trooper Obeshia took obvious delight in waddling out of her office to tell me that I flunked the test and couldn't retake it for two weeks.

Ω

As a Navy veteran, I receive from the Georgia Department of Veteran Affairs several little perks. These are nice gestures that are intended to show appreciation for our service and save the veteran a couple bucks. Free driver's license renewal is one, a savings of $20 per occasion. The other is benefit is free license plates, the charge for which would otherwise be $10.

Upon honorable discharge from active military service, all uniformed personnel are given a government form, DD-214. This is a one-page history of one's entire military career. It is the magical key to any and all veteran's benefits, from education reimbursement through government insured home loans, VA system healthcare, and ultimately, even burial at Arlington National Cemetery. When checking out of your final command, the yeoman or clerk who gives you your DD-214—somebody like M.A.S.H.'s Radar O'Reilly-- cautions you to make a bunch of copies and put the original in a safe deposit box. The copies are all you ever need. The original stays in the box. Back in the seventies, records were created and maintained on paper. Technology has changed that, but the principle remains. Copies are all you ever need.

Qualification for Georgia's veteran DMV benefits requires a visit to the county seat and the presentation of one's veteran status to the designated bureaucrat. I took my DD-214 to Canton, Georgia, on a steamy hot August afternoon and waited for a slow-talking Bubba type to return from lunch. He reviewed my form and then he completed, signed, and dated a DPS-516, the Georgia DMV's Certificate of Eligibility.

Some months later, a bank teller advised me that my driver's license had expired, so I visited the DMV Website to check the procedure for getting my free renewal driver's license. It said to bring my DD-214 and DPS-516 forms to any license station, and present them with the expired license, following which you stand for the snapshot and walk out with a free renewal, compliments of the Governor.

29

Not wanting to misplace or surrender control of the original of my DPS-516, I made a color photocopy and took it, along with a DD 214 copy to the station. I took a number and, after a wait of no more than five minutes, was called to the window. I handed the clerk my expired license and the two forms. She summarily returned them, informing me that the DPS-516 was a photo copy, and they required the original. The Web site hadn't indicated this, so I protested, but she wasn't about to be moved. At that point, I told her we'd need to get the station manager to authorize use of the copy.

When the manager came out from the door behind the counter, I politely indicated that, if he could show me anything official that stated a requirement for the *original* DPS-516, I would apologize for troubling him and be happy to go home, get the original, and return with same; however if there were no such documented requirement, then I expected his clerk to honor my photocopies.

"After all," I added, "Your form is issued on the basis of a copy DD-214. Nobody carries the original of that around. So a copy of your form should be adequate for its purpose as well."

He went back through the door, and I stood at the window, drumming my fingers while the clerk paged nonchalantly through a People magazine.

Several minutes later, he emerged with a reprint of the Web page and an instruction manual for DDS clerks. He stood quietly while I reviewed them. Both referred to the "Form DPS-516" without the word "original" appearing anywhere. Additionally, there was no specific mention of photocopies as being invalid for this purpose. I pointed this out to him.

"Naturally, any reference to 'the form' implies the original," he proclaimed as though he were infallibly grounded in dogma.

"That's your interpretation." I countered. "Until the wording is changed to specify 'original,' you'll need to accept this copy."

He wasn't budging, and I refused to go home and return with the original. It had become a battle of wits, but I was in a stronger position. He just didn't know it. I acquiesced, acknowledging that, since I was already there and it wasn't worth twenty bucks to go home and return, I'd pay the twenty, adding that I'd get authorization for a refund from someone with the required authority and they could credit it back to my card.

"Once we swipe your card, there aren't any refunds here," he cautioned, confident in his perceived upper hand.

I handed him my credit card, and he processed my renewal, sending me down to the photo station for the snapshot. While I waited for my license to spit out of the press, I called 411 for the Governor's office, got referred to the top License Dog, and told his assistant the old familiar, "if I had his job, I want to hear my story etc…"

She wasn't buying it. This woman screened her boss's messages very carefully. She wanted to know all the details, so I regaled her with the whole incantation of the misleading instructions and the resultant confrontation with the station manager. As we talked, she pulled up the Web site and instruction manual, ultimately adding that she agreed with me, but that she would check with the boss, who was in a meeting. I returned to the seating gallery, and she called me back on my cell phone in a couple of minutes. She advised me that she'd spoken with him and that the station manager would very shortly accept my photocopy and process my refund.

In a few minutes, the manager reemerged, paging me to the window. He handed me a twenty dollar bill and asked for my license and the two forms. We re-commenced the process without a word of reflection on what had transpired earlier. When you have to steamroll somebody to help them do their job, smugness serves no purpose. Worse, it can rear up and bite you, evidence my motorcycle exam encounter with Trooper Obeshia. Nonetheless, I suppose some of my residual frustration was evident as I quietly reflected, once more, on the fact that I shouldn't have to call the Governor's office every time I need the DMV to do its job. Little did I know at the time that there lay ahead a DMV experience to eclipse all others in depth of lunacy and obfuscation.

Recently, I decided to sell a DeTomaso Pantera that I'd owned for a number of years, so I placed an offering on eBay. Early in the 10-day listing, I was contacted by a man in South Georgia—almost to the Florida line—with an offer to trade my Pantera dead-even for a nearly-new 2001 Qvale Mangusta.

The Mangusta is a limited production Italian car made from 1999 to 2001. Two-hundred and thirty-eight were produced, and about half ended up in the US. I jumped at the opportunity to own one. The seller still owed $40,000 on the car, so I dealt with his small-town banker who held the note. Once the banker had ascertained the value of the Pantera and decided that it was good banker business to simply convert the loan from his client's yellow Mangusta to my black Pantera, the banker had me sign away my title and FedEx it to him. He, in turn, released the lien on the Mangusta and FedExed its title along with a notarized Power of Attorney, signed by the seller and his wife, who were the Mangusta's registered owners.

Several days later, the seller set out after work, driving my new Mangusta from his little town in South Georgia, arriving at my home around 11:30 that evening. We shook hands, each admiring the other's offering and giving one another a quick check-out on controls, switches, or anything unique to our respective models. He jumped into my black Pantera and headed south on his five-hour trip back home.

The following day, I took the Mangusta title, proof of insurance, the Power of Attorney document, and my checkbook to the nearest Georgia DMV office, expecting a slam-dunk registration event. The clerk, a chubby, middle-aged woman with all the apparent symptoms of DMV attitude, curtly informed me that I would be unable to register the car, insofar as the "current registered owners" hadn't signed the title. I offered the notarized document, signed by both owners, giving me their Power of Attorney in all matters pertinent to the Mangusta.

This POA was "invalid," it seemed, because while they could have assigned valid power of attorney to any other living adult human on the planet, who then would have had the DMV's blessing to sign the sacred title as seller, I was excluded from this vast pool because I was the buyer.

"What does that have to do with it?" I queried.

"The same person cannot be both the buyer and seller. That would be a conflict of interest."

"Whose interest is conflicted?" I responded, with mounting confusion. It seemed to me that this would be the ideal situation, insofar as both parties, of one flesh, were visible and present for the Sacrament of Transfer.

The DMV lady stared blankly into my face and, with a tone implying that only an idiot would need such a simple matter explained, relayed, "This title is a legal document. The seller is testifying to the correctness of the stated odometer reading. The buyer is agreeing to this reading. This is to protect the buyer from fraudulently misstated mileage. You know, sellers HAVE been known to lie about the mileage," she intoned with clear exasperation at having to explain the obvious.

"But I AM the buyer. I don't need to be protected from bamboozling myself. Anyway, the mileage was already written in. I don't see where the conflict of interest is," I pleaded incredulously.

Having concluded that my comprehensive abilities were hopelessly opaque, she gave up in her efforts to educate me, falling back on the ultimate explanation—a variant of the one we've all used with our children when their tenacity overcomes our patience: "Because I'm the dad and you're the kid," or in her case, "The same person cannot sign as the buyer and seller. It's the law."

"OK," I acquiesced in a tone of hopeless victimization. "So I've got to send this back to the sellers for their signatures?"

"Either that, or have them give Power of Attorney to your wife or somebody else to sign for them—as long as your wife's name isn't going to appear as a new owner," she offered, handing me my documents.

The epiphany struck as I crossed the Government Center parking lot. I had both parties' signatures on the Power of Attorney document. I was legally authorized to sign for them. I could render a reasonable likeness of each. There was a satellite DMV office not far from my home in the other direction. I'd go home, practice my best hand at forgery, sign their names on the title, scoot over to the other DMV location, and be done with it.

I arrived at the satellite location later that afternoon and took a number. After a relatively brief wait, I reached the head of the line. I eagerly watched the red LED sign announce my number, directing me to Window #5. Approaching the window, I was pleased to note that the clerk was a sweet little muffin not a day over twenty. This would be a piece of cake. Nonchalantly, I tossed the title, insurance card, and my driver's license onto the counter and withdrew checkbook and pen from my pocket.

The muffin poked at her keyboard, earnestly noting whatever it was that appeared on the screen of her monitor.

"Just a minute," she smiled and rose from her stool, walking back past Windows #4, #3, #2, and #1 to the rear corner of the location, through a door into another area of the building. With mounting interest, I watched the door for her reemergence. In several minutes, the muffin led a small procession back to Window #5. I sensed the formation of a Court of DMV Inquiry. In her company was a stern looking woman and an armed Georgia State Trooper who looked to be about seven feet in height, Smokey hat and all.

"Were you at one of our other locations earlier today?" inquired the stern looking woman.

"Yes," I replied innocently. "Why do you ask?"

"Who signed this?" she probed, pointing to my well-rendered signatures of Jeffery and Lou Ellen Hutcheson.

I had learned as a very young boy that one lie inevitably leads to another, then another, and ultimately disgrace, embarrassment, and humiliation. It had long ago become a rule of practical necessity to simply tell the truth. "I did," I offered with the assuredness and self-satisfaction of a frat boy who'd just won the fart lighting contest.

The trooper seized the title from the stern lady and gestured to it with his huge trigger finger. "So you forged these two signatures on this document????" he asked menacingly, fully expecting that my answer would result in the first-ever felony collar in a DMV office.

"Sure," I answered in my best Beaver Cleaver innocence. "I have Power of Attorney to sign for them. Isn't that what Power of Attorney means—that I can sign their names?"

"Where is it?" he challenged.

"Out in my car," I Beavered demurely.

"Go get it," he demanded.

I returned with the POA document, watching him with the smugness of a fourth grader whose big brother happens on the scene just as the neighborhood bully is about to start pummeling. He scrutinized it, mumbled something to the stern looking woman, and peeled out of the formation, retreating to the room behind the corner door.

Returning both documents and my license to me, she admonished, "You'll need to get the sellers to sign the title before you can register as the buyer." She turned on her heel and also stomped back to the door in the corner.

Most of the time, you can outsmart stupid rules or irrational policies, but not when the force of law underlies the stupidity. I crumbled into compliance. I lined out my signatures and FedExed the title back to the Hutchesons for theirs. They signed it and FedExed it back to me a couple of days later.

Armed with the officially signed title, I returned to the satellite DMV office. By luck, I drew Window #5, but instead of the muffin, the window was staffed by a middle-aged woman with a pleasant smile. Reviewing the front, then the back of the title, her smile vanished, furrows appeared across her brow, and she apologetically advised, "This document has a correction. You're going to need their affidavit explaining this first set of crossed-out signatures. Either that or the sellers need to apply for a new title."

"I was in here last week and some woman from back there," as I pointed to the corner door, "told me to have the sellers sign this document. That's exactly what I did. She didn't say anything about an affidavit or applying for another title. Can you please go back there and bring out the lady I talked with last week?"

She excused herself, my title in hand, and headed for the corner door. I could feel my pulse quicken. I was beginning to sense the onset of a major case of the redass.

The stern looking woman from the previous week's episode came out of the corner door and walked briskly to Widow #5 with Pleasant Smile chugging along in her wake. Before I could recite my verbatim recount of last week's instructions, she assaulted me with her quintessential gotcha.

"You can't submit a motor vehicle title with names crossed out. Look. It says right here in large red letters: NOTICE: ANY ALTERATIONS VOID THIS TITLE. Just below that it says SUBMIT A SIGNED AND NOTARIZED AFFIDAVIT EXPLAINING ANY ERRORS. Can't you read???"

"Look," I countered meekly, figuring to throw my seemingly illiterate self at her mercy. "All I want to do is register this car I bought. The bank acknowledges I own it. The sellers acknowledge that I own it. Notaries have testified to the legitimacy of all these signatures. The car is out there in your lot. Go look at it. Take it for a ride. Here is the key. Here is my proof of insurance. What do I need to do?"

The DMV likes to see us grovel. It validates their self-appointed superiority and reinforces their mastery over us. They alone have the power to elevate one's status from pedestrian to motorist, and they know it.

The stern looking woman, acknowledging her victory, adopted a demeanor of enhanced condescension, advising me that the Hutchesons needed to apply for a replacement title, or alternatively, submit a notarized Affidavit of Correction since, as far as the DMV was concerned, they still owned the car---signatures, paper, and possession not withstanding.

The thought of going back to the Hutchesons and asking them to apply for a replacement title, then getting it to the banker, then back to me seemed Herculean in scope. Suddenly, a flash of inspiration overcame me.

"Yes," I countered, but since I was their *"duly appointed attorney-in-fact to represent (me/us) before the Department of Motor Vehicle Safety"* I quoted, reading verbatim from Form T-8, *"and was,"* I continued reading, *"authorized to apply for original or replacement certificates of title,"* I declared my intent to apply for said certificate here and now and requested that the stern looking woman commence execution of the process. "How much will that be?" I enquired commandingly, reaching for my wallet.

She begrudgingly nodded to Pleasant Smile, and we consummated our title replacement transaction. I learned that the new title would be mailed to the banker in Baxley, Georgia, as that was the address on the original. Banker W. Marshall Anderson would again be required to sign release of the lien and forward the title to me.

Having read all the small print on the title and on *"Form T-8 Limited Power of Attorney/Motor Vehicle Transactions,"* I concluded that I could bypass the Hutchesons entirely in this next go-round. I could sign for the Hutchesons as Seller, as long as I wasn't signing the title as Buyer. I could grant Power of Attorney to my wife, who then could sign as Buyer in my behalf.

I took delight in the fact that I'd probably found a way around this convoluted logic that even the DMV hadn't yet contemplated. On the drive home I called the banker in Baxley, Georgia, and gave him a heads-up regarding round two. He committed to signing release of the lien and forwarding the replacement title to me the same day he received it.

While I awaited the reissued title to arrive from the banker, I took a stack of "*Form T-8, Limited Power of Attorney/Motor Vehicle Transactions*," to the wife of a dear friend, a neighbor, who also happened to be a Notary Public. Two were signed by my wife, Barbara, one of which gave Power of Attorney to me, one of which we left blank. Two of the forms were signed by me, one of which gave Power of Attorney to Barbara. The second one, similarly, was left blank, in expectation of a possible player to be named later.

The new title arrived on a crisp autumn morning. I may be a fool, but I wasn't about to make Mark One on this document. I would take the title and all my notarized POA forms to the DMV and have the clerk instruct me precisely what to write, sign, and indicate where. I wasn't going to fall victim to ignorance or misplaced logic on this go-round. No siree.

I reached the head of the line, and Window # 1 clicked onto the LED "Now Serving" sign along with my number. Window #1? A good omen, perhaps, and this one was closest to the line.

Pleasant Smile, tended Window # 1 today, and she remembered me. I handed her the unmarked title, and told her I had all the paperwork I needed to cover any eventuality, and wanted to ensure the form was correctly completed. She instructed me what to write into the "Seller" block, and to sign and print my name, adding "POA." She had me write the odometer reading in the appropriate space. Then she got to the "Buyer" box.

"Who's the buyer?" she asked.

"Well, I really am, but we're going to use my wife," I explained, offering her the Form T-8 document granting Barbara my Power of Attorney.

"Where is your wife?" Pleasant Smile continued.

"She's at work, but that's OK, because," I countered, "I have her Power of Attorney to sign in her absence." I laid the second notarized document before her, as a supplicant might lay precious gifts at the foot of a deity.

"But you're already listed as the seller. You can't be listed as the buyer."

"No, you don't understand." I slowed my delivery as though I were talking to a toddler. "We are going to designate my wife as the buyer. But she can't be here because she's at work in Alpharetta. Because of this, she granted me POA to sign in her absence. I'm not the buyer. She is--Barbara. I'm just the owner. Now please tell me what to write where so I can pay you and we can move on."

Her smile having faded, her brow again furrowed as she stared into the back of the title with enough intensity to burn two small holes, then shot darting glances from one Form T-8 to the other then to me. "You need to come back with your wife. You can't sign this for ANYBODY as buyer, as you've already listed yourself as seller."

"She works. She can't come here during your hours. Who else can sign it?"

"Anybody, as long as it's not you," she sighed.

"How about if you sign it then?"

"I can't. I am the approving officer. That would be a conflict of interest," she wearily explained.

"Can one of them sign it?" I asked, gesturing to the line of waiting customers, number chits in hand like eager patrons at a bakery counter.

"I suppose so," she reasoned hesitantly.

She hadn't quite finished the answer when I was waving a twenty dollar bill in the air, projecting towards the nearby queue in a tone worthy of Carnegie Hall, "Any of you folks want to make twenty bucks in thirty seconds?"

Near the front of the line, a young guy in a Braves T-shirt and jeans broke ranks and ambled up, asking "Is this for real? What do I do?" "Whatever she tells you," I answered, handing him the twenty and the notarized POA Form T-8 that I had executed without assignment.

Pleasant Smile asked to see his driver's license, and instructed him to enter his name on the Form T-8, and to print and sign his name on the back of the reissued title.

"What am I signing?" he inquired.

"Don't even ask, I sighed. "It's too complicated and not important." I wasn't about to tell him he was signing a legal document as buyer of an exotic Italian sports car. My explanation seemed to satisfy him.

The T-shirt guy returned to the line amid the laughter and acknowledgement of his line-mates, each of whom was probably thinking "You snooze, you lose." I wrote Pleasant Smile a check, and she handed me a license plate, year sticker, registration papers, and the cursory notation that the title would arrive within 10 business days. As I gathered up my hard won spoils, I had to recount, one final time, for my own enjoyment, the absurdity of it all.

"Here's a thought," I said to Pleasant Smile. "You guys had a valid Georgia title and signed, notarized documents from the registered owners and the lien-holding banker. You had in your presence the legitimate, designated buyer with proof that the vehicle had been paid for. You had the car in your parking lot. You had current proof of insurance. But you couldn't recognize the change of ownership until some random stranger, who still doesn't know what he signed, testified to the legitimacy of it all, and validated the odometer reading of a car he's never even heard of much less seen. And his signature alone makes it all legal and official? How do you feel about that?"

"It's the law," she muttered, looking away. "Next," she barked, clicking her switch to advance the number on the *Now Serving* sign.

THE CABLE GUY

I started out really liking The Cable Company. Shortly after moving into our home in a new subdivision north of Atlanta, The Cable Company began installing their infrastructure throughout the neighborhood. Their digging crews were immensely helpful in my landscape and irrigation project. I had a load of topsoil dumped at the top of my front yard near the street. Their guy with the front-loader spread it around, and their grader leveled it out, all for a case of beer. It only took them five or ten minutes, but it would have taken my wheelbarrow and me all day. They drilled under my driveway and allowed me to pull a PVC pipe through the hole alongside their cable for my irrigation system. The guy with their Ditch Witch cut the channel for my irrigation feed, again, for a case of beer. (Beer, by the way, is accepted as coin of the realm by workmen not self employed. The garbage men will haul away your old tin shed if you leave a case of beer on the trash can.)

The first provider, Summit Cable, was OK. It was only after they sold out to Time Warner that our relationship started to sour. Time Warner removed Speed Channel and HBO from my lineup. When I called asking them why, they told me that they had both been moved into premium package bracket, and if I wanted to continue receiving their programming, I'd need to install a box and pay an additional rate. Now, the rate increase wasn't outrageous—maybe five bucks or so—but it was the principle that I objected to. I couldn't suddenly decide to pay them a few dollars less each month. Why should they arbitrarily decide to charge me a few dollars more without boosting the value of their offering? If they were taking away something, I expected a reflective reduction in monthly charge. You can imagine how far I got with this rationale, logical and reasonable though it may have been. It was simply that they were The Cable Company and I was just a number on a monitor to the headset in the cubicle. End of discussion.

Time Warner Cable sold out to Comcast, and things began to change. First off, all the channel numbers got scrambled. It had taken me years to know the numbers of all the channels. Now, I had make a card to stick on the back of each remote and refer to it to find anything. That gave me the redass. Then, they had several price increases with no commensurate increase in service or product quality. Victimized, I simply pulled my dress over my head, as it were, and bent over. Then, like a fool, I reluctantly gave them my high-speed Internet business when my kids' school research for papers overwhelmed my archaic dial-up. Now they had me.

As Comcast converted more of their programming to digital, I started to lose access to channels. I refused to accept their digital box as long as they intended to charge me extra for it. Adding insult to injury, the high-speed connection worked intermittently at best. Comcast grew accustomed to my regular calls to their technical support group for help with Web service outage. These episodes occurred with increasing frequency, and on every occasion, their telephone support person could somehow access and reset the modem under my desk, restoring service. To a person, they refused to accept my suspicion that the problem was due to a faulty modem, which I rented from them. They insisted that the cause was something in my network cable, the ports in my hardware, buggy network software on both of my computers, or errant electromagnetic interference from a UFO hovering near my house—anything but their equipment. My valve finally blew when service went out one Friday in March. The phone tech couldn't get me back up, and their field service guy claimed an inability to get a tech rep to my home for "48—72 hours." Something about it being almost five o'clock, the reduced resource availability on the weekend, and other weak excuses that I wasn't about to accept. I told him to put me on hold and go talk to whoever he needed to, but to get somebody here by noon the next day. He had my account record there in his system, detailing all the angst I'd suffered with their support people, and it was now time to solve my problem.

After a half hour of elevator music, he returned with a promise to have someone here the following morning. Their tech put the system through a rigorous series of tests resulting in disclosure that the problem was indeed their modem. He replaced it, and life was again good—until a Comcast rep called in follow-up to my service issue. She said she was checking to ensure that I was satisfied-- a gesture that I thought was pretty positive for The Cable Company. Then she made me an offer I couldn't refuse. If I would switch my local and long distance phone service to Comcast VOIP, my total Comcast monthly invoice would actually come down. Since I was paying BellSouth and some fly-by-night long distance company about $40 per month for phone alone, I took the bait. I could dump both phone companies, keep my number, and pay Comcast $99 per month for all three services rather than the current $104 for TV and Internet alone. Besides, I'd always wanted to be able to fire

The Phone Company. They scheduled The Cable Guy to come out and hook me up.

He showed up as planned and climbed around my attic and basement for about an hour, stringing, disconnecting, and reconnecting wires. When he finished, he brought me some paperwork to sign, along with the explanation that someone at Comcast had failed to notify BellSouth to release my phone number. I would need to have a "temporary number" until the number swap could be accomplished—a week to ten days—at which time I'd get my old number back.

This was clearly unacceptable. That wasn't what I had signed up for. Clients had my land-line number. My family used it to send and receive faxes. My kids used it to call me at work if my cell was busy or turned off. It was the number on my business cards and stationery. I'm supposed to call everybody I know and give them my new "temporary" number for ten days??? And I'm supposed to be OK with this????

I told The Cable Guy to call Comcast and get me my number back or he'd have to put everything back together as before. Although it wasn't his fault that Comcast had screwed up getting my number released, I enjoyed watching his growing impatience as he was subjected to the frustrating IVR system and interminable hold times and elevator music I'd become accustomed to. Paid by the job, he was watching the day, along with his income, evaporate before his eyes. Ultimately, he was able to convince somebody at his company that, by making me a reasonable offer for my inconvenience, I'd probably accept the temporary number, they'd have a relatively happy three-service customer, and he could move on to his next service call rather than climb around in my 120-degree attic. A Comcast woman got on the phone and offered me a free month of service, so I told her to leave the number in place. I would notify my clients of the new number and create new stationery and cards.

The new phone service worked fine, and I was into my fifth month when I returned from ten days overseas to find that my Comcast phone line was out. I punched the number into my cell phone, and it rang in the earpiece, but my line was deader than Kelsey's nuts. No ring, no dial tone, no nothing.

I called Comcast on my cell phone and, after going through their annoying IVR menu and ten minutes of elevator music, got some guy named Quannas. I told him my Comcast phone service was dead. Quannas asked me my number, which I gave him. The exchange went something like this:

"May I have the number you are calling about?"

"770-559-3800"

"Is this Mr. Cooper?"

"Huh? No, this is Mr. Melka. Who's Mr. Cooper?"

"I show that account as a listing for Mr. Michael Cooper."

"Impossible! It's been my number for five months! How could somebody else have the same number???"

Quannas put me on hold, returning a few minutes later with an explanation that clearly satisfied him but clearly gave me the redass. Somehow, either "the system" or some distracted employee had, quite simply, assigned my number to a new customer, which discontinued my service entirely. But Quannas, being an action oriented kind of guy, was intent on getting me up and running. He would get me a new number assigned and have my service turned back on within twenty-four to forty-eight hours. While this remedy was clearly acceptable, perhaps even favorable, to Quannas, I was incredulous that he would even suggest it. My mood hardened and the exchange notched up a couple degrees in intensity.

"No! That is unacceptable. I've already printed new business cards and stationery and notified everyone of my new number. It's been in use for five months, and that's the number you'll need to reassign to my phone. Now what exactly are you going to do to get my phone working with my number and when will it be fixed?"

Quannas, cool as ever, explained that another department was responsible for connecting service, and still another department would assign the number—whatever it might ultimately be. He would send emails to both departments and get the ball rolling.

As one might imagine, this didn't go over very well. I made Quannas keenly aware of my concerns with his solution.

"Let me see if I've got this straight. You'll send an email, not to a person, but to a department, and we assume someone will review this email and decide to take action. This might be today or tomorrow or the next day, since you have no control when or if it gets read. Meanwhile, hoping that someone will act, you will wait for them to contact you with an answer as to when my phone is being reconnected. And then, you will contact me with the information. And meanwhile, I am expected to sit idly by, phoneless, and let all this transpire on its own with no participation or involvement other than wishing and hoping and waiting? How comfortable should I be with all that, Quannas?"

The fog suddenly lifted, and Quannas saw the world from my perspective. He was stymied, however, because that was the only avenue open to him, according to their established processes. I, not similarly bound by Comcast rules or process, instructed Quannas in an alternative.

"Quannas, I'm not going to sit here and hope. I'm taking control of this situation, but I'll need your help. I'll need to talk to the person who runs your customer service center."

"Mr. Melka, give me your cell phone number and I'll have my supervisor call you back."

"No. Put your headset on your desk, stand up, walk around, and go get your supervisor. Don't put me on hold. I'll wait. Have you got a pen? Write down this number just in case we're disconnected. But until we get this thing fixed, I am not going to hang up."

The supervisor, an eminently reasonable guy named Bill, agreed that I had been egregiously wronged, but unfortunately, the only way I could get my number back was for Comcast to contact Mr. Cooper and get his permission to release it.

"Wait a minute," I bellowed. "Nobody got MY permission, I didn't release it, and I had it for five months! This Cooper guy had my number less than a week! And you're telling me that you need to play mother-may-I with him to get it back??? Jerk it from him the way you jerked it from me."

Bill explained that Comcast would need Mr. Cooper's agreement, because, unlike my situation which resulted from somebody's screw-up, jerking the number from Mr. Cooper would be a conscious, purposeful act. Essentially, incompetence at Comcast is tolerated and forgiven; correcting the incompetence is not. Fortunately for me, my situation was unique enough that Bill would need to escalate it to the top of the Customer Service food chain. He was not empowered to do anything but make phone calls and send emails. By "phone calls" Bill really meant leave voicemails, because we all know that nobody answers phones anymore. The effectiveness of emails was anybody's guess. During my conversation with Bill, I had to give him a short course on getting through voicemail.

"Keep punching zero or other extensions until you get a live person, then ask whoever answers if they know what the top guy looks like. If they do, tell them that a matter of strategic urgency requires that they go find him and bring him to the phone."

When he asked what the matter of strategic urgency was, I told him to take notes.

"Tell him that unless he wants camera crews crawling all over his lobby while he answers news reporters' questions, I need a dial tone and my number back. This would make a great piece for a slow news day."

> *"How is internet phone service working out? Hear what happened to one Atlanta area businessman. Details at eleven."*

Also, tell him about all those government reports he'll need to fill out after the Georgia Public Utilities Commission and the FCC come poking around for answers, since I'll probably file formal complaints with both agencies. Then his bosses and Comcast lawyers will need to get involved for authorizations and releases, not to mention the PR resources doing damage control. That should get his attention.

Bill got the message. I shouldn't have to train and educate Comcast's people on how to be action oriented and customer focused, but they, like so many of their oxymoronic Customer Service counterparts, have been conditioned to believe that their job is to follow defined procedures and processes. They don't see their job as satisfying the customer. Rather, their job is to be supportively apologetic and dispatch internal voicemails or emails. The customer's satisfaction is not something within their control, but making the phone call and leaving the voicemail is. Mission accomplished. Meanwhile, there's still no dial tone when I pick up my phone.

I inquired as to how he'd get my number back if Mr. Cooper wouldn't cooperate. He had no plan, other than explaining to Mr. Cooper how he'd been given the number in error and asking him nicely to release it and accept another number. I felt that by this time Michael Cooper probably had grown to like what he thought was his new number, since it was even hundreds: 559-3800.

I had to explain to Bill how money works, suggesting that he go get some and be ready to spend it if necessary. Everybody has their price. I assured Bill that Mr. Cooper would release the number if the price was right. This whole discussion was an epiphany for Bill.

While Bill went off in search of Atlanta's Grand Poobah, I went to the Web as a militia might muster at the armory. For weaponry, I got the name, email address, and phone number of the top dog at

Georgia Public Utilities Commission, the Commissioner of the FCC in Washington (I use my landline for interstate business calls, so I figured I'd try to rope them into the fray), and the names and phone numbers of the news directors at the four network TV stations in Atlanta. My plan was to mobilize at 4PM. If I wasn't satisfied with Comcast's progress by that time, I'd start making calls and lobbing mortars.

I got the number listed for Comcast's corporate headquarters in Philadelphia from Hoover's Web site and placed a call to the office of Brian Roberts, Comcast's CEO. Naturally, I had no expectations of getting Brian himself on the phone, but when you call a CEO's office, you will in all likelihood get to talk to an assistant or designee, which in either case can be a powerful ally. If you're courteous and have a compelling story to tell, these people can pick up the phone and make the earth move; and as the soiled diaper is passed from one executive level down to the next, it grows in malodorous content, mass, and intensity. By the time it reaches Atlanta's Grand Poobah, it becomes the most critical item on his to do list. His boss wants an answer because HIS boss wants an answer, and so on, and so on, and so on.

Comcast was a tough cookie. They must have gotten wise to disgruntled customers calling their corporate switchboard, because their Philadelphia number recognized the inbound call's area code and routed my the call to the executive offices in Atlanta. But at least I was into the executive suite. I got patched into Darinda with a hyphenated last name, a highly professional and articulate manager who, as had Bill, concurred that I'd been screwed and asked for an hour or so to work from her end to fix my problem.

Apparently, when she got into her exploration, Bill had already lit the fuse around the Southeast based on our earlier conversation, and Darinda simply added her weight to the scramble already underway   Shortly after Darinda had asked for time, I received calls from a guy named Johnson in Mississippi who owned the technical piece, and a guy named Gerald in Atlanta who claimed to be everybody's boss, even, one might assume, the Grand Poobah's and Darinda's. They both sought to assure me that my case had their complete attention and that there were lots of people working to get it fixed. I thanked Gerald for his help and explained the three conditions essential to re-gaining my satisfaction.

1. A dial tone.
2. My phone number.
3. Something to make me whole, because we're still not even.

A couple hours later, my dead phone sprang to life and rang. It was Comcast checking to ensure that service was restored and that the number was correct. Soon after, Gerald called and offered me two months' free service. I told him I figured that was fair, and we parted friends. I made a note of his direct number.   I expect to be a Comcast customer long term, and I also have good reason to expect I'll have another occasion put that number to good use some day.

COME FLY WITH ME--NOT

Airlines are easily, if sometimes wrongly, victimized. I try to cut airlines a lot of slack for several good reasons. The people we, as travelers, deal with are generally well-meaning, dedicated, hard-working sorts who want to do a good job and keep us happy. They're just stuck in a bad place.

Also, I have a cadre of very good friends who are, or were prior to retirement, Delta captains. These are smart, savvy guys who probably could have done a better job running the company than Ron Allen and Leo Mullin, both of whom were forced out as CEO but managed to escape with fat pensions and a half-million per year consulting contract for the next eight years. My Delta buddies got their pensions whacked by two-thirds.

Lastly, I myself am a pilot and understand the nature and nuances of aviation and the air traffic system, and how it doesn't always go your way. I have no problems with delays or cancellation. It happens. What gives me the redass is that small percentage of airline people who screw up at the customer's expense and get away with it because most of us don't know how to call "Foul."

I should acknowledge that I, being older than dirt, personally recall a time in air travel when everything about the airlines worked a lot better, except perhaps for the planes and pilots. Airliners used to fall out of the sky on a regular basis. Fortunately for the traveler, the FAA, NTSB, aircraft manufacturers, and airlines have done a great job improving the safety of air travel.

But back to the point. I started traveling by air in high school during the sixties. It was a whole different world.

- A male wouldn't even THINK of boarding an airplane without a coat and tie.

- It was OK to call a flight attendant a stewardess. That's what they called themselves, and they were proud of it. They were all young, attractive, single (by company mandate), and were subjected to monthly weigh-ins as a job requirement. My sister was an American Airlines stewardess, and she knew girls who were married on the sly. If the company found out or a colleague ratted on you, you were fired. The married ones didn't dare make enemies; they had to be nice to everybody—even people they didn't like—for fear of being outed and losing a great job.

- Baggage systems were manual and visual. Guys manhandled bags between carts, planes, chutes, racks and the occasional carousel, and bag tags were little cardboard tickets on strings, color coded and annotated with the three-letter airport code. The color blind need not apply.

- You selected and were assigned your seat from a sticker-chart of the flight's seating on the wall behind the gate counter. The agent pulled your chosen sticker off the chart and stuck it onto your boarding pass. If you wanted an exit row and the sticker was still there, you got it. The agent wasn't required by law to ask you if you could hear thunder, see lightning, and eat a banana. He could look at you and judge whether you had the sense and strength to open the door.

- All airline VIP lounges were by invitation. There were no fees or charges associated. By being a regular customer and writing a nice letter of request to the airline CEO, membership was generally granted. Delta had a program called Flying Colonels, which bestowed upgrades and automatic admission into Delta's Crown Room lounge. Otherwise, Crown Room admission required having one's secretary call in advance and arrange admission for that specific trip.

Almost a secret society, the Flying Colonels' very existence was rather low profile. Admission requirements were generally acknowledged to be an executive level position, somewhat regular travel on Delta, and an ability to bring value to the airline either by being in a position to influence the travel choices of others or simply on the basis of one's favorable, high-profile. A guy like Ted Turner was solicited and simply sent Flying Colonel credentials. I had to have my travel agent write Delta a letter.

Then sometime in the mid-to-late-seventies, airlines ran into the PC buzzsaw. Women and minority activists took issue with the race and gender profile of the anointed ones, which, not coincidently, mirrored the race and gender profile of the typical airplane full of people at the time. Logic notwithstanding, the crybabies whined and shrieked and threatened to make a scene, and Wham! The door slammed shut and you know the rest.

What has happened to the world of air travel has happened by degree, and the "ratchet effect" has gradually notched up our pain threshold and lowered our expectations to a point where, had the changes been imposed abruptly, we all would have rejected them summarily and gone back to taking the train.

I have spent over thirty years flying around internationally and domestically on business, often logging five legs per week. I fully understand the airlines' challenges and constraints, but too many of the painful experiences are well within the field people's ability to address or eliminate, if the company would simply remind them occasionally that good customers pay their salaries, give them the latitude to make rational business decisions, and encourage them to initiate action when warranted. Delta subscribed to this philosophy until the nineties, when restrictive, inflexible systems, cost cutting measures, and mind-numbing federal regulations usurped the autonomy of bright, energetic, customer-focused people. Delta, right along with the other major carriers, shot itself in the foot.

Here is what gives me the redass.

Reward Programs: Airline reward programs were fabulous when they were first introduced in 1981. My initial experience was with Eastern. I was living in New Jersey and flew Eastern out of Newark every week. These were the days of paper tickets, which my travel agent sent over every Friday for the following week's travel. One Friday, the ticket envelope arrived in a handsome brown, suede-like wallet, embossed with a gold Eastern Airlines logo. There was also a pad of chits, resembling a checkbook, each printed with a seven digit number and my name. Also inside was a plastic card, much like a credit card, with the number and my name in raised letters. The card proclaimed in bold, golden font, *EXECUTIVE TRAVELER.*

My secretary, which is what they were called then, told me that the chits were to be turned into the gate agent at check-in. Eastern kept track of the mileage, and as it accrued, it could be redeemed for free travel. What a fresh idea!

I dutifully turned in my tickets at each check-in and received a statement at the end of the month. I had already earned a free ticket. I had been turning these in on a regular basis when, one day, I approached the desk after checking in, just prior to boarding, and asked if there was possibly a seat with more legroom. I handed him the plastic Executive Traveler card in what I thought was a subtle effort to add some weight to my request.

"Certainly, Mr. Melka," he said, handing me a boarding pass for First Class. My eyes widened, and I thanked him graciously, not understanding until I recounted the story to Judy, the travel agent, that the Executive Traveler status was exactly for that purpose. If there was an unsold seat in First Class, the holder of an ET card was automatically upgraded.

This status was available only through travel agents, and credentials were rare as hen's teeth. Judy told me that her office had been granted an allocation of only ten, for six agents and hundreds of clients. The agent completed and submitted the application forms, and that was it. For the first year or so, general awareness of the program was minimal, somewhat like a secret society. As it became more widely known, everybody wanted to be an ET, but the numbers remained restricted enough that I was upgraded to First almost universally. Not only that, mileage point credit doubled for ETs, so until Eastern went under in 1991, I flew them almost exclusively, always in First Class on coach tickets. I earned enough mileage points to take the four Melkas to Boston for Christmas, Cape Cod for summer vacation, and San Diego for

Easter—that's twelve tickets per annum—every year until they parked the planes for good.

Shortly after Eastern announced its program, Delta jumped aboard the Frequent Flyer juggernaut. Their program initially required that the traveler maintain the passenger receipts, which were turned in for credit along with a paper form one completed to accompany the submission. In a matter of months, the system was automated with SkyMiles numbers. Credit accrued automatically, provided one's number was included in the flight record. Since I flew Delta infrequently, usually only when Eastern didn't serve a particular destination, my points didn't accrue in significant amounts until Eastern went away. Then they started piling up like trash at the church picnic. I continued using the freebies to fly my family around, because the miles were as good as dollars. You called Delta, booked the flight, and told them to take the miles from your account to pay for the tickets.

Delta enhanced the simple program with a status based system called Medallion, which featured varying levels of earnings and achievement. Silver, Gold, and Platinum Medallion status was awarded for twenty-five, fifty, and a hundred thousand base miles annually. The status resulted in earnings bonus of twice or three times the miles per trip. Early in the program, Platinum members got giddy with the points, not to mention the virtual assurance of a First Class upgrade. I was fortunate to be among the giddy.

Then things began to change, and I started to get the redass. Platinum members seemed to grow exponentially in numbers. Upgrades were becoming less routine, based on the numbers. Platinum status was granted on the basis of 100,000 miles, or 100 flight segments annually, insofar as the minimum miles awarded for a segment was 1000. I live in Atlanta, Delta's principal hub. I can get virtually anywhere in a single hop. A guy living in any other southeastern city, say Greenville or Birmingham or Macon, needs to go through Atlanta, requiring two hops to get anywhere. Because of this, he earned 4000 miles on a Chicago round-trip while I was restricted to only 2000. He needed only twenty-five trips per year, while all of us in Atlanta had to fly fifty to earn the same Platinum benefits. I had a lively discussion with the one of Delta's SkyMiles program executives one day, explaining how unfair this was to their Atlanta passengers. She said they were looking at it.

They looked, and what they found was something even more insidious. Now, mileage credit is based largely on what you pay for your ticket. This is positioned as "rewarding our best customers." I, along with my friends who travel, regard it as "screwing people who buy low fares to save their companies money." At first, upgrade selection was based on when you bought the ticket, which is fair. Now, ticket price is the determining factor in upgrade priority.

The real kick in the ribs comes when you want to use some of these miles. They are no longer good as cash. Generally speaking, cash will buy you any or all of the sixty-seven remaining empty seats on next week's 8:10 to San Diego. Try to get one for your miles. There are no seats "available" for the 25,000 SkyMiles required for a "free roundtrip ticket anywhere we fly." Instead, they'll make one "available" for 50,000 miles, or what Delta calls "SkyChoice," which is effectively twice the cost of the program we all signed up for. Easy come, easy go, I suppose.

Interestingly, Delta's SkyMiles program has mutated from handsomely rewarding loyal customers to handsomely enhancing profits. Now, carry the right credit card or "lock-in" with the right natural gas provider and you earn miles with every banana you buy at Kroger and every bratwurst you grill on your patio. The Delta partner pays a fixed cost per mile dispensed. Delta sold that mile to MasterCard or Scana Energy for a fraction of what it will cost them in redemption. Cha-ching! Delta is reported to generate roughly a billion dollars annually to businesses offering SkyMiles to their customers. There is a tenet in the loyalty marketing world called "slippage," which refers to the predictable percentage of chips that never get cashed. When you couple slippage along with the seat that would have gone to Cleveland empty, the redemption cost is ridiculously low: a bag of peanuts, a Coke, and about three cents per mile for the incremental fuel, or about thirty-five bucks for a roundtrip from Atlanta to Cleveland. This stacks up pretty well against the $500 to $1000 they collected selling the miles required for that free roundtrip seat. I applaud and admire Delta for figuring all this out, but it still gives me the redass. Miles were like green, folding money when I earned them; and now that I want to spend them, they're chump change. That's not what I signed up for.

<u>Legroom Seating</u>: I am 74" tall, with legs that already go all the way to my butt, so I can't screw them up a few inches when I fly. I have knees that suffer the effects of a bad skiing accident in my twenties and thirty years of jogging on hard surfaces. The last series of aircraft configured to accommodate my long, creaky legs were the DC-8 and the L-1011. These final vestiges of civility in air travel have given way to psychosis at the hands of airline financial executives, policy and system bureaucrats, and low-level government hacks who justify their existence by creating silly new regulations. A classic example: on a recent return from Boston, I booked the flight on-line but had to call Delta to get the exit row. Regulations now mandate that she read the qualification requirements and secure my verbal acknowledgement that I understand and meet them.

Soon after this requirement was implemented, probably my fourth or fifth encounter, I interrupted an interrogating agent, noting, "You don't have to read it all. I know the requirements and I meet them all. I've been requesting exit rows for thirty years." She admonished me soundly. "Oh no, I have to read the complete list. It's the law. If you were an FAA agent, we could be fined if I didn't go through it all."

The agent recited the entire verse as I listened dutifully and acknowledged that I understood and personified every attribute on her spec sheet. That done, she assigned me my exit row seat. Then when I checked our luggage at the counter in Boston several weeks later, the agent noticed my seat assignment and went through the very same litany. I knew better than to interrupt her. I listened politely and affirmed my compliance. Minutes later, I provided my boarding pass to the agent for admission to the Crown Room. She scanned the pass, validating me as a member, and noting my seat assignment, she sought confirmation that I was aware of my exit row seat. Withholding my true sentiments, I simply answered, "Yes."

Upon boarding, the scanner that validated my boarding pass triggered a signal, requiring that the boarding agent ask me if I knew that I was in an exit row. Numb by now, I stared at her blankly and nodded. Then just prior to departure, the flight attendant stood in the aisle, asking each of us in the exit rows whether we were aware that we were seated in an emergency exit, making eye contact with all twelve in succession, intent on gaining individual acknowledgement from each we were prepared to exercise our responsibilities accordingly. Alice had it easier in Wonderland.

Today, any aircraft in airline livery has configured its coach seating such that thousands of tall people suffer the torture of jammed knees, stiff backs, and deep vein thrombosis. Delta, my hometown airline, is the worst. Their 757 is renowned for its lack of legroom. The seat rows are jammed together such that my knees suffer interminable pain from the metal rod atop the seat pocket in front. I had a sadistic nun in grade school that punished classroom infractions by making us kneel on a mop handle. At least that torture lasted only a few minutes. Try kneeling on a mop handle from Atlanta to San Francisco. That's me on Delta's 757 in coach.

And their 737-800...now there's an airplane I won't even board unless I've gotten a legroom seat or first class. I recall my initial encounter with this variant when it was first added to the Delta fleet. As a Medallion customer, I early-boarded with several other men of similar proportion. We squeezed into our coach seats and cast incredulous glances at one another. The seating configuration was a joke. The back of the seat in front of me was, by reasonable estimate, fourteen inches from my nose. If the person in front reclined and I remained upright, I could perhaps slide a pizza box into the remaining space. Use of a laptop on this airplane was a physical impossibility. The geometry of the tray table and its seat back was such that the screen could not be opened sufficiently to be read, unless one's eyes were in one's nipples. I suspected for a moment that this was a Candid Camera sequence and Alan Funt was about to pop out of the biffy.

Boarding continued; the nightmare was real. I felt consigned to unremitting hell. Half way through the flight from Chicago, I fantasized about marching into Delta's Atlanta headquarters and confronting the single individual who had final sign-off on the coach seating configuration for this batch of newly delivered Boeings.

These airplanes have rows of holes on the floor, running fore and aft. Boeing will drill the holes, into which they bolt the seats, wherever Delta tells them to. Where the holes are drilled determines how many seats the plane can sell, and how much money a full airplane will generate. Some person in Delta's executive group actually approved the decision governing how they'd tell Boeing to place the seats on their 737-800.

I would grab this guy by the belt loops, jerk him into a full wedgie, and drag him back to the airport and down a jetway onto an empty 737-800. I would force him to sit in one of those seats for enough hours to satisfy my lust for revenge, finally demanding to know "What were you THINKING, you moron?" There is no rational justification for subjecting your customers to the agony of a two-hour ride in that airplane—unless the customer is a child, small woman or a midget. Any man of average or larger stature is condemned to unrelenting agony for the duration of the flight.

The typical jet airliner has perhaps 10—20 coach seats that can comfortably accommodate anyone over six feet in height. These are the emergency exit rows and some bulkhead seats. But, just try and get your butt assigned to one of them when you make your booking. The forward bulkhead seats are "held for airport assignment," in the event a wheelchair-bound passenger shows up for the flight.

I find this ironic, insofar as the entire coach section seems to have been configured for double amputees. The exit rows go in a hurry, so these are generally taken. And when I board the flight, prepared to shoehorn myself into a standard coach seat, I notice that, invariably, many of the "choice legroom seats" have been wasted on short people. This really gives me the redass.

Delta knows me. I've given them over two million miles of my travel. They have my cell-phone number in their system, and their digital lady even calls me to inform me of a delay in my departing flight. Why can't they add one more characteristic to each frequent flyer's profile: height? It should be a fairly simple coding job to divert seat selection of the "legroom" seats to persons over six feet—or whatever is determined to make sense. If there is a short-people's lobby, they'd probably whine that the policy was discriminatory, much as the fat people's lobby sat all over Southwest for their eminently reasonable efforts several years ago to charge the morbidly obese for two seats. While I guess fat people could argue, under the Americans with Disabilities Act, that they are entitled to special seating requirements, there is no constitutional protection I know of that affords short people access to bulkhead or exit row seats.

I am in Maui as I write this, having recently arrived from Los Angeles. I booked an exit-row in coach, but tried to get moved to the center section first row bulkhead at the gate. These are some of the choice seats "held for airport assignment." Aside from the center entrance row, there is more legroom in 10C and 10E than any other seat on the 767, including first class. They had already been assigned. After boarding, I observed with interest as three elderly Indian women, complete with flowing silk and red dot, settled into 10C, D, and E. None was over 4'8". That really gave me the redass.

Another legroom issue, particularly significant because an international flight in a typical coach seat is excruciatingly painful, is the matter of US regulation vs. European regulation. A couple years ago, a client sent me to Paris to work with their European practices. Their executives traveled coach or used their own points for upgrades, so, since they paid my expenses, I took my cue from this and attempted to book a coach ticket and upgrade to business class. There were no mileage upgrades "available," at that time. They had 38 business class seats they could sell me for money, but none that I could buy with the million-plus reward points I'd earned for being a good customer. OK; I'd stand by, hat in hand, hoping that at some future moment prior to departure, a business class seat became "available" for SkyMiles upgrade. But in the event the upgrade didn't go through, I would need to be assured that my fallback coach seat had legroom. Delta was unable to provide me this assurance. Although NONE of the exit or bulkhead seats had been assigned, all were held for "airport assignment." I tried the old, "I understand if you don't have the authority or ability to access one of these seats. Who does, and would you please transfer me?"

It seems that no one in Delta's chain of command could over-ride the system. I couldn't risk the possibility of not getting one of these legroom seats if my upgrade didn't clear, so I called Air France, Delta's codeshare partner on the Atlanta-Paris route. In a codeshare agreement, two airlines literally share a flight. The airplane and crew are provided by one, but both companies designate a flight number and can sell their own tickets and assign seats. The Air France reservation agent was happy to take my money and put me on hold while she talked to someone in Paris or Montreal or New York who knew the magic code to grab the seat I wanted: an aisle bulkhead, center section, in the first row of coach. On a Delta's Boeing 777, this seat is a virtual lounge chair, with four feet of forward space. It struck me as bizarre that an Air France agent was able to assign me this seat on a Delta airplane, something no one at Delta could do.

I called Delta back and asked to talk to a Customer Service Coordinator. These are special people in Salt Lake City whose job is to pull strings and find ways to correct customer grievances or find ways to solve problems for good customers, as long as the request is reasonable. I relayed my experience, asking "Why did I have to buy an Air France ticket on your airplane and give the revenue to them so they could get me the seat that nobody at Delta was able to do for a two-million mile customer?" Not coincidentally, this was at the time when Delta was in the heat of their financial struggles, flirting with bankruptcy, losing senior captains to early retirement, and suffering other assorted woes. It was also at a time when a groundswell campaign was underway to boycott all things French. I would have much preferred to give my money to Delta.

The Customer Service Coordinator was incredulous that an Air France agent could access a restricted seat on a Delta aircraft. She promised to investigate and call me back with some answers. As committed, she called back, but with all the wrong answers. The simple reason: federal regulations require that bulkhead seats are held for the possible arrival of persons with disabilities and emergency exit seats on international flights are assigned to specific persons observed on-site to be capable of performing certain functions in the event of necessity. Delta's system prevented any assignment counter to these rules, and no one could over-ride the system. Air France, unbound by these "Nanny Regs," was not subject to their adherence, and therefore was free to behave in a reasonable, logical, customer-centric fashion.

I made two more trips to Paris that year. In both cases, Delta's dysfunctional seating practices prevailed and, although I flew on a Delta aircraft with a Delta crew, Air France got my money.

Airline Beer: Running an airline is a complex matter. Equipment, fuel, logistics, baggage, passengers, regulations, safety, human resource issues. . .each is enough to challenge the most experienced team of consultants. Putting enough beer on an airplane, or keeping the beer on the airplane cold—that shouldn't be a struggle for English speaking adults, right? Wrong!!!

Delta's MD-80 series were the worst. Their stowage was apparently limited, and it was not uncommon, particularly on late summer afternoons, to experience a beer crises in coach. It got to a point in the summer of '94 that, upon boarding a MD-80, I would routinely ask the senior flight attendant if they had plenty of beer and whether they would start the beverage service from the rear or the front.

On the MD, the galley was in the rear, and it was the Lead Attendant's choice whether to push the cart to the front and work back or work from the rear forward. The more practical of the two was to start from the front, since the biffies were in the rear. Starting cart service in the rear blocked bathroom access to much of the coach section for a large portion of the flight. By starting in the front, passengers with a need could see the rolling blockade coming and handle matters accordingly.

The starting point of service was important because, if one's seat was back aft and they started forward, it was going to be a dry flight, and vice versa.

I recall on one occasion, I was traveling with Susan Deeney, a business associate, from Philadelphia to Atlanta on a warm summer evening. Our seats were in the very rear of the coach section. I asked the flight attendant upon boarding whether they had an adequate supply of brewskies and whether they would be starting service from the front or rear. Her answers were both wrong. She indicated that they'd all but sold out of beer in coach on the inbound and they'd be starting our service from the front. I asked if they would be getting any more beer aboard, since we would be at the gate for another thirty minutes. She indicated that this flight wasn't "catered" in Philadelphia—in a word, "no."

Taking action in exceptional circumstances was something that, apparently, they never thought to do. Perhaps making customers happy was beyond their perceived scope of responsibility. Or maybe they thought it was OK to run out of supplies. She dismissed the matter, explaining that "all that stuff is handled by in-flight-services and there isn't anything we can do."

I walked back up the jetway to the gate counter and asked the agent to page the Station Manager or, in his absence, whoever was senior Delta manager on duty. When he got to the phone, I explained that I was simply a good customer trying to help them do their job, noting the impending out-of-stock. I asked if having no beer on a two-hour flight was an acceptable situation, or if it was unreasonable for me to expect that he, as SkyChef's customer, ought to be able to direct his vendor to get a supply of frosty cold ones to gate E-7 in the next 20 minutes. Remember, all those little trucks with the scissors jacks have radios and they can zip around the ramp at will. It's not hard to get beer to an airplane when you've got a fleet of manned trucks within two-minute's access to a virtual liquor store. He thanked me for the call and said he'd see what he could do.

We hadn't quite leveled off when the chime sounded and the flight attendants rose from their jump seats, commencing their service preparation. The one with whom I'd spoken earlier came down the aisle, her hands cupping five cans to her abdomen.. Reaching our row, she extended her beer-laden arms, saying, "I don't know who you are or what you did, but this is all the beer on the airplane and I'm supposed to give it to you."

I'd failed to solve their problem, but at least Mrs. Deeney and I got ours, and the price was right.

Another problem, not unique to the MD-80 series, was beer that was not cold, but merely cool. It got to be so bad that I routinely asked the flight attendant to allow me to feel the can before she opened it. I learned that the standard beer chilling protocol on Delta was to put the cans in the drawer of the cart, then lay a bag of ice atop the drawer. Naturally, unless the ice is in actual contact with the can, you're going to get a warm beer. When asked about their beer chilling problem, you'd be amazed at the high percentage of Delta flight attendants who profess ignorance with "I'm not a beer drinker."

You don't have to be a beer drinker to remember high school physics. Amazingly, both of these situations have improved somewhat in recent years, but this may be my jaded perspective resulting from longer flights, hence more time on the 767 which has larger galleys. I'd like to think it's also due, in part, to my tenacious email campaign. Flights seem to have adequate supply, it is much colder now, and several years ago they added Heineken to their standard domestic offerings. Maybe my emails were getting read.

Baggage issues: I continue to marvel at the batting average of the airlines getting it right with my checked baggage. In my two million Delta miles and a million-or-so with Eastern before they augered in, I could count on one hand the times my bags didn't show. And whenever that happened, the bag or bags were delivered, either to my hotel or my home, in a timely manner at little or no inconvenience to me. Of course, I rarely check a bag, and when I do, it is with acknowledgement that I have no urgent need for anything contained therein. If I have need of it, no way I'm going to check it. That's what carry-on is for.

I carry (or roll, as has become the norm) my bag aboard most of the time-- all of the time if the trip is outbound international. There is a reason I have a bag that fits in the overhead, and that reason is because I need it to BE in the overhead when I land at my destination. If I arrive late at the gate and the overhead is full and I am traveling coach, I dutifully surrender my bag at the jetway door without a whimper. Those are the rules. Odds are, it will beat me to the carrousel anyway. After all, it's reasonable to conclude that they're not going to put it on the wrong airplane, since I have personally delivered it to the right airplane, ten feet from the cargo bay's hatch.

But if I'm flying first class, I unfailingly expect there to be overhead space to accommodate my bag. Do the math. There is sufficient bin space in the first class compartment for the number of seats, barring somebody traveling with a surf board. The problem, when it occurs, is that the cabin crew often put their roll-aboard bags in the first class overhead bins.

There have been occasions, when traveling in first class, that I have been advised that all overhead space is full and that I must surrender my bag on the jetway. Invariably, I explain that I will be able to find a spot because there is probably a crew bag occupying my space, and we'll simply need to find alternative arrangements for it. As you might imagine, this proclamation is as well received as a fart in church. The dialogue generally flows along the lines of: "No, I don't want to wait for my bag at the carrousel. That's the reason I don't check. I travel with a carry-on so I can carry it on. I understand the problems with overhead space in coach when the flight is full, but there's plenty of space in first."

"I'm sorry sir, the overheads in first are full."

"That can't be, unless some coach passengers stowed their bags in first, or there may be crew luggage up there. Let's check."

Reality suddenly strikes. I am actually suggesting that a flight attendant remove her bag and "ramp check" it rather than inconvenience a first class passenger with the whole carousel adventure. (A ramp check is what they do with child seats and strollers. They are stowed in the baggage compartment, last on, and returned to the jetway, first off, upon arrival.) In a service business, this makes eminent good sense.

We usually come to an impasse. Someone is going to be inconvenienced. Let's see. . .who should it be? Should we inconvenience the customer (the GOOD customer....the Two Million Mile customer) who pays everybody's salary, or should we inconvenience the hourly employee? Hmmmm. . .that's a tough one. . . .Let's think about this. . . .

Trying to get some prima donna flight attendant with thirty-year seniority to comprehend the rationality of my position is hopeless. If it comes down to a pissing contest, the prima donna usually wins, but I give it a good fight.

I had, on one memorable occasion, an encounter that one such prima donna won't soon forget. I boarded late in the process, and the attendant advised that I'd have to check my carry-on bag, as all the overhead space was full. I told her that I was in first class and that we'd be able to find space. She insisted that this would be impossible. I countered that there was probably a crew bag that we could check.

She stared at me incredulously as I explained that if someone must go wait at the carrousel, it made more sense that it be an employee rather than a customer. "Or does that sound unreasonable?" I added.

Rather than answer the question and either agree with me or appear unintelligent, she countered with "Would you like to speak to the Captain," glaring at me with eyebrows raised to her hairline.

"Sure," I responded.

She disappeared into the cockpit, reappearing shortly with a smug "He'll be out in a minute," as she turned and stomped back into the galley.

Within moments, the Captain emerged from the flight deck and stepped out onto the jetway. As luck would have it, my Captain that day was a good friend and neighbor, Pete Brennan.

"What seems to be the problem, sir?" he inquired, fully in Captain character and not acknowledging that he knew me.

"I was explaining to your diva here that I'd rather not check my bag, and insofar as I'm in first class, we could probably displace a crew bag to make room for mine since I am the customer."

"No problem, sir," Pete played it to the hilt. "Let me have your bag.

I'll personally give it back to you as soon as we land."

With that, in full view of my erstwhile adversary, he snatched the roll-aboard from my grip and scrambled out the jetway door and down the steps to the ramp. I smiled at the Gestapo and asked for a Heineken as I passed the galley. She was speechless.

As soon as the aircraft bobbed to a stop in Atlanta, Captain Pete was out of the cockpit and waiting for the gate attendant to position the jetway and open the door. Like a five-star bellman, he hustled down to the ramp and returned, bag in hand. By now, the flight attendant was clearly apoplectic. The fact that some jerk passenger had bested her in a pissing contest and had her Captain slinging bags like a skycap was more than she could countenance. Pete later told me that she slowly built pressure, not mentioning the incident for several more legs, then, unable to contain herself, she erupted. Something about undermining her authority, a delusional notion at best, insofar as Pete was the Captain and had absolute authority over everything and everyone on his aircraft. He explained his accommodation on the basis of our long standing friendship, but that didn't mitigate her volcanic fury. The woman clearly had some anger management issues, because he said she didn't get over it for the remainder of the trip. In retrospect, I'm just thankful that she didn't dump a hot cup of coffee in my lap.

$$\Omega$$

When checking a bag is necessary, the most frustrating problem I encounter is untimely retrieval. We've all experienced it. Bags appear through the hole in the center of the carrousel as they're ejected onto the gravity feed, and we eagerly scan each emerging piece in anticipation that the next one will be ours. And we wait, and we wait, and we wait, with a sense of utter helplessness.

I can excuse this delay if there is a breakdown or mechanical problem. Machinery fails and technology burps. I don't like it, but I can live with that. What I can't live with is indifference or apathy among the people tasked with providing service.

I met my sidekick Scotty at the Atlanta airport for a trip to Chicago one winter evening. We stayed a little too long in the Crown Room and consequently boarded after all the overhead space had been exhausted. We dutifully surrendered our roll-aboards at the aircraft door and settled into our seats for the uneventful ride to Chicago.

In Chicago, the walk to baggage from all Delta gates passes the Crown Room. Scotty and I, figuring it would take several minutes for the bags to arrive, dropped in for a quick snort to brace ourselves in anticipation of Chicago's mid-winter air. We got to baggage a few minutes later, and the carrousel posted for our flight was motionless and empty. Several dozen passengers stood around, waiting for something to happen. We joined them. Fully thirty minutes later, Scotty and I went to Delta's baggage service office to check on the situation. My first question of the guy in charge was whether they were encountering some kind of labor action—maybe a work stoppage or slow-down resulting from a union grievance. I'd had enough experience with unions in Chicago to know that things can go sideways in a hurry if a union gets its pants in a wad.

A response in the negative brought my next question of the guy in charge: Why has it taken forty minutes thus far to get the bags 200 yards from Gate L3 to here? He said he didn't know but would check.

He came back a few minutes later and announced to the waiting crowd that the bags would be up momentarily. He explained that they were short handed and some of his crew had been on break. You can imagine how well that went over.

Sure enough, bags began to trickle through the hole in the wall, parting the plastic flappers that keep Chicago's Arctic cold or tropical humidity out of the baggage area. Scotty and I watched eagerly as each emerged, chugging along the serpentine conveyor and ultimately back into the exit hole and out of sight for another cycle.

One by one, passengers grumbled about the delay as they retrieved their bags and shuffled out the door to the cab line. Shortly, the conveyor was empty and the crowd had dwindled to Scotty and me and maybe two or three others. At this point, we assumed that our bags were on their way to Dallas and broke for the baggage service office. Suddenly, both bags parted the flappers in rapid succession.

We grabbed our respective black roll-aboards off the belt, and Scotty headed in the direction of the door. I jerked him back by the coat sleeve.

"Wait a minute," I said. "We're not done yet."

Returning to the baggage office, we noted the supervisor and one counter attendant along with several parka-wrapped, ear-flapped bag slingers who'd come inside to get warm.

"Can anybody here tell me why it took fifty-three minutes to get this bag from L-3?" My question, thought perhaps to be rhetorical, got blank stares and silence. I wasn't giving up.

Delta Platinum Medallion holders receive, in their annual renewal reward kit, a new ID card, Crown Room membership, and several robust, high-gauge poly, virtually indestructible, baggage tags, approximately two inches wide and seven inches long, fluorescent green in color, with the word "PRIORITY" in bold black letters.

"Can anybody tell me what this tag means?" I asked, tugging at it for dramatic emphasis.

More silence.

I directed my next comments at the supervisor. "Your people need some training. Delta provides these tags to their very best customers—people who fly at least a hundred times a year. The idea is to make sure their bags come off the plane FIRST, not last. That's what 'PRIORITY' means."

By now, several other ramp rats had entered the office through the

back door. They were gathered in a crescent, listening intently to my explanation as the supervisor looked on.

"Tell that to your buddies out there," I said, now addressing the blue parka crowd directly. "People with these tags give your company a lot of money. You guys should treat them like it. There's a reason why these tags are acid green and so big. It's so they stand out and you'll notice them."

Scotty and I left the baggage office and walked the short distance through the terminal and out into the cold.

"Melka," Scotty said as we stood in the taxi line. "Those people in there think you're nuts."

Ω

Unnecessary delays: I have absolutely no problem with delays that are beyond people's ability to control. Weather presents safety issues, equipment fails, the Air Traffic Control system becomes clogged and needs a breather. This is all perfectly OK with me. I don't give it a second thought. I have learned to deal with it and plan accordingly. If I absolutely, positively, HAVE to be there, I'll fly in the day before, have a workout and a relaxing dinner, and remain in control of my own schedule. If I'm returning home, late arrival— even the next day-- isn't critical. Unpleasant and inconvenient, yes, but not a crisis.

What gives me the redass is when the delay is based on somebody's screw-up. Like when they forget that the flight needs a cabin crew, because the scheduled crew is stranded in Chicago or has gone over permissible time. Or when some bimbette decides to stay home with her boyfriend and calls in sick at the last minute.

Or when the flight crew is delayed to the point of going illegal, and the company hasn't planned for this eventuality and brought in a reserve crew until after learning, from the gate agent, that there's nobody there to fly the airplane. Or when the load is so light, they cancel your flight and double up on the next one because the equipment isn't needed at the destination and they can save some money. It's all happened on multiple occasions.

Bad Information: Wasting my time doesn't have to only apply to flight delays. I also get the redass when I drag my butt down from the Crown Room to the gate because the monitor shows departure in twenty minutes, and the equipment hasn't arrived yet. In some cases, it may not have even departed the previous airport. So I drag my butt back to the Crown Room, and go through the same drill based on an updated posting that is also wrong. So it's back to the Crown Room. Normally, these monitor postings are entered by company dispatchers in the tower. I'm told that some purposely avoid advancing the departure time as a psychological stimulus to the ground crew to hustle harder. Otherwise, they reason, the ground personnel figure, "Oh, cool. We just got an extra twenty minutes."

Regardless of who owns the keyboard or what their motivation is, somebody at Delta must know what the best estimate for the new departure time is, based on the airplane's location or ETA. Let's call her on the phone or give him Web-based access to the monitor system and have THEM note the revised departure. My wife and I were returning from Cape Cod a few weeks ago, and we made the trip from Crown Room to gate four times based on bad information. I've sat in a gate area in Newark, looking at a posted departure time twenty minutes prior for a plane that is still deplaning passengers from the arrival. I don't mind delays. I mind bad information.

Back in 1995, FedEx was a client and they hosted me on a tour of their hub in Memphis. In 1995, every FedEx package, even one addressed to the office across the street, went into and out of the Memphis hub. As millions of packages raced at breakneck speeds, flipped and shunted and sorted into hundreds of staging areas along miles of conveyer belts, there were huge TV monitors stationed throughout the acres of orchestrated chaos. These pink-screened monitors bore only four large, continually changing numbers. The numbers, for example 0247, changed constantly, jumping up and down every few seconds. They represented the exact minute the system calculated that the very last package would be loaded aboard the very last airplane of that night's global load. This information was used to make immediate decisions regarding maintenance, equipment, staffing, routing, and other critical operational requirements.

If FedEx could reliably estimate this departure time, influenced by millions of packages and hundreds of inbound and outbound aircraft and updating it on the fly every few seconds, an airline ought to be able to estimate the time my airplane is going to push back from the gate, right?

They have the technology and systems. It's a people problem. I learned from Denny Waldron, a retired Delta Captain buddy, that they have a data link which automatically records and communicates the "out time" when the cabin door is closed, the "off time" when the landing gear struts extend on liftoff, and the "on time" when the gear compresses on touchdown. The pilots also send an Estimated Ramp Time (ERT) report if there are delays enroute. On approach, the ERT is updated according to the queue for approach and taxi depending on the runway assignment. With all this information and years of experience learning how long it takes to empty, clean, stock, and board a B-767-300, you'd think they could get it right.

Don't blame the crew. They have their own cross to bear. Denny told me that despite all the above information and despite the pilot calling, upon landing, to confirm the gate assignment, nearly half the time there is no agent and/or parking crew to accept an early arrival. The crew, having all done their jobs professionally and competently, now have several hundred angry passengers, many of whom are watching their connection window shrink by the minute, fuming in their seats as the aircraft stops and waits, 50 feet from the gate.

Sometimes, delays are a matter of fate simply compounded by airline policy and employee adherence to standard operating procedures. But their SOP are not necessarily my SOP. When things go sideways, a passenger can sometimes step in and make a difference. Back in 1991, I was returning to Atlanta from Dallas with several business associates. There were thunderstorms raging across the Southeast, and Atlanta shut down operations while we, along with a slew of inbound flights, were airborne enroute. We, along with everybody else in the sky, ran racetrack patterns waiting for the weather to break. The only alternate not experiencing local thunderstorms, was Montgomery, Alabama. The captain announced that we would need to divert temporarily to Montgomery to take on fuel. We would remain there until the line of storms passed and Atlanta reopened.

This was fine with me. No sane pilot is ever going to knowingly fly a perfectly good airplane into a thunderstorm. A Southern Airways DC-9 stumbled into one in 1977 and had its windshield and both engines trashed by a virtual wall of water and hail. It glided powerless to what would have been a perfect landing on a straight, narrow country road in New Hope, Georgia, had it not been for telephone poles, a gas station, and general store. I'm always OK with weather delays, particularly due to thunderstorms.

We landed in Montgomery and taxied onto a crowded ramp not far from the comparatively small terminal building. Montgomery, being a small regional airport, had no jetways. Delta's gate space had already been taken by two or three parked airplanes, so we lined up, wingtip to wingtip, with other diverted planes on the ramp. The Captain set the brakes, powered down the engines, and lit the auxiliary power unit to maintain cabin lights and ventilation. He told everyone we were free to "move about the cabin." My friends and I were traveling in coach, so we headed for the rear galley, where both flight attendants were tending bar. Drinks were on the house, and business was brisk. A passenger or two helped with the bartending, and the plane took on a cocktail party atmosphere. Within minutes the Captain, seeing that several of the other planes had lowered their airstairs, dropped the 727's rear steps and announced that we were free to stretch our legs, make phone calls, and use the terminal's restrooms, cautioning us to remember which plane was ours and that it was up to each to get back on board prior to departure.

Mark, one of my travel mates, and I took our drinks and descended the stairs into the warm, muggy night air. Dozens of people wandered among the airplanes to and from the terminal. It was quite surreal, like a scene straight out of Fellini. It was also anybody's guess when we'd get out of Montgomery, so my colleague thought we might be wise to book a rental car, just in case. We beat the crowd to the Budget counter and reserved a Town Car for drop-off in Atlanta. Keys and contract in hand, we calculated the break-even time as our decision point. We were three hours driving time from the Atlanta airport. Allowing an hour for block-to-block airtime, we reasoned that unless could launch out of Montgomery within two hours, we'd be better off leaving now in the car. We needed a professional assessment to help us with the go/no-go decision.

We had passed a "ready room" off the corridor between the gate areas and the rental counters. The room had some desks, counters, teletype machines, and computer terminals; and it appeared as though a pilot's convention had gathered there to wait out the delay. I strode in, cocktail in one hand and rental car contract in the other, asking no one in particular which one of them was the skipper of Dallas-Atlanta 884.

"Anybody here got eight-eight-four," one of them boomed into the milling sea of uniforms.

"Right here," responded a four-striper several steps away. I told him that we needed his best estimate when we'd be airborne, explaining our rental car situation. He said that the line of storms had passed, Atlanta airport had re-opened, and that the determining factor now was fuel. He pointed out the window at what looked like fifteen-or-so planes, adding, "They all need gas, and it's anybody's guess when we'll get ours. Could be an hour, could be three."

I acknowledged with a nod, and we edged our way through the crowded terminal, past the lines at the restrooms and pay phones, and out onto the ramp. A fuel truck was parked at the wing of a DC-9 several planes up the line. By the time we reached it, the fuel guy had finished reeling up his hose and was flipping through pages on a clipboard.

"Is there any particular order you need to follow in gassing these things up," I inquired.

"Naw," he intoned with a slow Alabama drawl. "I'm just gonna take 'em one at a time until the truck's empty, go fill 'er up, come back and do some more."

I peeled a twenty off my money clip and extended it to him with one hand, pointing to our plane with the other. "How about doing that one next?"

"Sure," he smiled. "No problem."

Mark took the car keys and contract back to the Budget counter, and I returned to the pilot's lounge. Our Captain was standing in a small circle of associates, sipping from a Styrofoam cup. Conversation stopped as I approached the group and said, "Let's go, Skipper. The fuel guy is doing us next."

The Captain blinked with a start, then looked among the group, noting, "It's good to have friends in high places."

He had a brief conversation with a Delta ground agent while his First Officer retrieved their hats from a rack by the door. An announcement soon rang through the airport's PA, "Passengers on Delta Flight 884, Dallas to Atlanta, please board the aircraft for immediate departure."

A Delta ground crew was attaching a tug to the nosegear as we climbed single file up the rear stairway.

That was the way air travel was on the old Delta, before the TSA, the Nanny State, and a herd of radical Muslims who are intent on killing us all.

<u>Surly employees:</u> We didn't used to have these when they were called stewardess, but some time in the seventies, unions, radical feminism, government, and probably some senior citizens' lobby forced the airlines to retain anybody who wanted to stay. Many remained beyond the point where they now like everything about their jobs except passengers. Based on the numbers, encounters with this breed are relatively infrequent, but when you get one, it'll ruin your day. I was flying from Boston to St. Louis on a Sunday in July, connecting with a small commuter carrier's twin Beechcraft (seven passengers, with one sitting in what is traditionally the co-pilot's seat) for the short hop to Lake of the Ozarks' Four Seasons Resort. I was scheduled to attend a meeting that started Monday morning, and my attendance was required. We were late departing Boston, and it was evident that our new arrival time would miss my connection by a few minutes. About forty minutes out of St Louis, I rang my call button and gave the flight attendant a piece of paper with my commuter carrier's phone number in St. Louis, the flight number and departure time, my name, and requested that she ask the flight deck to radio TWA St. Louis on the company frequency and have someone notify the commuter that I was inbound and ask that they hold the flight. This was a reasonable request, given the timing of both flights and the excellent flying conditions. Cockpit workload is heavy if the flight is encountering bad weather, system delays, holding patterns, sequencing, traffic backups, etc.; but on a clear day with routine traffic, the crew pretty much sits there and monitors gauges. Additionally, the six other passengers on the commuter flight were all colleagues of mine who expected me, so holding the commuter hop was a certainty.

The Dominatrix refused to consider my request, dismissing me with a curt, "There will be uniformed gate agents to help with your connections."

"You don't understand," I implored. "Gate agents aren't going to be able to help. It'll be too late. This is a seven seat airplane and it's the last flight of the day. They'll wait for me if they know I'm coming. Ask the skipper to call. He'll do it, no problem."

She wouldn't budge, so I asked to speak with the lead.

"I am the lead," she hissed, "and I'm not going to do it. Talk to the gate agent. That's their job."

As predicted, the Beech had departed minutes prior to my arrival. I summoned a gate agent and asked her to page the Station Manager or whoever had the TWA watch at the moment. A portly gentleman soon appeared and extended his hand. I relayed the story of my Dominatrix encounter, handing him the note she had refused to accept. He concurred that my request was eminently reasonable and that she had screwed up. She should have presented my request to the Captain and let him make the decision. He apologized on behalf of the airline and said he'd get me straightened out. At that point, he had nowhere to hide when I told him I'd need his help finding and paying for a charter. There were no more flights and I wasn't about to launch on a three hour drive over dark mountain roads because his woman didn't do her job. I reminded him that the problem wasn't me, it was Ms. Menopause in the TWA suit.

He led me to the TWA operations office at Lambert Field and lined up a chartered Beechcraft Baron. The charter company called a pilot away from his Sunday dinner. He brought his ten-year-old son along for the ride. The short hop cost upwards of five-hundred dollars, and I'm not sure how TWA paid for it, but they did. Sadly, none of this would have been necessary if the flight attendant had simply noticed the "customer service" part of her job description.

In his nineteen-eighties international best seller *In Search of Excellence,* Tom Peters cited Delta as one of the best run companies in America. This was largely due to the friendly, customer-focused attitude and performance of its "family" of employees. In the "good ol' Delta," customer-facing employees were not only empowered, they understood the customer's role in the business model. Make the customer happy, and he gives the company money, which gets split up and passed along to all of us. Make the customer unhappy, and he will either stop giving the company money or give it begrudgingly. In the former case, there is no company and we all starve. In the latter case, we all grow to hate our jobs and our customers, and thus become miserable. It seemed simple, and they all got it. The new Delta had too many employees, and probably managers, who thought the money *originated* from the company. The customers were an unpleasant reality that came with the job, like having to park at the airport and use public restrooms.

Ω

As I said earlier, Delta has maintained and continues to hire scores of top quality people who are a credit to the airline and a delight to transact with, but on any given day, if your Delta dice come up snake-eyes, it can make for a stressful day.

I took a West Coast redeye a couple years ago, landing in Atlanta around 5:20 AM. I was meeting some colleagues in Providence later that morning and was booked on an outbound just after eight. In Atlanta, Concourse E hosts all international traffic, and so their Crown Room Club also serves as the Business Class lounge for any Delta international traveler, Crown Room member or otherwise. Adjunct to the Crown Room, Delta has a facility, as do many international Business Class lounges, that features showers with private dressing rooms in which arriving or departing passengers can freshen up prior to whatever comes next on their busy agendas.

I changed into jeans in San Francisco's Crown Room john, figuring that I would shower and suit up in Delta's Atlanta lounge for our meeting in Providence. I was a Crown Room member, Two Million Miler, plus I was a "Platinum Medallion," Delta's *ne plus ultra* of certifiably good customers. That particular morning, I strode into the Concourse E Crown Room, dragging my roll-aboard behind me, and presented my Platinum card at the desk. A slim, gracious, forty-something woman with Glenn Close *Fatal Attraction* hair glanced at my card and asked if I needed a boarding pass. I advised her that I'd just arrived on a redeye and was connecting to Providence in a couple hours, but would like to use the showers to freshen up and change.

"I'm sorry, Mr. Melka. Those are reserved for international business class travelers."

Acknowledging that I now understood the policy, I asked if she could grant, or could help me secure, an exception to policy this one time, insofar as I'd made the reservations with this layover/shower as part of my plan, I was obviously a very good customer, and I promised not to break or damage their facilities.

"I'm afraid I can't admit you to the business class showers. You must be traveling international on business class."

"Who has the authority to grant an exception," I queried.

"I am the senior manager in this lounge, and there is no one else to ask," she responded. Her gracious smile had evolved from natural to forced contrivance.

"Well, can you get your boss on the phone then?"

"His name is Mr. Brown, and he is due here at eight o'clock," she said, neatly penning his name and number on one of her cards. "You may call him then."

"OK," I said, spinning a one-eighty, roll-aboard in tow, and headed towards the door.

Delta has a well-manned service counter at the main intersection in Concourse E, and I marched briskly up to the first unengaged station.

"I'd like a fully refundable first class ticket on the next flight to Toronto please," I said, laying my Green Soldier and Passport on the counter.

We went through the charade of selecting return flights and seat assignments, and in about ten minutes I was back in Major Domo's face, slapping the ticket on her counter, and in my best Jack Nicholson said, "Now, I would like to make use of your international showers, please."

She scrutinized my ticket and, raising her entire head so she could enjoy watching my face, intoned, "I'm sorry, but the showers are reserved for trans-oceanic travelers."

"No problem," I countered, gathering up my ticket envelope and heading for the door.

I liked the agent at the service counter, and I returned to her station. "Here," as I handed her the Toronto ticket. "I need to trade this in on something to Brussels."

She gave me a quizzical look, and I figured it would be best if I came clean. "All I want to do is take a shower. I came in on a redeye and am out in a couple hours, but the woman running the Crown Room won't let me unless I have an international business class ticket. Toronto doesn't count. Just make sure the Brussels ticket is fully refundable, because it's coming back in thirty minutes—unless I decide to go."

She laughed, shook her head, and pecked away, sparing us both the work of choosing seats and selecting return travel. Even so, the transaction took about five minutes.

Stretching my 74 inches to full capacity, I sauntered up to the desk, slapped down the $7000 Brussels itinerary, and glared silently as she examined the contents of the ticket jacket.

"Follow me, please," she said. Her superficial cordiality might have led an observer to conclude this was our first exchange of the day, but I knew better. This was killing her. She led me several paces down the concourse to a locked mahogany door, into a marble hallway with a dozen-or-so doors on either side. Opening one, she switched on the light and, with frozen smile, pointed out the assortment of amenities, hair dryer, and other elements of the facility. I thanked her for her help, and she left.

I returned to the Crown Room a few minutes later, freshly coiffed and dressed in complete change of wardrobe. After some juice, coffee, and a granola bar, I returned my Brussels ticket to the service counter, got receipt of the credit back to Amex, and headed to Concourse B and my Providence departure gate.

Late that afternoon, my colleagues and I were in a cab, headed back to the Providence airport. My cell phone rang. A man introduced himself, announcing that he was with Delta Airlines. I sensed that his call had something to do with the extraordinary financial transactions early that morning. My combined Amex charges and credits totaled well over ten thousand dollars, for which Delta would, I was certain, have to pay Amex transaction fees that could total several hundred. I braced for a scolding and possibly worse.

Instead, he was very gracious in his apology for what Delta had done to me that morning. He said that I shouldn't have had to go through the trouble of buying the bogus tickets, adding that the entire office enjoyed a good laugh over my creativity. He simply wanted me to know that they had learned from the experience and would find ways to allow their people more latitude when dealing with reasonable requests from good customers, and thanked me for my business and for making their day. I wish I had written down his name.

Ω

Sometimes you find it necessary to correct the poor judgment of lower echelon employees who make expedient decisions that, while simplifying the attainment of their immediate mission, are clearly illogical, poorly conceived, and result in a customer relations disaster. At times like these, it is good to have the name and number of a senior executive, or at least the corporate switchboard number, in your cell phone.

Several years ago, during Mayor Bill Campbell's reign, Atlanta's airport was run like a third world country, complete with corruption, ineptitude, and generally subjecting Atlanta travelers to the unremitting hopelessness one suffers when customer service is marked by indifference. His Honor was ultimately brought down by his own alleged misdeeds and is now appropriately housed in the federal hoosegow along with many of his political cronies. Our new mayor, Shirley Franklin, has some competent people running the airport, and this, coupled with the reconfiguration of the security area and the handoff of security responsibilities to TSA, has made traveling in and out of Atlanta somewhat less onerous.

But back in the Campbell era, the passenger backup on Monday mornings snaked through the terminal atrium and into the ticketing area like Disney's Space Mountain line on a July afternoon. Quite literally, one might spend well over an hour creeping through the bottleneck as City of Atlanta employees of questionable literacy scrutinized each victim's ID and ticket or boarding pass. There were usually just three or four ID checkers directing travelers to fifteen screening lanes. Do the math. There was no backup in the x-ray lanes, just at the ID checkpoint. Delays at peak periods were preordained, but nobody in authority seemed to care. The gate agents responsible for getting flights out cared, so they were forever paging checked-in passengers who were in the security lines instead of the departure area. They cared, but they had no influence over the security debacle. Equally impotent were the people who had to reroute stranded travelers on later flights. They cared because their workload tripled, as all those originating passengers appeared at the concourse service counter after their flights had departed, but they had no influence over main terminal security. Passengers cared most of all, but we were the necessary nuisance in the daily equation. After all, it was all those passengers who caused the problem, right?

The security people directing traffic and checking ID's and sniffing shoes and grandma's handbag couldn't have cared less. They were there until their shift ended, all the same. And they weren't even interested in finding terrorists. They were interested in finding articles—you know, nail files, pen refills, cuticle snippers, nose hair trimmers, and the occasional 40 mm projectile which, upon careful inspection, is really just some mortified lady's traveling companion, Mr. Buzz-Buzz.

Fortunately, Delta had a "short cut" to the security lanes that was restricted to all but Silver, Gold, and Platinum Medallions or anyone flying first class. While these priority travelers underwent the same scrutiny in the x-ray lanes, at least they avoided the snail-tail line that crept through the atrium for an hour or more.

On one memorable Monday morning, Scotty and I approached the "short cut" and found its entrance cordoned off. A hand-lettered "closed" notice was taped over the pedestal sign at the entrance. I asked the nearest Delta badge why the short cut was closed. He neither knew nor cared. He had a walkie talkie, so I asked him to page the person in charge. A minute or so later, a jacketed gentleman ambled up, the obligatory ring of several dozen keys jingling on his belt. He said he was responsible for the entire check-in and ticketing area. I asked him who closed the shortcut and why. He claimed credit, citing the length of the line and its interference with the smooth operation of his check-in area. I suggested that he reduce the length of the line to manageable numbers by paring back on the entitlement, e.g. replacing his "Closed" sign with "Platinum and Gold Medallion Only."

He had, by his bonehead maneuver, caused hundreds of his best customers to miss their flights, connections, meetings, birthdays, or whatever their reason for flying that day. I explained how he could salvage the mood of his best customers, one of which happened to be me, by stratifying the restrictions based on the relative size of the crowd. He could dial the line up or down, thereby maintaining order while equitably granting privilege to the privileged. Throughout our brief but spirited exchange, Medallion travelers continued to show up at the short cut, many of whom had a burning interest in our lively dialogue.

When it became obvious that he didn't care and was not to be moved, I pulled out my cell phone and called Delta's corporate headquarters. I asked the switchboard to connect me with Vicki Escarra's office. A small crowd had by now gathered, the sentiment of which was growing increasingly hostile.

Vicki Escarra, who didn't know me from Adam's housecat, was responsible for all matters involving customer interface. I knew her name because her signature appeared on all frequent-flyer marketing correspondence and her picture regularly appeared in a PR column in Delta's monthly in-flight magazine. I harbored no delusions about actually talking to her; these folks seldom sit at their desks taking unexpected calls. But, they all have bright, powerful assistants, one of whom came on the line. A brief explanation of the situation, supported by my reference to the gathering crowd of deteriorating mood, and the assistant asked to talk to Mr. Jingles, who stood nearby listening intently to my exchange. I handed my cell phone to him. His side of the conversation consisted of several "Yes, buts" followed by acknowledgement and resigned submission. He mumbled something into his walkie-talkie and, when one of his minions arrived, he uncordoned the shortcut and slinked away into the masses. He was not about to endure the possibility that my legion of followers might carry me in on their shoulders.

Ω

Whenever you are victimized by an egregious error in customer service judgment, remedy is usually at hand. The key is knowing how the system works and being certain that you are right and they are wrong. My kids think that this is my vocation—to fix the world's service problems. In reality, I'm merely intent on pointing out a stupid problem when I see it and helping businesses improve their service so they can meet reasonable customer expectations.

I was returning to Atlanta from Cleveland one night, arriving at the terminal ticket counter shortly before 8 PM for an 8:30 flight. My standby request for upgrade had cleared, and the agent printed a First Class boarding pass. I breezed through security and stopped into the gift shop. My college-age daughter collected city souvenir shot glasses, and I wanted to buy her a "Cleveland."

This was prior to the relatively recent changes in pre-departure timing regarding gate and boarding requirements. Back then, as long as you were checked in, ten minutes was the rule. Your seat was subject to loss if you missed the ten-minute cutoff. I arrived at the gate just after eight-fifteen and attempted to board, but the scanner at the jetway entrance rejected my boarding pass. The agent said I would have to check at the counter.

A young brunette, stunningly attractive and mid-twenties at most, was stressing over the final counts, pecking away at her keyboard and doing whatever gate agents do in efforts to ensure an on-time departure. As Bob Seger would say, she had been born with a face that would let her get her way.

I approached, studying her perfect features, and handed her my pass with a "Hi. What's up? Your buddy over there said to check with you."

She looked at my boarding pass, tapped a few keys, and her printer spit out a new card, which she shoved at me with neither utterance nor eye contact. I noted that I'd been reassigned a new seat, in coach. Heaping insult upon injury, it was a center seat.

I maintained my cool, explaining that this wouldn't work. I had a designated, reserved seat in First and my butt was going to be in it. She would simply have to advise the most recently cleared standby that his clearance was granted prematurely, the seat's rightful owner had arrived, and that he must vacate and take his assigned seat in coach. This is not an uncommon occurrence. It has happened to me on occasion, and I moved. Those are the rules.

"You were late, so your seat was reassigned," she shrugged.

"No, you are wrong." I countered. "Look, it's only 8:21 now, and I've been here a good four or five minutes," pointing to my impeccably accurate Rolex Perpetual Datejust.

"I go by my watch," she proclaimed indifferently, "and you were late. We are going to close the door. If you want to go to Atlanta, you need to board."

I camouflaged my growing case of the redass. "Well, the rest of the world and I go by Greenwich Mean Time," I replied calmly. "Your watch is wrong, and I'm going to Atlanta in the seat reserved in my name. You'll need to ask the guy in it to move."

"Suit yourself," she muttered, and disappeared with a sheaf of paper into the jetway, latching the door behind her.

My pulse quickened as my amygdala, now on full alert, dispatched a call for adrenaline and sent a "fight" impulse coursing through my sinews. I tried to think peaceful, serene thoughts as I watched the jet push back and start engines. When she returned, I calmly approached the desk and asked her to page the Station Manager, which she did.

I returned to my seat in the empty boarding lounge, casually flipping through an abandoned newspaper that may as well have been printed in Slavic. When the Station Manager arrived, The Face motioned to me and went about her work closing out the flight.

The manager asked me to accompany him to a nearby gate, and as we walked, I explained the situation, detailed with the chronology of events. He opened a vacant terminal at the empty gate and reviewed the record, verifying my check in-time and the time the coach pass was printed. It was clear that his beauty queen had screwed up, and he admitted as much, explaining her misguided rationale as pressure to get the departure out on time.

"She was wrong," he conceded. "She shouldn't have reassigned your seat when she did. When you showed up, she should have asked the other passenger to move. I'll talk to her about it. All that aside, what do you want me to do?"

I told him that I didn't want her fired or even disciplined, but I hoped that someone would help her understand the customer's place in the value chain and that she cannot ride roughshod over the source of her income when the customer is right and the company (in this case, she) is wrong. Also, since Delta had no more flights to

Atlanta that night, I told him that a reasonable compromise was to send me back on the next available flight on another carrier, first class. He got me onto a United flight leaving in about an hour. He also thanked me for my business and gave me a $14 meal chit, which I spent in the concourse bar.

The irony is, she was pretty enough to have used her smile, an apology, a shred of personality, and those big, brown eyes, and I would have folded myself into that coach center seat like a worn out roadmap.

THEY HAVE
PROCEDURES

For a guy without a whole lot of money, I seem to spend a lot of time dealing with banks. Lately, much of it has not been altogether pleasant.

My first exposure to banking was as a newly commissioned Naval Officer. I opened a checking account at the Bank of America branch in Coronado, California. This was back when Bank of America, while an in-state behemoth, operated only in California. I deposited my check, paid a nominal monthly fee, and transactions were uncomplicated. We had a great relationship.

Returning to civilian life, corporate moves required changing banks. Florida, North Carolina, Georgia, New Jersey, and, in 1983, a return to Georgia. Each new relationship was smooth and painless. The tellers and manager in each respective branch knew me, and everything seemed to work. In the '80s, legislation permitted the formation of Regional Interstate banks, and mergers started to form as big banks got together and swallowed each other. Then in 1995, the Riegle-Neal Interstate Banking and Branching Efficiency Act unshackled the industry, allowing well-capitalized banks to acquire others anywhere in the United States. Bankers started lighting cigars with my money, and it went slowly downhill until the hill became a cliff in late '08.

I started with Bank South because it had a branch near my office. It became NCNB, then NationsBank, and finally Bank of America. Every time the crane wheeled up to change the sign, I sensed an erosion of the simplicity and personalization I'd come to expect. It started with the first statement under the new logo. The statement contained a sheaf of paper printed in a font so tiny, (probably to discourage reading), that I'd have needed a jeweler's loupe to comprehend the section headings. I correctly concluded that these were the new bank's rules, disseminated in my statement so when they started nicking me with new fees, they could claim that I had been warned.

When I formed my corporation in 1992, I was required by law to open a business checking account. I had no trouble keeping my two accounts separate, but apparently the bank did. My first clue was when I asked to have my ATM card re-issued to allow access to either account. It seemed logical to me. You plug in your card, the screen asks which account you want to access, you choose A or B, and go from there. The teller, then the branch manager, and finally the supervisor of the telephone customer service department told me this couldn't be done. It seemed to me a fairly simple request. I felt that the bank's technology could handle the complexity, but the solution proffered by the bank was easier and more profitable for them. Why not carry two identical ATM cards?

Every financial institution in the country seems to be locked in a great land rush to capture real estate in my wallet. If I maintained all the credit cards that show up in the mail, not to mention all that I have been "pre-approved" for, I'd need to carry a man-purse. I wasn't about to carry two NationsBank ATM cards. And I mean ATM cards. I am adamant about my ATM cards serving in that capacity only. If I'd let them, the banks would automatically attached debit card capability to my ATM cards. I insist that they provide me a card that only works in ATMs and does not bear a Visa or MasterCard logo. I remain convinced that debit cards are among the greatest frauds ever perpetrated upon the consumer, and for years I steadfastly refused to participate in their scam. I ultimately lost this war, however, when Bank of America was able to concoct a scheme to muscle me into submission. After decades of no-fee checking, a thirteen dollar service charge suddenly showed up in my business account. I called the customer service line to have it removed, whereupon a very professional agent named Toni told me that the Bank had decided to start charging all business accounts the monthly service fee, regardless of the balance maintained.

Subjected to my immediate and vigorous protest, she offered a means of escape. If I would accept one of their debit cards and use it once or more each month, that month's fee would be "offset" by a reward of, coincidentally, thirteen dollars. I was hopelessly pinned, so I tapped out. Victorious, Toni refunded the previous month's fee and graciously helped me to my feet. I use the card monthly to buy a two-roll pack of bumwad, which I donate to the gentlemen's lounge at my favorite Irish pub, thereby gaining some small satisfaction in the appropriateness of its application.

Don't get me started. Debit cards really give me the redass. I cannot imagine why anyone would use a debit card rather than a credit card. In the first, the bank uses your money until you swipe the card, and most of the time, the transfer is virtually immediate. Your money is gone. In the second, you use the bank's money, for FREE, until you pay the bill every thirty days. Banks have positioned debit cards as a more convenient alternative than checks. Granted, they are more convenient for the consumer and everyone behind her in the grocery line, but they are mostly more convenient for the bank. With checks, banks must endure the costs to manually handle, enter, record visual imagery, copy, and store. With debit cards, all this "inconvenience," along with the attendant cost, goes away. Cha-ching!

Do banks reward the consumer for saving them all this money? Amazingly, it's just the opposite. More and more banks are charging the consumer a transaction fee each time the card is used and the PIN is entered. In a survey by the New York Public Interest Research Group, 89% of the banks surveyed tack on a point-of-sale fee of anywhere from 10 cents to $1.50 for PIN-based debit transactions. Cha-ching!

Just as with credit cards, retailers usually pay the bank a fee for the processing of a debit card transaction. Normally, a flat fee of 7.5 cents to 10 cents is paid when the PIN is used and the transaction is processed "online." If the customer signs for the purchase, it's processed "offline" and the fee can be as much as 2% of the transaction. On a two hundred dollar grocery order, that's four bucks. Cha-ching!

With a credit card, the bank has some exposure. With a debit card, the bank has little or no exposure; it's all borne by the consumer. Does the bank share the benefit of this protection. Not unless you call overdraft penalties sharing the wealth. These can be as high as thirty or forty dollars—not to mention the twenty-five percent interest rate the bank collects until the deficit is paid back. Cha-ching!

Little wonder the banks love to pass out debit cards. Granted, credit cards require discipline, which a prudent person exercises with a debit card anyway. Keep track of what you spend and pay the entire bill every month on time. Write one check instead of fifty and avoid fees and penalties. What could be easier? If you aren't up to the challenge, go ahead and throw yourself to the bankers. They saw you coming.

When NationsBank acquired Bank of America, things got worse. Gone was the old BofA I had known in California. I knew we were off to a bad start when, soon after the name change, I slid my card into my usual ATM in Kroger and it asked if I wanted to transact in English or Spanish. We've all by now resigned ourselves to this question, but back then, I was floored. I did a quick scan of the store for a level-set. Yep, I was still in the USA. Like Dorothy, I just wasn't in Kansas anymore.

Some months later, a colleague and I finished a meeting in Cincinnati and were returning to our rental car in the client's parking garage. I noted an ATM just outside of the elevator lobby. I was low on cash, so I took the opportunity to punch up a few bucks to handle my currency needs until returning home. As always, I fed in my card, selected "withdrawal", entered one-zero-zero-zero-zero, and waited.

The machine churned, accompanying by the routine hums and clicking sounds. My card reemerged, and the printer spit out a normal looking receipt, indicating a withdrawal of one-hundred dollars and the adjusted balance, but no money. Like a fool, I felt the empty cash slot, squatting down to peer into the dark, vacant hole.

I reacted as a New Yorker might if a pigeon suddenly swooped down and stole his Yankees cap: first with shock, then dumbfounded incredulity, followed by a strong expletive.

My sidekick Mark, in efforts at consolation, offered an empathetic "Wife beat you to it, eh?"

"No, look," I insisted. "I've got six thousand dollars in there," waiving the receipt in his face.

"Holy crap," he said. "It says you withdrew a hundred dollars. You got hosed."

The machine, placed by a bank I'd never heard of, bore a toll-free number, to which I placed an immediate call. The woman I finally connected with took the machine's location and my name, but was unable to do anything but report it. Since I wasn't their customer, I doubted there was any satisfaction to be gotten from her bank. I called the 800 number on the back of my ATM card, expecting MY bank to be more sympathetic in providing remedy. After what seemed an inordinately long wait for human intervention, my BofA customer service representative said the withdrawal hadn't yet appeared on her system, but that she would make a note in the record. Until the withdrawal appeared, there was nothing she could do.

The following day, I called again, hoping perhaps that the withdrawal would never appear, since it had never actually happened. No such luck. The mysterious hundred-dollar non-withdrawal was now a matter of record. The rep on the phone told me that he would commence an inter-bank investigation of the matter. He said they would request the other bank audit the machine, and if it bore an extra hundred dollars in inventory, they would effect the digital transfer and credit my account. What he didn't say, but what I heard clearly, was that if I were lying outright or the machine happened to give my Benjamin to some other person, or the auditor counted wrong, or any other untoward eventuality, I was hosed. I took a deep breath and asked to talk to his boss. I got no further with her. I was, after all, just a number on the screen and a voice in her headset—a voice that was building a case of the redass.

I took my ATM receipt to the little branch in my neighborhood Kroger, where the tellers and the manager all knew me by name. The manager said his hands were tied. There were procedures that must be followed. Now I really had the redass. I told him to get his boss on the phone and we'd have a three-way. With his district manager on the phone, I launched into a rant.

"I've been a customer here through four name changes, I've never bounced a check, I have two checking accounts with hefty balances, you guys have been using my money for free, and there's nothing in my history to suggest that I would suddenly try to fleece your bank out of a hundred bucks. Now, you put my money back and go conduct your investigations six ways to Sunday, I don't care. I want my money and I want it now—or do I need to call somebody in Charlotte?"

She consented to credit the account back the hundred while they investigated. She said she would call me with the findings. I told her not to bother and that for me, the matter was closed.

Several days later, she called anyway to tell me that the ATM did, in fact, turn up a hundred in excess. I told her that I was happy for her bank, because it was their money, not mine.

She went on to stress that no one doubted me, but that they had procedures. She also was dying to explain what happened. It seems that somewhere on the network phone lines, possibly a thunderstorm or electrical surge, the signal hiccupped at the precise moment between my electronic transaction and the machine's disbursement. She said it was a one-in-a billion event. I told her that I really didn't care what the system did and that the customer service rep should have been empowered to immediately credit my account over the phone, considering my record, which they had in minute detail covering twenty years. She countered by reminding me again that they have procedures.

Maybe they have so many nameless, faceless employees who handle so many nameless faceless customers that they need androids rather than thinking, rational, human beings, but some of their procedures border on the ridiculous.

I had been carrying around a small third-party check in my wallet for several weeks. On a Costco run, I noted a BofA branch neighboring the box store. Remembering the check, I swung into their lot and went into the branch to cash it. Not having either of my checkbooks with me, I laid my ATM card on the counter along with the check, asking the teller to cash it for me. She used the card to bring up my account data, and asked to see my ID. I handed her my Georgia driver's license. She scrutinized the license, looked at me, then back at the license, then back to me.

"This license has expired," she noted, handing it back.

"Oh, so it has," I replied, seeing the expiration date of my birthday several weeks prior. "I'll have to get it renewed. Thanks."

"I can't cash this check," she said with a hint of apology in her tone. Then more eagerly, "I can deposit it, though."

"No," I said, "I want to cash it."

"I can't cash it without a valid ID."

"But this is a valid ID," I explained. All that's expired is my right to drive. It still says that I'm me. I didn't expire. The driving part is expired. The ID part is still good."

"No," she maintained, "I need a valid ID to cash a check, and that one's expired."

"What's the purpose of that rule," I asked.

"To prevent fraud. It's for your own protection," she replied, beginning to show signs of growing impatience.
"Who are you protecting me from," I asked with mounting intolerence, "myself? I don't need protection from me cashing my own check. Isn't it obvious that I'm really me? Here," I said, flopping my wallet full of credit cards on the counter. "I have a bunch of credit cards, and if you want to come out to the ATM in the lobby, I'll even show you that I know my PIN. That's because I am this guy," I said, tapping the expired license for dramatic effect.

"Oh, I don't doubt that this is you," she replied, gesturing to the check. "It's just that I can't cash it without a valid ID."

She had dug in, so I asked her to call the manager over. At this point, my frustration was developing into a solid case of the redass.

The three of us were soon bonded in solid agreement regarding my identity and the check's validity, nonetheless, the manager's best solution was to deposit the check, which didn't require any ID, then step out to the lobby ATM and withdraw the cash in two transactions. The absurdity of the dialogue reminded me of the Monty Python skit in which John Cleese struggles to convince the pet shop owner, "This parrot is dead."

In utter defeat, I allowed the teller to complete a counter deposit slip, and I withdrew my cash from the ATM. The manager graciously apologized, noting that they had procedures that must be followed.

Ω

My neighborhood Kroger is very convenient. It's near my home, it's next door to my gym, it's open 24 hours a day, and it accommodates my unorthodox hours. It's nice to be able to buy groceries on a moment's notice, since I never know from one day to the next whether we'll be eating out or I'll be playing chef. Also, when Chris is home from college he eats like a backhoe.

NationsBank had a contract with Kroger's Atlanta division to operate branches in most of their stores. They had convenient hours, from 10 AM until 7 PM, and 4 PM on Saturdays. Kroger did not renew the arrangement with BofA when the lease expired, so now a visit to the bank involves a seven mile round-trip rather than a short hop from the checkout lanes. But at least they left the ATM.

One evening last summer, I stopped in to pick up some essentials and elected to pay cash. Flipping through my money clip, I was down to seven or eight singles. There was no one in line behind me, so I told the cashier I'd punch up some cash at the ATM which was no more than ten feet from her register. I fed in my card while she watched. Instead of the usual English/Spanish election and PIN screen, a screen which I'd never seen appeared, announcing that my card was being retained due to some reason that the bank and their machine thought warranted snatching it. All I recall now was that there was some unsettling terminology in the notice, with words like unauthorized or invalid or restricted. I didn't really care at the time WHY the machine ate my card, but rather THAT it ate my card. I returned to the checkstand, paying with my Amex card and suffering the embarrassment of what must have, to the checkout girl, looked like insolvency. (For some reason, I care what checkout girls think, OK? Maybe it's a personality disorder.) I returned to the machine with my cart, seeking a number to call regarding this obviously errant unit. I wanted my card back.

I dialed the 800 number and, unable to enter my account number, tried to break though the bank's onerous IVR system since none of the menu options were remotely related to the purpose of my call. Ultimately I was connected to some customer service headset who looked into my accounts and could find absolutely no reason why her machine had eaten my card. She transferred me to their Fraud Division, insofar as she suspected that they might be able to explain the phenomenon. The night watch in Fraud knew even less. End of discussion. Call back during business hours.

I called the following morning and worked my way up to a supervisor in their ATM department. Like those before her, she had no idea why the machine retained my card. I told her that I would meet their tech at the store to retrieve it; just tell me what time to be there. She countered that once a machine snatches a card, it disables the data stripe, rendering it useless as teats on a boar. My card was history.

I told her that I didn't like being without my ATM card and asked her to have another one overnighted to me today. This was, she said, impossible. She would enter a request for a reissue card, and they could mail it or I could pick it up at the bank in seven-to-ten business days. They required three to five days to produce the card, then the shipping and handling would take several more days. Now I had the redass.

I protested pretty vigorously. They had wrongfully snatched my card, they were unable to explain why they had done it, and they expected me to wait patiently, hat in hand, and endure their routine card replacement procedures. I told her that, if the right, person REALLY wanted to, they could force their card makers, whether outside vendor or in-house, to produce one today. That was what I expected to happen, insofar as it was they, not I, who created the problem. I expected them to step up and go beyond their standard operating procedures to get me back my card. I didn't lose it. They screwed up and took it.

She finally got my point and put me on hold. When she returned, she said they would produce a replacement card the following day and overnight it to my home. No one ever uncovered why the same ATM I had used for years prior and since suddenly chose to disable and retain my card.

The card episode with Bank of America drove me to request a backup ATM card at Washington Mutual. When my mother passed away several years prior, the executor managed the estate account in a Washington Mutual branch near San Diego. I received several sizable checks, and insofar as there was a new WaMu branch near my home, I took the checks there and opened an account, solely for the purpose of immediate transfer from the estate account into my own. I didn't want to wait for checks to clear, nor did I entirely trust the executor's lawyer, who, as her husband, might be subject to conflicting interests. My intention was to open the account, then transfer the assets soon thereafter and probably close the account.

I was impressed by the general tone and ambiance of this WaMu branch. Their free standing teller stations were un-banklike. Their casually attired tellers didn't dispense cash, rather they issued a ticket that one took to a station in the wall, much like a mini ATM, which then dispensed the currency and change. I left some money in my new WaMu checking account, just to have a fallback banking relationship in place if BofA ever stepped over the line. So, wallet real-estate shortage notwithstanding, I stopped into my WaMu branch and requested an ATM card. It was comforting to know I had a backup. And it was a good thing I did.

I have an old fruitcake tin with Euros, Pounds, Yen, Yuan, and currency left over from any country I've traveled to. I try to break even just prior to returning home, but rather than give whatever remains back to the Thomas Cook window and taking a major hit on the exchange rate, I bring any remaining cash back with me. I always gave the coins to my kids and kept the currency for future trips. This gets me my first beer or taxi upon arrival, and I use ATM s exclusively for the remainder of the visit. You can save hundreds in fees over time as opposed to using currency exchanges, and ATMs are more plentiful in Europe than in the US. It seems there are two or three at every major intersection in downtown commercial areas. Even in Japan, while our ATM cards don't work in the standard machines scattered everywhere, one only needs locate a US bank, which are plentiful and all feature twenty-four hour ATMs in their entrance lobbies.

I was in Kiev, Ukraine with a couple friends last winter, using my Washington Mutual ATM card at the numerous machines located through the city. One night, I stopped at one to punch up some cash. The machine notified me, in English, that it was unable to process my request. I figured the machine was out of money. I tried a machine across the street. Same message. Around the corner, same thing. Then I slid in my BofA card and had no problem. I found this puzzling.

Soon after I returned to Atlanta, I called Washington Mutual in search of the individual responsible for my near-disaster in Kiev. Had it not been for my Bank of America card, I'd still be sitting on a box on Khreschatik Boulevard. Ukraine is a cash economy. While the Premier Palace Hotel, I am certain, accepts American Express, all the bars, restaurants, retail shops, and taxis expect cash on the barrel. Without access to cash, a tourist is out of the game.

Granted, I could have probably found an American Express office and gotten an advance, but that should not have been necessary. I had a valid ATM card with several thousand dollars to sustain it, and I ought to be able to use it.

The WaMu customer service rep reported that there was a fraud hold on my card. That was all she knew, so I asked to be transferred to their fraud department. I reached Corporate Security, and after navigating several layers of IVR asking me to choose which "for information about" I sought, I reached the Security Help Desk. I asked my appointed fraudbuster why they had placed a fraud hold on my ATM card. He took my account number and, in the blink of an eye, was able to cite the fact that their monitoring technology had detected two withdrawal transactions in the Ukraine, as though this was a big "Ah ha!"

I told him that I already knew about the two withdrawal transactions in the Ukraine, insofar as it was I who made them. Speaking more slowly this time, I again asked him why they had placed a fraud hold on my ATM card.

"Well," he explained, "our detection systems didn't know it was you."

"I thought that's what the PIN number was for—to tell your system that it IS me and not just some guy who found my card" I shot back with mounting frustration.

Sherlock had it all figured out. He began to expostulate about "that part of the world" and how transactions originating there raised more suspicion than, say, England or France or - - -.

He had gotten to his second country when I cut him off. "Transfer me to whoever runs your fraud division."

He hadn't the foggiest notion of who that might be, so I called their corporate headquarters switchboard in Seattle and asked again to be transferred to whoever ran Fraud. The corporate operator didn't know either, but she patched me into the "Executive Response Team," where a patient and fairly knowledgeable manager named Jeannie presented the bank's rationale.

Jeannie said that I was notified in the printed material I was given when I opened the account that I should advise the bank whenever I travel abroad. Translation: "It was really YOUR fault, because everybody knows you're supposed to read all print, fine and otherwise, on all the paper and mail you get from the bank."

The bank's standard procedure, which they followed in my case, was to attempt to contact me via phone, then notify me in writing that there was "unusual activity" on my account. Being unable to reach me and receiving no response, they shut down the card. Sure enough, there had been the bank's message on my voicemail—the one where my greeting stated that I would be out of the country with limited access to voicemail—and their "unusual activity" letter was in my mailbox.

"Wait a minute," I said. "Let me see if I have this straight. If you reach me at home or I respond to your letter, you'll conclude that I'm not in Kiev and shut off my card. Conversely, if you can't reach me at home and I don't respond to your letter, you'll also conclude that I'm not in Kiev and shut off my card?"

Jeannie went on to advise me that, all of the above not withstanding, I must remember that these sophisticated procedures are in place for my own protection, and for that I should be tolerant, or even grateful.

I corrected her. "If some Ukrainian technogeek hacks into your bank and steals money from my account, you'd have to replace it, because it's really YOUR money that was stolen. Explain again to me how this is for MY protection?"
Jeannie had some difficulty explaining this, and I cut her off mid-struggle. Having had all the answers I needed, I thanked Jeannie for her time and patience and told her she'd been drinking the bank's Kool-Aid way too long.

I got over the redass and kept my WaMu account, primarily because I actually enjoyed occasionally transacting with their people and because they never charge an ATM transaction fee regardless of whose machine I use.

Washington Mutual's field retail people, like most banks,' are well trained in dealing with customers. They almost universally provide efficient, friendly service, even on the first encounter. Almost, because occasionally, a dud can slip through the net and display a demeanor of indifference that would drive most customers away. This is particularly egregious if the offender is a manager.

My daughter had recently changed jobs, taking a sales position with a pharmaceutical manufacturer. Her compensation package included a lovely new Volvo. She had also recently bought a new Infinity G-35. As much as she loved it, the monthly payments and insurance coverage were hard to justify, so she listed it for sale and the car sold immediately. She asked me to help manage the transaction.

The buyer's mother lived on Long Island and lent him the $32,000 purchase price. We all know that in this day of photo quality desktop printers, cashier's checks are not the bulletproof instruments they once were, so I insisted we meet at his bank. Since both the buyer and his mom banked at Washington Mutual, I suggested we meet at my local WaMu branch with his mom's check and I would bring the car. He could have the check made out to himself, and the bank could simply transfer the funds to my account upon his endorsement.

The buyer, a nice young guy named Amir, lived in an Atlanta suburb diametrically across town from me, about an hour away. He left after work and Atlanta traffic had slowed his progress to the point where he was running up against the bank's closing time of 5:00. I told him I'd go to the bank at our prearranged meeting time, 4:45, and he could call me when he drew close, advising me of his ETA. I figured that I could reasonably arrange for the manager to admit us if it was only a matter of five or ten minutes after closing. After all, I reasoned, the manager and teller staff don't exactly file out of a bank at 5:00 like a factory shift.

I waited in the parking lot, and Amir called me at 4:55. He was ten minutes away. I entered the branch, and a cheerful young woman smiled and asked if she could help. I told her that I'd probably need to talk to the manager, since I had a special request. She directed me to a shirtsleeved, tieless guy in his late twenties. He was seated at a desk facing the open atrium of teller stations, peering into a monitor, wiggling a mouse. I approached his desk, and, looking up from his monitor, he said, "Can I help you?"

I thought it odd that he didn't rise and extend his hand. Maybe WaMu was really into the Northwest grunge scene and common business courtesy was viewed as uncool. At least he didn't address me as "dude." In any event I told him of the situation and asked if he could admit Amir a few minutes after closing so we might complete our transaction.

He looked at me like I had asked him to paint my house. "I'm not gonna stay open and keep a teller available after closing. He'll have to come back tomorrow."
While I lived only five minutes away, I explained that Amir was driving from Lawrenceville, and it would be a shame to make him do the two-hour round trip twice.

"Sorry," he said. "I'm not gonna do it."

Starting to get the redass, I replied in a tone of obvious derision, "Well, I guess the days of the personal banker going the extra mile are over, huh?"

"Yep," he replied. "Guess they are."

I turned on my heel and headed for the lobby. He went back to his monitor. The cheerful young woman shot me a wincing little smile and mouthed "Sorry," as she locked the door behind me. Amir was, at that moment, pulling into the parking lot.

We executed the same plan the following day with better timing.

The next day, I was still suffering enough of the redass to call another Washington Mutual branch and asked the manager for the main number of their regional or district headquarters. I got the number and spoke to some vice president's assistant, advising that I'd had a "very unsettling episode with one of their branch managers and that if I had her boss's job, I'd want to hear about it."

She advised me that she knew her boss well enough to predict that he would refer it to the manager's immediate director, adding that it would be better if the director heard the story from me. I identified the branch, and she assured me that she'd contact the director and have her call me. Later that day, a very personable, professional sounding woman called my cell, and I factually recounted the details of my encounter, waiting until the end to add my editorial contribution about her man's relationship-building techniques.

She was sincerely apologetic, concurring with me that it was unconscionable for him to deny such a simple request. She said that "it would be nothing for him to let the two of you in for the time that transaction would have taken." She really appeared mortified at her man's behavior, apologizing so profusely that I felt sorry for her and began to mitigate the seriousness of the offense. When she said that she'd handle it with him, I told her I didn't want to get the guy fired over this, but felt that there were three clear training needs: knowing the difference between a reasonable and unreasonable customer request, how to say no without being a jerk, and comprehending the customer's role in their business model.

Of course, at times one might conclude that banks only need customers so they have somebody to fleece. Walk 'em to the door with a smile and a handshake, one hand around their shoulder and the other hand in their pocket. This is evident in residential mortgage's recent implosion, wherein bankers were complicit in knowingly trapping unsuspecting victims into financial arrangements that were, with virtual certainty, destined to line the fat cats' pockets and turn the struggling customer out of his home and onto the street. I'm not saying that the major banks are participants in larceny, but simply driven by unconscionable greed. The direction that banking and credit card fees have taken recently has mobilized me into a crusade of resistance.

I use an American Express card almost exclusively. I have the earliest "Member Since" year of anyone I know. I have profound respect and admiration for Amex, as I'll explain in a later chapter.

Unfortunately, acceptance of the Green Soldier is not universal, so I carry a Visa for use when the establishment advises, "I'm sorry, we don't take American Express." No problem, that's what Capital One is for. I don't like it, but I'm not going to get the redass over it.

I provide my son Chris, a senior at Auburn, with a Bank of America Visa card, primarily for gas and emergency use. My wife and I used GM MasterCards extensively when that program was introduced. It worked for them and it worked for us. We bought our daughter Katie and Chris each a new GM car solely because of the value we had accrued in our GM accounts. Combined, we were able to deduct almost $10,000, same as cash, from the final price of both cars.

We've never paid fees or interest, because we treat our Visa and MasterCard accounts the same as American Express. We pay the entire bill each month. On the rare occasion when I misread the bill, screw up my math and leave a balance unpaid, or the statement is lost in the mail, my quick review of the following month's statement immediately discloses the error. I call the 800 number and invariably get the fees credited back, but only because my history and my compelling explanation identifies the situation as an obvious and forgivable error.

An example is something that happened with Capital One a few months ago. I pay Chris's college tuition on line with my Capital One account. The Auburn bursar's office has my card data in their system, so I get an email when there's money due, and I go to their site and literally two clicks later, I've paid for lab fees, copies, parking tickets, and tuition.

I also use the CapOne card for the occasional business expense where the establishment won't accept Amex. To keep my accountant happy, I split the total monthly payment across two checking accounts, personal and business. One particular month, I had a couple small business expenses and a honking great tuition charge on the card. I did the math in my head (a mistake), and generated two payments on-line from my two checking accounts. The next month, the statement included an interest charge of almost a hundred dollars on the miniscule shortfall error. I annualized the interest on what they were charging me to use their money for 30 days, and it came out at almost 2500% APR.   .

I called the Customer Service number and got an explanation. The finance charge is calculated not on the payment shortfall, but on the average daily balance. Since the tuition is just south of ten thousand a semester and the payment was early in the cycle, my five dollar shortfall was churning their finance meter at warp speed.

In addition to finance charges, past-due fees if your payment is received a day or more late, and minimum payment fees, missing the minimum payment by a cent or more can add another $78 in penalties for the month. Cha-ching!

To their credit, CapOne happily credited the finance charge in light of what was clearly a simple error, but these guys seem to me in business not so much to provide a service as to operate a loan sharking operation. They'd love for me to get into the $10,000 credit line available for cash advance. . . .at a mere 23.59% APR. Do I LOOK like an idiot?

I received a mailing from BofA last week announcing "important notice of change in terms" regarding the Visa card I provide for Chris. It was four legal size pages, printed both sides in tiny font, detailing God only knows what. I wasn't about to invest the time to read it all, insofar as I don't pay fees or interest or penalties. One aspect of this notice struck me as interesting however. Buried in the text was a paragraph pertaining to cash advances via ATM, Debit Card, Overdraft Protection, and those flimsy paper checks that show up with the bill, hoping to seduce you into cashing one. This particular section of the eight page document announced an increase in the Annual Percentage Rate charged on those cash advances to 24.99%. It went on to say that I could reject this APR increase by writing a letter of specified wording by a specific date, whereby my APR of 19.99% would remain in effect. Huh?

This looks for all the world that they're setting their customers up for a "Gotcha," as I doubt that many will even read the mailing much less write a letter to say that they'd prefer paying less than more.

Bank of America, doesn't have a monopoly on fees, penalties, and usurious interest rates. I also bank with Wachovia, which has branches in Auburn. Neither BofA nor WaMu have branches there, so I set up Chris's checking account with Wachovia. Additionally, my wife has banked with Wachovia since it was called First Union. She now has a couple of checking accounts with them as well as savings accounts for the kids and some CDs.

Recently, Chris called at the start of fall semester and said he needed four-hundred dollars for books—like yesterday. His checking account was light, as the month's end was approaching and I restock it on the first. My normal practice is to write a check from a college account my broker set up for him, and drop into my local Wachovia branch. I have no deposit slips, but the teller takes the last name on my check, brings up a screen that displays all our Wachovia accounts, and deposits the funds in the account with an Auburn address and a ten dollar balance.

On this occasion, I figured I'd better deposit cash so he'd have instant access with his ATM card. I withdrew cash from the ATM and laid it on the counter at Wachovia. I told the teller to deposit it into Chris's checking account, which she did. I confirmed with her that he would have immediate access to the funds, and leaving the bank, I called Chris on my cell phone to report mission accomplished.

The next day, Chris called to tell me that his account was overdrawn although he was certain there should be almost fifty dollars left. I went on-line and looked at the transaction detail for his account. I showed several ATM withdrawals as well as three fees or penalties totaling sixty-four dollars.

Rather than call the 800 number, I printed off the transaction detail, grabbed my deposit receipt from the previous day, and headed to the Wachovia branch on my way to the gym. I didn't know what the fees were for, nor did I care. I simply knew they were invalid for whatever reason and I wanted them refunded to the account.

Wachovia has a station in the front of the bank with a customer service rep who directs traffic to the various offices depending on the customer's needs. Customers wanting teller service need not check in, bypassing this greeter and heading for the counter. As I entered, she asked if she could help. I said that I doubted it, but that in any case, I wanted to talk with the manager. She responded that he was not in the branch, adding that she might be able to help if she knew what it was.

I laid out my transaction printout, my deposit slip, explained that I'd deposited cash the previous morning, and that these fees were in error and I needed them put back. She said that only the manager could credit back fees and that he was doubling today at another office. I asked for his phone number, and she said that she would contact him and have him give me a call. I explained how that wouldn't work in this case, because I wanted to talk to him now and get the matter settled. It was obviously a bank error. She refused to give me his number, saying only that she would have him get back to me.

I asked to know what branch he was managing, and the game ended. Unable to justify withholding that information, she told me where he was. I got back into my car and headed for the branch.

When I got there, I told the resident traffic director woman that I needed to speak with the manager. She invited me to have a seat in the lobby. I stood. Soon, a young, personable Asian gentleman came out of an office and introduced himself. We exchanged business cards. His name was Joe.

I explained my position in four succinct points.

1. I added four hundred dollars cash to the twenty already in my kid's account yesterday morning
2. He has since that time withdrawn only $380.
3. Your bank has nicked him $64 in bogus fees and penalties
4. I want the $64 put back into his account NOW

He took my two documents, the printed transaction sheet and the deposit receipt, and read through both with apparent concern and interest. Then he walked to a computer terminal and commenced to poke at the keyboard and wiggle the mouse.

I said, "Look, Joe, just put this kid's money back and you can explore what went wrong on your own time."

"I can only refund the fees if they are due to a bank error," he replied. "That's what I'm trying to find out."

"Of course it's a bank error," I said. "Look, here's the deposit and here are the $380 withdrawals. One, two, three," as I vigorously tapped on the printout. "These other three are your fees, and they put him in the hole," I noted with three more taps. "Just put the money back now and find out why later. I'm in a hurry."
"I can't do that, Mr. Melka," Joe again confessed.

Here we go, I thought. "OK," I said. "I understand if you don't have the authority to put it back until you've found the cause of the error. Let me have your boss's name and phone number," I demanded, withdrawing the phone from my pocket.

"I can't give that out. Can she reach you at this number?" he asked, fingering my card. "I'll have her call you."

Now I had the redass. "Never mind," I said, snatching up my two documents. "I'll have Charlotte fix it." Heading for the door, I made a mental note to replace the stuff in my safe deposit box with a frozen mackerel.

Charlotte, North Carolina, is the financial capital of the South. Both Wachovia and Bank of America are headquartered there. I went back to my office and pulled up the CEO's name and the corporate switchboard number. When the operator answered, I asked for Ken Thompson's office. Although I had no expectations of Wachovia's CEO becoming involved in a retail customer problem, I was confident that a call to his office would get me routed to someone who had the clout to fix it.

A very nice lady answered, and I apologized for the intrusion, but explained that I had a retail banking problem that her field people couldn't seem to solve, and while I didn't want to bother Mr. Thompson with it, perhaps she could steer me to an executive who could help.

She said that they had a group of senior managers comprising a special department called "The Office of the President," any one of whom was certainly equipped to address any retail banking issue. She transferred me, and a marvelous, professional manager named Mary listened to my story, brought up the account record, and within a few seconds found and fixed the problem. The teller had deposited the four hundred into Chris's *savings* account. When he withdrew $380, from the ATM, it nicked him for a $44 overdraft cash advance fee, (Cha-ching) then overdraft protection kicked in and transferred the money from his savings account, which generated a $10 transfer fee (Cha-ching) which put his account into the red, which generated a second $10 transfer fee. (Cha-ching) Since he didn't withdraw any funds beyond that, he wasn't fleeced for another $44 cash advance. Remarkably, that would have followed next if he hadn't punched up a balance and called me for help. What we have here is a circular conundrum, wherein application of a fee generates the application of fee, which generates the application of a fee, etc.

The next morning, a woman named Theresa called me. She said that one of her managers, Joe specifically, had left a message for her to call me.

"You're late, Theresa," I told her. "I called Ken Thompson's office and got it fixed."

"What was the problem?" she asked with some concern.

I couldn't resist. "Call Ken," I said.

Ω

Sometimes, even bank executives get to experience their company's lunacy. I did some work for a client and sent them an invoice. Six weeks had passed, so I asked my sponsor to check on their payment. He talked to his Chief Financial Officer and was told that the invoice had been processed and was in line for payment by "the end of the month," which was a week-and-a-half hence.

Three weeks later, I hadn't received the check, so I called the company's accounts payable clerk. She indicated that the check had gone out two or three days earlier.

I waited another week and called my sponsor again. He was embarrassed, feeling perhaps personally responsible that I was getting the runaround from his company. It doesn't take two weeks for Kansas City mail to reach Atlanta, and it was clear that something was fishy. He committed to get to the bottom of it all.

He again called his Chief Financial Officer, this time including some strongly worded editorial regarding what appeared to be the old "check's in the mail" routine. The CFO checked their records, noting that the check had in fact been posted and cut over two weeks prior. When he relayed this news, we both concurred that his company would stop payment and issue a replacement check.

He relayed this request back to the CFO, who passed the instruction on to his controller, and thence to the clerk. He called me back a couple days later, in a tone somewhere between flustered and confused. He asked me where I banked.

"Take your pick," I said. "WaMu, Bank of America, Wachovia. I got 'em all. Why?"

He said that when they tried to cancel payment, their bank told him that the check had been cashed by Bank of America. The CFO had a faxed image of the cancelled check. He didn't say it, but his voice implied that, while he was not questioning my integrity, perhaps my short-term memory would benefit from ginko biloba.

While not taking lightly to the implication of senility, I concentrated more on the image of some felon living it up on twenty-thousand dollars that belonged to me.

The check had been drawn to my corporation and therefore, by law, could only be deposited in a business account in that name or registered as "Doing Business As" that name. I was incensed that some postal employee had the audacity to open an account in my name so he could scam my check.

I called the CFO and requested he fax me his image of the check. I was on three missions. I was intent on nailing the perp, so I'd need to get the FBI on it. I was ticked that Bank of America would allow someone to open a business account within their system, regardless of geography, with the same name as an existing account. Lastly, I needed to reposition the theft, shifting the CFO's mindset away from "they stole your money" to "they stole MY money." After all, I reasoned, until I take possession of the payment, it isn't mine—is it?

Concluding that interstate bank fraud fell within their jurisdiction, I called the Kansas City office of the FBI. I reached an agent who, although he wouldn't tell me his name, seemed thorough and exacting in his questions. I concluded that he was entering all my detailed information into an advanced case file management system: names, addresses, telephone numbers, dates of birth, date business incorporated, and bank account numbers. When he asked me the amount of the check, he folded up like a lawn chair. I heard the unmistakable sound of a page being ripped from a lined pad and wadded up into a little ball.

"Oh, we don't get involved in anything under half a million—maybe two-fifty. A federal prosecutor wouldn't get out of bed for twenty thousand."

Incredulous, I could sense onset of the redass. "Wait a minute," I protested. "Somebody stole a bunch of money from me, it involved defrauding a bank, and the FBI isn't interested? Who am I supposed to call then?"

"Try local law enforcement," was his best professional advice.

I tried to envision Barney Fife and the Lenexa, Kansas, police department marshaling a task force to go chase my case. On second thought, perhaps it made more sense to go see my bank. After all, somebody at Bank of America had some 'splaining to do. But first, I'd call the CFO and suggest that, while they undertook efforts to recover the money that had been stolen from them, they go ahead and FedEx me MY check, since I hadn't been paid yet.

He opened the discussion by telling me that the GOOD news was the money was still there. It hadn't disappeared. It was in a Bank of America lock box. He had gotten this information from his banker, who had apparently gotten it from BofA, based on the markings on the back of the check. I wouldn't have known a lock box from a lunch box. At first I thought he was referring to the safety deposit boxes where people stash their diamonds and lottery winnings. He told me it was a special kind of account maintained by businesses for automatic disbursements.

With that, I decided to take my fax copy of the cancelled check, march into my BofA branch, and get my money from them, since they enjoyed handling my business account and it looked like they had my money safely locked in one of their accounts that was called a box. I took my fax to the branch and asked to see the manager.

An impeccably dressed young man named Paul met me in the lobby and led me into his office. He listened intently as I relayed my saga. Maybe there was something to a bank that dresses its managers in suits.

"Shouldn't be a problem," he said reassuringly. "We ought to be able to do an internal transfer," as he picked up his phone and dialed.

I enjoyed watching his obvious annoyance as he poked his way through several layers of IVR and ended up in a queue. We continued making small talk while he listened with one ear to elevator music interspersed with the occasional break-in announcement about loans, CD rates, and the prestige and freedom of carrying another credit card.

When someone answered, he introduced himself with a litany of BofA code-speak about his position and branch location, then explained that there was an account, he thought in the Midwest from the number, into which had erroneously been deposited a check intended for another account, the holder of which was his client and was sitting in his office at that very moment. Squinting at my fax, he recited to his telephone mate the information on the back of the check. He listened intently to a reply from the other side, following which, his face fell.

I suspected that the money had evaporated.

"Well, could you transfer me to them, then," he said disappointedly into the handset.

Still alive, I thought to myself.

Paul went through the same exercise for a second time, poking away at the phone's number pad, waiting in another queue, and apologizing to me for the delay as the music played in his other ear. Eventually, he brought whoever answered through the identical litany. His counterpart must have been in the right department, because Paul entered a series of numbers and clicks into his terminal keyboard, and, voila, there on his screen appeared a photo simile of both sides of my check. I drew comfort from the fact that we seemed to be closing in on my money.

We learned that the account belonged to an office supplies distributor in Chicago. His conversation ended somewhat abruptly when his counterpart on the other end told him that he'd need to be transferred again.

More waiting, menu choices, music and queues. We conversed in small talk as he waited. "Lockbox is a weird end of the business," he said. "It's nothing like retail."

He soon had a live person, to whom he again relayed the circumstances surrounding his call and asked how they would go about making the transfer. I only got one side of the conversation.

"What do you mean we can't do it?. . . . . But they're both our accounts. . . . . .Well it's obviously our mistake. . . . . . Well, we put it in there.. . . . . But it wasn't made out to them.. . . . . . Why can't we? . . . . But it's not theirs. . . . . .Are you sure? . . . . My client is not going to go along with that. . . . . . No, we need to find another way. . . . . Oh. . . . . . Wait, I'll ask him."

Cupping his hand over the receiver, he reported that the lockbox was inviolable. The holder of the box alone could release funds. I would have to contact the holder of the lockbox and ask them to send one of us, either me or my client, back a check for an equal amount.

"Huh?" I said. "So I've gotta go to some company in Chicago and ask them nicely to give me back my own money that they don't even know they have because your bank put it in their account?"

"Well," Paul offered, "you could also ask the maker to issue you another check and have them get the money back from the box owner."

"Wait a minute," I said. "Some Bank of America clerk opened an envelope and took out a check written and addressed to R. H. Melka Associates Inc. in Atlanta and deposited it into an account belonging to Joe's Office Supply in Chicago, and I'm supposed to be OK with that????"

"I'm afraid that's our only option" he replied apologetically.

"But it's not their money. It's mine," I insisted. You guys take money out of accounts all the time. What about all these fees banks are always snatching? Just have somebody poke at their

133

keypad and snatch it. You mean you can't correct your own mistake?"

Paul was flummoxed. Like me, he was a captive cog in the clockwork of megabanking.

I decided at this point to shift to Plan C, reasoning that I could easily get another check from my client. They bore most of the responsibility, having apparently mailed my check in the same window envelope as a payment to their office supplies house; and since they were the supplier's customer, they could comfortably demand return of the misapplied funds.

"I'm sorry, Mr. Melka," Paul commented as he walked me to the door. "Lockbox is a whole different business. They have some weird procedures."

RESTAURANTS, BARS, AND SALOONS: WHY CAN'T THEY GET THE EASY STUFF RIGHT?

If I were in the food and beverage business, I would hire me to periodically swoop in and tell me what I am doing wrong. This is because, having pursued a career in sales management and remaining a bachelor until age thirty-five, I have spent an inordinately large share of my life in restaurants, pubs, taverns, saloons, dirtbars, and joints. Through countless and widely varied adventures, the benchmarks of hospitality excellence have been tattooed across thirty-five years of recollection. Once you experience something good done right, expectations are established. As a consequence, disappointment comes easily when the encore falls short, particularly when the most common disappointments are so easy to identify, address, and correct. I'll never understand why so many bars and restaurants get the simple things so profoundly wrong.

I don't claim to be an expert in the restaurant or bar business, nor would I want the job of running one. Getting the hard parts right would be too frustrating and difficult. But as a customer, I am well beyond expert. I have developed these skills to the level of a fine art. In this pursuit, I have ascertained that most places get the hard stuff right and the easy stuff wrong.

I should also add that I don't expect perfection. My standards, as a customer, are not unreasonable. In fact, my demands are few and small. There are only a few things about restaurants or bars that give me the redass, but those that do are all inexcusable blunders. One simple demand is that they get the beer right. Incredibly, most of them don't.

Beer, like food, is an important part of my life. I could live for a while without it, but would rather not. I don't consume it to excess, despite the claims of some, all of whom are non-beer drinkers. Some would maintain that a few daily beers is excessive. Most doctors tell me that a guy my size can drink beer every day and live to be a hundred, provided he pick the right parents and always wear a seatbelt. And non beer drinkers—what do they know anyway? That's like a nun trying to lecture high school girls about sex.

But before I get into what it is about beer in restaurants and bars that gives me the redass, you should understand the origins and evolution of my beer crusade.

I started drinking beer at age four. My mom and dad would give me a chug or two whenever I asked. I can see them under the maple tree in our back yard, sitting in white Adirondack chairs on summer afternoons, frosty fishbowls on the broad armrests. I'd run up from whatever my sister and I had been playing and ask for a taste.

Obligingly, they would allow me to help myself, reaching to snatch it away as my little head tilted back for a third gulp.

When I was in high school, I worked summers in the DuPont paint warehouse in Cleveland. Not having a car of my own, I took the bus downtown each morning and back to Cleveland Heights each night. I'd get home about six, bone-tired after a day of slinging sixty-pound paint cases onto and off of trucks. With the support and blessing of my parents, I would relax on the screen porch with the Cleveland Press and some icy Carling's Red Cap Ale. We had a pact. I was allowed to drink at home, but must refrain from ever drinking out with my friends. I respected my parents and appreciated their trust enough to honor that pact until college, when it was dissolved by mutual consent and several hundred miles.

There were no women at Notre Dame, unless you considered the St. Mary's girls across the road. They were few in numbers and sheltered in convent-like restriction through the evening hours, so there was little to do, particularly during Indiana winters, other than study or drink beer in the South Bend bars. Alcohol on campus was a capital offense, so we limited our consumption to town. Five bucks secured a reasonable counterfeit draft card—not that you really needed it. Local law enforcement winked at underage drinking. Students weren't allowed to have cars unless they were twenty-one and lived off campus. Logic therefore dictated that all underage drinkers had to walk home; hence any potential risk of drunk driving was self-negating. The University didn't care, as long as we staggered home in groups and saw to each other's safe return by sign-in curfew.

Drewery's was a popular Midwestern brand at the time, brewed and bottled in South Bend. It was universally available in quart bottles for twenty-five cents. You could go on a bender for a buck. But none of us drank Drewery's unless we were really strapped for cash. Quarts of Bud, Stroh's, Pabst, Old Style, High Life, Falstaff's and Hamm's were only fifty cents. Meister Brau and Hudepohl came in big, brown, half gallon bottles for a dollar. I don't think I ever saw anyone drink a twelve-ounce bottle of beer in four years, including Sister Mary Jeanne in my theatre workshop summer class. When she went to Frankie's with Kelly and me after rehearsal, she ordered a quart of Bud like everybody else.

In the South Bend bars, the only viable alternative to the quart bottle was a pint draft, which typically went for a dime. Billy's Coney Island at Michigan and LaSalle sold half-pint drafts for a nickel, but then you felt obligated to buy a hot dog or two, a mistake that normally led to intestinal distress. In grad school, our house brew of choice was Pabst. We'd party on the porch roof of our duplex with a half-barrel, procured for the princely sum of fourteen dollars.

Although I guzzled enough beer through my five years in South Bend to float a Nimitz class carrier, I never advanced beyond the rank of amateur. College was measured in quantity.

My four years as a Naval Officer helped refine my appreciation and hone my taste. Coors was, at the time, only available west of the Rockies. It was a rare and exotic treat. Olympia was a nice addition to the menu as well. Living on Mission Beach, I was introduced to Buckhorn, a favorite of the resident surfer crowd. It sold at Safeway for eighty-eight cents a six-pack. And Anchor Steam, at the other end of the price and quality spectrum, was a whole new world. I also tried my own hand as braumeister, working up a batch in a big plastic garbage can in my bedroom. I used a bit too much corn sugar. Yeast converts the sugar into alcohol until the batch reaches about twelve percent alcohol by volume, at which time the alcohol kills the yeast spores and fermentation ceases. The brew is potent, but flatter than Kelsey's nuts. The trick is to catch it before fermentation stops—say ten or eleven percent -- and bottle the batch quickly. Hence, the last bit of fermentation takes place in the bottle, trapping the carbon dioxide gas and giving you the snappy bubbles and head if you catch it just right — or a series of small explosions and glass shrapnel in your kitchen closet if you bottle too early.

The healthy dose of corn sugar gave this batch an alcohol content of around eleven percent. I bottled it in quarts, having collected several cases of empty bottles and their screw-on caps. I introduced it at a tasting party. It was quite pleasing and people liked it, but everybody got roaring drunk. Two bottles and you couldn't walk. There was one guy there, a fellow Naval Officer of slight stature named Arnie, who'd run the Mission Bay marathon earlier that day. Still a bit dehydrated, he attempted to rehydrate at the party. Arnie pounded three quarts and went from sober to silly to stupid to comatose in a mater of minutes. We all thought he was going to die. Albert Barret's girlfriend was an RN. She checked and monitored his vitals, which alleviated our fears, but not the raging hangover he suffered for several days.

Throughout my twenties, I guzzled with the abandon of a frat boy. Although young people sometimes fail to develop true appreciation for anything, I was eager to try any and all beers that offered a new experience. This was well prior to the burgeoning development of the micro-brew phenomenon, so my exploration was generally limited to imports and regionals. Prior to the micro-brew explosion, I had the uncanny ability to recall with distinct precision the time and place of my first experience with any of the hundred-or-so beers in my recollective library. It wasn't until I had matured, probably in my late thirties, that my taste as beer critic began to develop. Although my evolving discernment lacked the sophistication of a wine connoisseur, I enjoyed the variety of colors and flavors and body, and as far as I was concerned, they were all good.

In addition to an educated pallet, my assessment process had developed two mundane requirements as well. It should be cold, and it should be big, or at least fill the glass. To consistently meet these two criteria, the dispensing establishment must understand their importance. That's not a lot to ask, is it? Cold, big, and consistent? Most places get it wrong, and that gives me the redass.

Having experienced the effect of draft (I know it is more properly spelled *draught*, but I like the simple spelling) beer in a glass or mug stored in a freezer or refrigerator, I established the chilled glass as a baseline standard. I apologize to the beer connoisseurs reading this who correctly maintain that beer should not be icy cold, but rather chilled to around forty degrees to allow the subtle flavors and aromas to fully emerge. And if any of them want to buy me a beer, I'll drink it at whatever temperature they choose. But if I am paying the freight, I expect to make the rules. I like my beer really cold, just north of turning to slush. When ordering a beer in an establishment for the first time, I routinely ask a simple question: do you chill your glasses? An affirmative response triggers the second question. What do you have on draft? I need to hear the breadth of the publican's offering. For me, it is like deciding which tie to wear. I need to review the entire assortment, then choose on the basis of some indefinable, momentary whim.

Oddly, the quality of the establishment doesn't necessarily imply a quality beer selection. One Valentine's Day several years ago, my friend Marcus and I took our wives to one of the most highly regarded restaurants in Atlanta. Marcus made the reservations in October. They had no beer on draft, and only offered four brands in bottles. I almost fell out of my chair. The stuffy waiter responded to my incredulity with some irrelevant commentary about their wine list. He arrogantly claimed it was the most extensive in the Southeast, implying that I might wish to take my business to Cheshire Bridge Lanes, where I could find lots of beers and perhaps bowl a few frames as well.

Somebody once asked what my favorite beer was. I realized, when first challenged with this question, that I had none. If I had to settle on one beer for all time henceforth, I'd probably switch to rum.

It is question number one, however, that takes me, and often my companions, down a critical path which is likely to give me the redass. Frozen or chilled classes are an absolute necessity. If the establishment doesn't chill their glasses or offer to chill one for me, I'll make a metal note not to return. Next, I ask for a beer glass full of ice water, heavy on the ice. It only takes a matter of moments for the glass to cool down to 32 degrees Fahrenheit. Next, I take or send the glass to the bar, or hand it to the bartender myself if I'm already bar-side, and request that he fill the glass that I had to chill myself, thank-you-very-much.

One of my favorite pubs, Churchill's in East Cobb, stores their pint glasses in a freezer chest behind the bar, as do many of the bars in Atlanta. While in middle school, my son attended a tennis clinic two nights a week. Churchill's was several blocks away, and rather than make an extra round trip home and back, I stopped in to kill the two hours and have a beer. I knew when I walked in that it was my kind of place. They had a big bin of peanuts, the shells of which patrons were expected to toss on the floor. The bar was a U-shaped facility, complete with brass foot rail, in the middle of a large room surrounded by booths. Big-screen TV's covered three of the walls at the ceiling. My kind of place. I grabbed a handful of peanuts and strode up to the bar. An attractive, personable, bare mid-rifted bartender introduced herself as L.B. I asked if they chilled their glasses, and she said they chilled the twelve ounce mugs but not the pints. She instantly perceived my concern and grabbed a pint glass, thrusting it into her ice bin in one smooth motion.

"It'll just take a second. What would you like?"

I surveyed the tap handles, and spotting Bass Ale among them, indicated my choice. In a minute or two, she withdrew the glass from the ice, replacing it with another, and drew me the freshest coldest Bass I'd ever had. Her kegs sat out in the open under the bar, the ambient air of which was probably sixty degrees, but the radiator-like coils snaked through a huge vat of ice, emerging at the tap about twenty-nine degrees. I was struck by the establishment's commitment to excellence and L.B.'s customer focus, and I instantly became a loyal patron.

From that night forward, L.B. would immediately jam a glass into the ice vat whenever I crossed the threshold. Some years later, Churchill's expanded their freezer chest and began storing their pint glasses in the freezer as well. And although L.B. has moved on, her replacements, Lisa, Jamie, and Katie, have continued the practice of having an icy Bass working the moment I break the plane.

I learned years ago that it doesn't work to pour beer into a warm glass, then transfer it to a cold one. It's a simple matter of physics—thermodynamics in particular.

I am not a student of physics, or any other science for that matter. I attended a Jesuit prep school, heavily focused on Greek, Latin, oratory, literature, and the humanities in general. I took one course in applied physics, and while I've forgotten most of the formulae, I've retained most of the theories. Don't ask me to explain wave propagation or calculate the friction coefficients of objects at rest, but I definitely recall that there is no such thing as cold, only the absence of heat. And that heat migrates by conduction or convection from the more hot to the less hot.

For this beer drinker, thermodynamic principle decrees that when you pour a cold beer into a warm glass, the heat in the glass is immediately drawn into the beer, raising its temperature commensurate with the pre-pour differential, the mass of the glass, and the amount of beer relative to that mass. If the glass is "heavy" and at room temperature—say 75 degrees—a beer at 34 degrees becomes a beer at 40 degrees before it reaches your lips. This may not matter to some, it certainly doesn't matter to Joe the bartender or Mary Sue the waitress, but it gives me the redass.

Heineken wants you to chill and drink their beer at 45 degrees. That only works for me if Heineken is picking up the tab. If I'm paying for the beer, I'll want it chilled to my taste, which seems to me altogether reasonable. I visited the Heineken brewery in Amsterdam last year. Upon beginning the tour, each guest is given several green poker-chip-like tokens to exchange for quarter-liter drafts at little pubs stationed along the tour. The tour is led in groups of about two dozen, departing their corporate lobby at spaced intervals. Naturally, there are members in the party who are non beer drinkers, so extra tokens are freely available for the asking. The beer, fresh and delicious, is served at Heineken's mandated 45 degrees, or whatever is its Celsius equivalent. Although I felt it was warm, it was fine with me. Heineken was buying.

143

Worse than an unchilled glass is the boneheaded screw-up of serving a beer in a glass fresh from the dishwasher. Any bartender worthy of the profession should know this, but it has happened to me on multiple occasions. By my count, once is too often. A few weeks ago, a friend was visiting from Los Angeles. He arrived around nine PM Atlanta time, and after the four-hour flight with no food, he was ready for dinner. By the time we got to my stomping grounds, all the local area kitchens were closed except for Taco Mac. It might sound like a fast food Tex-Mex, but it's really a local chain of excellent sports pubs, with thirty-eight TVs, an extensive menu of pub food, and, so help me, one hundred and eight beers on draft and two hundred sixty more in bottles. If the beer has a name, Taco Mac stocks it.

It has a great ambiance. Booths and tables in a large dining area, and booths and high tables in the bar area, with a bar that winds its way along the wall of taps. We ambled up to the bar, and I requested an Abita Purple Haze. The bartender, a nice enough young guy, maybe very early twenties, set the glass before me. I picked it up, and the bottom was still HOT. The sides of the glass were cold, having given up their heat to the beer, but the bottom, due to its concentrated mass relative to surface transfer area, held more heat and thus was slower to cool. Here's a tip: At a table, you don't know where the glass has been. If the place offers cold glasses but you suspect that yours was sitting out in the air rather than in ice or a cooler, check the bottom. It's the last part to cool and a dead giveaway. The same applies to the handle on a mug.

"Whoa," I balked upon picking up the glass. "This glass just came out of the dishwasher."

"I know," he replied. "We've been slammed all night and we don't have any cold ones," as though this explanation mitigated the travesty.

"I don't want it then," I said. He swept it from before me with a clear case of attitude. I ordered an iced tea, with a clear case of the redass.

A conscientious, professional bartender would have no more served a beer in a hot glass than one with a turd in it. When I rejected the beer and ordered iced tea, the professional would have said, "Sorry sir. I'll chill a glass down with ice water. It'll just be a minute." This guy didn't have a clue. Is it his fault? Not really. It's the chain's fault for hiring a dim bulb and, given that, failing to train him in the art of perception and customer care.

I've had enough good experiences at Taco Mac that this one disappointment won't keep me from going back. But it shouldn't have happened. There can be no excuse for consciously heating your customer's beer. Think about it.

My daughter recently bought a condo in a new multi-purpose development in a happening area near downtown Atlanta. It features a "Main Street" plaza area like Disneyland, retail under residential. There's a well crafted Irish pub-like restaurant, and Katie was proud to take her mom and me there for dinner. They have a sizable selection of draft beers, and knowing how much I like beer, Katie ordered a me sampler. It came served in a wooden tray with little round cutouts, each holding a miniature mug, about four ounces, of six of their beers. I semi-enjoyed all six mini-mugs through the dinner, not mentioning to Katie that the beer was warm.

As is typical of a well managed establishment, the manager stopped by our table, asking how everything was. I complimented him on the physical plant, the staff, the food and service quality, but I felt compelled to help with the sampler. Explaining the principle of heat transfer, I showed him, by hefting a mini-mug, the mass of the glass and demonstrated that a mere four ounces of cold beer quickly absorbs whatever ambient heat resides in all this glass. Yeah, the glass gets cold to the hand, but you have six little mugs of warm beer before it gets to the table. This was an epiphany for him. He noted that they chill their sixteen and twenty ounce glasses, but not the mini-mugs. He gave himself a virtual slap on the forehead and thanked me profusely for bringing this obvious faux pas to his attention. Katie and Barbara were mortifyingly embarrassed as I led him through my physics lab, but I made the world a little better, and many people, in some small way, will benefit. It's my calling.

The lack of chilled glasses is one easily corrected but common fault. The temperature of the keg refrigerator and the length and insulation of the lines is another. What good is it to pour the beer into an icy glass if the beer's temperature at the tap is 45 degrees? The beer gives up some of its heat to the glass, but this cannot overcome the fact that it wasn't cold when it came out of the tap.

There's an Outback near my home that does an excellent job all around. Importantly, the keg cooler is about fifty feet from the bar. Long lines, unless they are well insulated or chilled, allow the beer to warm once it leaves the keg. Outback runs its lines through a closed circuit conduit with circulating chilled ethylene glycol, so it comes out at the tap near freezing, and they serve it in a frosty mug. Outback understands that their customers want their beer cold, and they have a foolproof solution in place to ensure that this expectation is met or exceeded. I love it.

Dave Howard, a good friend and neighbor, has built a successful restaurant business, starting with his first location back in the eighties. He knows the business, hires good people, trains them well, treats them well with things like full health coverage, profit sharing for managers, 401(k) plans, and he and his wife Anita are really great people to work for. Naturally, Dave's first *Chicago's* prospered, and he opened several more in measured succession, all of which do very well.

In the mid-nineties, he opened a seafood restaurant, *The Bitter End*, around the corner from our neighborhood. My son Chris, fifteen at the time, applied for a job as food runner. Food runners deliver any table's order the moment it comes up, since the server for a particular table might be occupied at another table. Chris couldn't drive, so I dropped him off at night and returned to pick him up at closing. Dave's place had comfortable little bar with a nice selection of draft beers and served them in either the standard, straight sided pint glasses or a curvy, taller, twenty-two ounce glass, both chilled. On opening night just after closing, Dave was winding down and offered to buy me a beer, which we enjoyed at his new, granite topped bar. We both remarked appreciatively how cold the beer was.

Several weeks later, I waited for Chris to finish up at closing, per my usual routine, in the nicely appointed bar area, watching the flat screen. Sipping on a large Sweetwater 420, I noted that the beer wasn't quite cold enough.

I mentioned this to the bartender, and he indicated that he'd straighten it out.

The following weekend, I waited at closing time for Chris to finish, ordering my usual. The beer was still warm. Mentioning it to the bartender, he said that he had called their beer distributor, who was responsible for repair and maintenance of the system. He said that the technician couldn't find anything wrong, but that he'd tell him to check it again.

Next week, same tune. Getting defensive, he told me that the tech told him everything was in perfect order. I couldn't stand it. Cold beer is not rocket science.

I called Dave the next day and reflected on the excellent beer we'd enjoyed some weeks prior, noting that the standard had fallen in recent past. I complimented the bartender for his apparent efforts at responsiveness, but we both agreed that he hadn't gotten the job done. Dave was appreciative, understanding that I wasn't complaining, but rather had his interest at heart. He's also known me long enough to have confidence in my assessment of all matters concerning beer.

Next weekend, I ordered my usual Sweetwater 420 as I waited for Chris, and to my pleasant surprise, it was crackling cold. I called Dave the next day to report our success. He said, "I know. I turned the cooler down a couple notches."

He went on to relay that the bartender was defensive and a more than a little embarrassed that the owner had to get involved, protesting that the distributor's own guy said he checked it and monitored the cooler's temperature, and that everything was as it should be. Here was another case of the guy responsible for customer satisfaction "making the phone call" rather than solving the problem. Dave offered some quick training, advising him that the customers, not the fridge tech, decide whether it is right or not. Customers want cold beer, and it was the bartender's job to give it to them. Any questions?

Bottles are a whole other matter. Bars that know how to serve bottled beer keep it in big tubs of ice, buried up to the neck. Churchill's and Montana's, my other neighborhood watering hole, both keep their bottles in ice. The barbacks carry in a five gallon pail of ice every half hour or so to keep the bottles buried to the caps. God bless them.

The depth of burial is critical. My good friend Mikey and his wife were marrying off their only daughter a couple years ago. The wedding and reception were held in the gardens at Greystone Mansion, a magnificent venue in Beverly Hills that has been used for location shoots in countless films. It was a warm September evening, and the open bar had a big rectangular Rubbermaid tub with a nice assortment of bottled beers. Mikey shares my love of beer, so he got the selection right. Too bad the catering staff got the rest of it wrong. The ice in the tub was only about two inches deep, leaving the top half of the beers exposed to ambient, eighty degree Los Angeles air.

Let's think about this. The bottom half of the beer is thirty-two degrees, the temperature of melting ice. The top of the beer is eighty degrees, the temperature of its surroundings. The cold beer, being denser, stays in the bottom of the bottle. The warm beer, being less dense, stays in the top. There is an isothermal layer between the two temperature differentials that prevents fluid at rest from mixing until disrupted. Naturally, they mix when you tilt the bottle back for the first swig or pour it into the glass. The net result, once blended, is a beer at about fifty-five degrees. Fifty-five degrees is cold enough to kill you if you're tossed overboard in the North Atlantic. Fifty-five degrees is warm enough kill a party by ruining an otherwise excellent Sam Adams Boston Lager.

I went to red alert, grabbing one of the staff guys and explaining that we needed a five gallon pail of ice, STAT. That done, I took the bartender aside and tried to educate her. It was obvious that no one else had ever bothered, and unless she planned on retiring from bartending that evening, she really needed to learn how and why beer needs to be cold. I explained the temperature differential thing, and she hung on my every word with the rapt, if mindless, attention of a dog watching television. My wife was unsympathetic to my mission, lambasting me quietly through tightly clenched teeth for embarrassing our host and injecting disruption into his gracious affair. From my perspective, I'd succeeded in a critical rescue mission. Mikey was a good friend, and I would hope he'd have done the same for me, had the situation been reversed. On the surface, my concern was for the benefit of all his guests, but at a higher, transcendental level, I was driven to right an inexcusable wrong. I should not have been called upon to do it. The catering company staff should know how to make beer cold. They got the difficult stuff right; it was the easy part that eluded them, and probably still does. My guess is that, despite my best efforts, their bartender remains oblivious. My hope is that she has switched professions.

Ω

If a bar or restaurant doesn't have draft beer, I routinely ask whether they keep their beer in ice or in a cooler. It has been my experience that most bottled beer taken from a cooler is not cold. Think about it. Every time the door is opened, warm air is admitted, surrounding the beer in air significantly warmer than the requisite 32 degrees. The more beer they sell, the more time the cooler door spends open. Compounding the problem is the fact that, if they move a lot of beer and have to restock on the fly, the bartender dutifully puts the warm beer in the back of the cooler so he's sure not to serve it to the customer. What they don't recognize is that the heat in the restocked beer, if its temperature is to drop, needs somewhere to go. Some of it goes out the rear vent in the form of warm air. The rest of it goes into the cold beer in front, warming it up. How dumb is that? It happens in thousands of bars across this great land of ours, each and every day.

Recently, I meet some friends at a marvelous restaurant and bar in Atlanta's Phipps Plaza, an upscale shopping mall complex with all the right stores and trendy shops. The ambiance was perfect, with lots of dark-stained oak, beveled and frosted glass, brass fixtures, plush carpets in the dining area, and a beautiful bar that invited beautiful, exciting people to pull up a stool and drop anchor. The food and service was excellent, served by attractive, personable staff. The bottled beer, kept in a handsome cooler under the backbar, was predictably warm. Here was another place that went to major efforts to get all the hard parts right. It's the easy part, like making beer cold, that they screw up. Go figure.

Lest we lose all hope, I should note that there are pleasant, although limited, exceptions to the bottle-beer-from-the-cooler problem. Taco Mac, in addition to their broad selection of draft, maintains several hundred brands of bottled imports and micros in a huge, glass-door cooler at the end of the bar. This industrial-strength device gets the job done, much to everyone's satisfaction. Similarly, Gilly's, a cozy little sports pub in Dunwoody, maintains their imports and micros in a large glass-door cooler. I enjoyed several Stellas and a Red Stripe there just last week, and they were crackling cold. It CAN be done.

A few years ago, I shared happy hour with some friends at a nice little restaurant/pub across from Lenox Mall in Atlanta, The Bucket Shop. They offered a nice selection of draft, but a limited selection of glasses: all warm. My friends ordered drafts, and I made my usual request of a warm-glass emporium: a beer glass of ice water. Once the glass was icy cold and sweating profusely, I drank the water and poured the ice into an empty glass sitting on a bussing tray nearby. I summoned the waitress, handed her the cold, empty glass and requested that she go have the bartender fill it with Newcastle Brown. She promptly deposited the glass on the bussing stand and bellied up to the servers' station at the bar, calling "one Newcastle please." I don't think she heard me pounding my forehead on the table. When she delivered the Newcastle, I politely instructed her in the life-principle of heat transfer. I was trying to help her, explaining why I had asked if they chilled their glasses, why I had ordered the ice water, and why I had asked her to bring my Newcastle in that particular glass. She listened politely, gazing through me with the vapid stare of a mannequin. My friend Alan Factor, embarrassed for me since I am incapable of embarrassing myself, laid his hand on my arm and said, for the table to hear, "Bob. She doesn't care."

Ω

So much for the beer being cold. My second, simple demand is that the beer be big, or at least, full.

At the top of the hill are the Germans and the Mexicans. The Germans have those huge, one-liter Oktoberfest steins. I have a collection of a dozen or so of both varieties: clear, heavy bubbleglass and gray earthenware. The Mexican restaurants in Atlanta earn my respect because most among the dozens located throughout Atlanta offer a thirty-two ounce mug, normally frozen to a glaze, or at least chilled to sub-freezing. Most Mexican restaurants limit their draft selection to Bud, Miller, Coors, their light variants, and Dos Equis. While limited in their selection, they're served ice cold and big. One place in particular, Tijuana Joe's near my home, features a stunning little Columbian bartender named Natalia with the lithe, sinewy body of a ballerina, a winning smile and personality, and Bass and Guinness on draft. This is a rarity—to be able to get Guinness or Bass in a thirty-two ounce mug. I taught Natalia how to swish a little water around the bottom of the frozen mug before starting the pour. This, a trick I learned from Jorge at El Jenete's around the corner, prevents the beer from foaming up in the glass. Natalia has been indebted to me ever since.

Other than Mexican restaurants, the only other Atlanta area bar I know featuring thirty-two ounce mugs is the Fire House. A biker joint in Woodstock, Georgia, Sunday afternoons find the parking lot crammed with dozens of Harleys. An outdoor area and the noisy interior draws everything on two wheels from Rolex bikers to the genuine article, complete with pony tail, Billy Gibbons beard, and the requisite "Born to Lose" tattoo. The Fire House also serves bargain priced thirty-two ounce mugs on Sundays, but only for Bud, Miller, and Coors products. I tried to order a thirty-two of Guinness once and met with prompt rejection from the bartender, an attractive, if slightly worn, woman in her early thirties with an impressive array of colorful body art.

"They're only for Bud, Miller and Coors," she said.

Concluding that price was the obstacle, I offered her what I thought was a.logical way around the restriction. "I realize you'll have to charge me more, but that's OK. I brought money."

"Sorry, the Guinness only comes in pints," she maintained.

"Look," I pressed. "You guys are in business to sell stuff. The more you sell, the better. Charge me whatever you want."

"I can't. I don't have any way of ringing it up," she reasoned

"Well, there are two pints in a quart. Pretend there are two of me and ring me up for two pints of Guinness."

"Oh, OK," she said, fully acceptant that problem solving did not number among her strong points.

I later learned from the manager that they restricted the quart mugs because of a prior experience wherein a big ol' boy had several mugs of premium priced import and, pointing to the promotion banner, expressed uneasiness at the amount he was charged. In a biker bar, it doesn't take a lot to turn a lively discussion into a full-blown riot, so, not wanting another destructive incident, they limited the assortment rather than add a footnote to their promotional signage. I promised not to break furniture or glassware and was granted a permanent dispensation.

When it comes to big beers, I prefer the German bubble glass or Oktoberfest steins to any other beer glass. When frozen, the mass of glass is great enough to keep the beer cold through a whole quarter of college football. I have a collection, most of which I found on eBay, and I maintain several in my freezer at all times. One I acquired at the Paulaner brew pub in Shanghai. A group of my colleagues decided that we'd get together after work at a very impressive little French shop that featured wines and cheeses. The shop had a little sidewalk café, where patrons were free to take the samples of cheese they'd selected and a glass or bottle of wine, enjoy the evening air, and watch the passing people. As it happened, there was a German owned Paulaner Brauhaus around the corner on Fen Yang Road, not fifty yards away. I like wine, but given a nice German lager, I'll take the beer, so I went around the corner to get one. The place was cranking, filled to capacity with a rowdy, robust crowd of beer lovers. I ordered a liter and paid the six bucks equivalent in yuan, then approached the hostess with my stein.

"Is it OK if I take this outside for a few minutes? My friends are having a little party at the cheese and wine shop around the corner. I promise I'll bring it back."

She looked at me like I was from Mars. Her English was excellent, but I'm certain that no one had ever made such a request since Nixon opened China. She said she would have to check with the manager. She returned with a guy who appeared to be in his mid-thirties, although you can't really tell with the Chinese.

He was apologetic but emphatic. He couldn't let it out of the restaurant, being responsible for it. "I am responsible," he kept reminding me.

I wasn't about to chug it, I couldn't leave it undrunk, and I didn't want to abandon my colleagues at the wine shop—nor could I stay in the Brauhaus and let them worry that I'd been Shanghaied. I offered to pay for the stein. The manager was offset by my request, as this was probably a first for him as well.

He said something to the hostess. She responded, and a couple of the staff standing nearby leapt into the fray. They all had their respective say, after which the manager said, "How much you pay?"

I didn't want to get into a bidding war, so I offered the equivalent of about twenty bucks. He said that would be fine, and all the staff participants smiled, cackling simultaneously in Mandarin as they nodded their heads in agreement.

I took my trophy and its contents back to the cocktail gathering, returning to the Brauhaus about twenty minutes later for a refill. I made sure that the front-end staff saw the returning stein as I entered, thereby avoiding another round of barter upon my exit. I figured had no credibility there, or they would have trusted me to borrow it in the first place.

I ultimately trucked that stein halfway around the world, to its current home in the door of my freezer.

At the other end of the glass-size spectrum sits Japan. Beer, like everything in Japan, is small. The Belgian monks taught the Japanese the art of brewing in the early nineteenth century, the history of which is recounted in a lovely museum at the Sapporo World Headquarters. During one of my stays in Tokyo, I toured the brewery and enjoyed samples of each Sapporo offering. The samples, dispensed by an incredible array of self-serve robotic devices that dispatched a glass, filled it, and skimmed the thick, creamy heads from the glass tops, were fabulous. Sapporo, Asahi and other, smaller brewers craft excellent beers, but throughout Japan, the standard glass is only about seven ounces. Their standard bottle, approximately 10 ounces, fills the glass once and a half. Like the Germans, their draft has a rich, foamy head. As a consequence, a draft, which sells for about five dollars, is roughly five ounces of beverage. Talk about a stubby! It's almost enough to give me the redass, but it's their country and that's the way they like it, so I can live with it.

I had stopped for a week in Tokyo after leaving Shanghai. I stayed at the New Otani Hotel, an upscale property in Tokyo's popular Akasaka area. The hotel featured a Trader Vic's among its four or five restaurants, and I set up my after-work base of operations in the Trader Vic's bar. I had gotten to know the manager, a delightful

Japanese American named Nick. He was from San Diego, and we shared many stories about the good old San Diego and how growth has spoiled everything but La Jolla.

It was my third night at the bar, and after downing a tiny beer, it struck me that I didn't have to put up with these wimpy little glasses. After all, I had the liter Paulaner stein in the luggage up in my room, and I was friends with Nick the manager. I beckoned Nick over to the bar and explained my aversion to the tiny glasses, adding that I had a German stein I'd acquired in Shanghai that I'd like his bartender to fill, if it was OK with him.

Nick said sure and had a brief discussion with the bartender. I took an elevator jaunt to my room and returned in minutes. The bartender filled the stein with ice water, swished it around, then drew from his Kirin tap to the liter mark, allowing the thick, foamy head to grace the remaining three or four centimeters of space. It was cold, crisp, and delicious.

Nick and I were soon joined by a doctor from Chicago and an affable Tony Soprano type from New Jersey. The four of us enjoyed some lively, entertaining conversation about a range of subjects as I held court with my enormous beer and enjoyed the admiring gaze of the bar's other patrons. It was like having the only Bentley in the Safeway parking lot. I ordered a refill, accompanied by more lively discussion. Eventually, we all asked to settle up. My tab was eighteen thousand yen, or about a hundred and sixty dollars. Eighty bucks for a beer!

I brought it to Nick's attention, suggesting that it might be a bit much and perhaps his guy missed something in the conversion.

"No," Nick answered consolingly. "We have to charge based on the volume computed by the tap dispenser. It meters and tallies the charge like a gas pump. That's the same as you've been paying all along."

I unquestioningly accepted Nick's explanation, due in large measure to the two liters of Kirin Ichiban that had by now kicked in. I was mellow enough at that point to have bought into anything. I later did the math and realized that I'd been snookered by a factor of two. I don't suspect Nick or the bartender. The Japanese are a scrupulously honest culture. I must have broken or confused the tap meter, and none of us caught the error.

Aside from Mexican and German restaurants and the Fire House, big mugs are hard to find. Most bars and restaurants feature the standard, straight sided, "pint" glasses. Only most are not really pints—or at least you don't get a pint of brew in them. Sixteen fluid ounces will barely fit, crowning the top of the lip such that surface tension alone holds it in the glass. It certainly couldn't be picked up or carried. So when you're served a "pint" in one of these glasses, you're really getting twelve ounces or less. I've had this discussion with numerous bartenders around the country, and the truth comes as a surprise to most.

Next time you're in a bar, pour a standard bottle of beer into one of these glasses. When the foam settles, that's twelve ounces. You'll have less than an inch of void remaining. When the bartender draws you a draft, a foam head thicker than that void means that you are getting less than twelve ounces, or as my beer buddies call it, a "stubby." Stubbies give me the redass. Germany and the UK addressed the stubby issue eons ago. Universally, liter, half-liter, or pint markings etched in the respective glasses serve as the minimum legal measure of a full pour. Any pub keeper worthy of the profession will ensure that the head sits at or above this mark. It is beyond me why our federal, state, or local governments, anal about so many inconsequentials, routinely permit twelve ounce pints or worse. The Huns and the Brits got it right centuries ago, and we're still selling stubbies.

Look at the bottom of your glass. If it is more than three-eighths of an inch thick, it is probably not even a "crested pint" glass, probably something more closely approximating thirteen or fourteen ounces at most. Pour a bottle into one of these. You will be able to tell whether the void will accommodate four more ounces. If not, do the world a favor and call "Tilt." If the menu publicizes pint drafts, the manager will be very interested in learning from you that the state's Department of Weights and Measures could shut down the whole operation, or at least hit them with a fat fine. It's no different than a butcher with his thumb on the scale. That's why they have those stamps and seals on gas pumps. Beer should be no different.

In their defense, every time I've encountered this, the manager was blissfully ignorant that his glasses weren't of pint capacity, amazed that a twelve ounce bottle virtually fills it up. There is only one bar I know of that actually serves a genuine pint in a genuine imperial-pint glass. That would be the Vortex, in downtown Atlanta. Michael and Kristen, the Vortex's owners, got it right, and I love them for it.

The bottom feeders of the bar and restaurant business are those loathsome establishments that try to get away with idiot mugs. These are mugs with a thick lower lip that elevates the bottom about a half-inch off the bar. The bottom glass is almost three—quarters of an inch thick. The sidewalls of the mug, particularly near the bottom, are as thick as your finger. The mug, which sits about seven inches in height, only holds ten ounces when crested over the top. With a normal head on the beer, you end up with seven or maybe eight ounces due to the virtually conical shape of the mug's interior. This really gives me the redass—not so much because it's a stubby and I'm being taken, but because I am grossly insulted that somebody thinks I'm stupid enough not to know it. Worst of all is the idiot mug that isn't even chilled. Thick glass, sitting out in seventy-five degree air, holds a lot of seventy-five degree heat. This is why, not coincidentally, the cooling fins on your car's radiator aren't a half-inch thick. Thin material can't hold much heat, and it dissipates quickly. Thick material heats or cools more slowly, but it also contains more thermal units, all of which end up in my beer. I don't care how cold the beer going into the glass is. The glass becomes cold to the touch because it's transferred all its heat to the beer. If I find myself in an establishment that serves idiot mugs, I order bottles. If the bottles aren't kept in ice, I order Jack Daniels and make a mental note never to return.

I was hosting a meeting for my managers several years ago, and, being young guys with big thirsts and inclined to get noisy, the eighteen of us descended on an Applebee's pub not far from the hotel. The staff put several tables together, and we were seated at once. A cute little waitress started at one corner of the long, rectangular table assembly and took drink orders. Naturally, everybody wanted a beer, of which they had a number of popular brands on tap. Ten minutes later, she returned hoisting a huge round tray with eighteen mugs. She passed them out, and by the time she had distributed the last of them, those served first were empty. I noted with unbridled derision that they were idiot mugs. I asked her if they had larger sizes, and she told me they didn't. I asked if we could have six pitchers then. She said that they didn't sell pitchers. We ordered a second round, and while she was fetching them, I asked the hostess to send the manager over.

He approached the table, and I rose to talk privately with him.

"Look," I said. These are a bunch of sales guys, mostly just out of college, who drink a lot of beer. These little mugs don't cut it. Don't you have any pitchers back there you could use?"
"No," he said. "I can't sell pitchers."

"Well then, can you get some big kettles from the kitchen and fill them up. We can dunk into them like a punchbowl. I'll pay. It's not the money, it's the fact that your girl can't keep up with these little mugs. How about serving us in iced tea glasses and double charge me?"

"No," he repeated. "The mugs are all I have for beer."

This guy was a robot, and I had the redass. My guys started ordering their beers three at a time. We made it through the meal, lousy service, warm beer, and all, but I didn't set foot in the place until years later, when a new franchisee took over and changed the beverage policy.

There is one more thing about a bar that is high on my list of priorities, although not as critical as cold beer and big glasses. The bar must have a rail that encourages one to stand, should one desire. It should also feature tall pub tables, so each person in a group can elect whether he wishes to sit or stand.

I am a stander. I haven't sat at a bar, other than to eat, in thirty years. This presents a slight problem if there is no place to reposition the stool previously assigned to my spot, as anyone passing behind me has to navigate around an empty stool adrift on the floor. My friends all know I don't sit at a bar. When anyone asks, "Is he gonna sit down," they know to say, "He never sits."

When asked why I stand in a bar, I normally explain that John Wayne never sat in a saloon and neither do I. The real reason, quite frankly, is that I cannot drink well sitting down. It feels strange, foreign, and awkward. Standing at a bar feels comfortable and natural. This was, I believe, an acquired condition, contracted over the first fifteen years of my social career and reinforced out of habit such that, after thirty-some years, sitting to drink would feel as weird as standing to take a nap.

It all began when I was in the Navy. My friends and I regularly attended the cocktail parties and receptions that are part of a naval officer's social life. Standing preserved the starched creases in dress whites. Also, there were the weekly pick-up gatherings on Friday night that drew women to the Officer's Club from a fifty mile radius. The crowd milled about like a huge amoeba. I'd go hours without sitting. The place was so crowded, there was nowhere to sit, unless you went out to your car, which was not an uncommon occurrence.

Later on, in civilian life, each transfer landed me in a strange new city with no family, no friends, and importantly, no women. I'd find the most happening area and the most happening bars and go make some friends.

Here was my theory. When a guy gets off his stool and walks any distance to make contact with a woman, if she is warm and receptive, he can remain there and transact, basking in the approving gaze of all present. If, on the other hand, she summarily dispatches him, he is forced to slink back to his home turf, ego scraped and bruised, in full view of the herd. I only needed to suffer this indignity once or twice to conclude that, by being mobile and unencumbered, I could strike targets of opportunity at the bar or anywhere else in the place and simply keep moving if I got a wave off. I wasn't exposed to the public humiliation of rejection.

Six moves as a bachelor prior to settling into marriage conditioned me to drink on the hoof. It served me well, insofar as I found the love of my life and the mother of my wonderful children in a bar. She was on a stool, and I was on the hoof. Old habits die hard, but although I long ago gave up the hunt, I still need to stand when I drink. When I absolutely MUST sit, I hate it.

Occasionally, a client group might want to go to a bar after work. It's not uncommon to pull tables together and everybody sits, like guests at a wedding. This is especially true if there are women in the group. Women don't like to stand. Maybe it's because they wear fashionable shoes that make their feet hurt. So I sit with them because they're clients and I like the people, but I hate sitting at a table in a bar. In such a case, a very acceptable solution is the tall, pub table. Others can sit, I can stand, and we are all level with one another. Any bar that has tables should have tall, pub tables.

To summarize: my bar expectations are that the beer be cold, big, and full, and they make it easy to stand. Not very complicated.

Ω

With restaurants, it's all about the culture and attitude of the staff, the skill to remove food from the grill, and an expectation that I won't have to train their help. In that order.

Restaurants seldom give me the redass. I cut them a lot of slack, because running a restaurant well and getting everything right is complicated and takes a lot of hard work on the parts of a lot of people. People make well-intentioned mistakes, and that's OK. But when people do stupid things that demonstrate indifference or lack of customer focus, it's hard not to get the redass.

Again, as with bars, I don't ask much. When I get seated, I like somebody to come to the table within a minute or two to see if we'd like a drink. It amazes me how often I've waited ten minutes or more before they allow me start spending money. It says that they don't get it on two counts: that the customer begins to grow impatient and the dining experience is already headed south, and perhaps more importantly, that they have failed to impart on the help one very important concept. The place exists to sell stuff to customers. That's the main thing, and they aren't, in the words of Jim Barksdale, keeping the main thing the main thing. When I'm part of a group of four, six, or eight customers just sitting there, waiting for someone to acknowledge our presence and no one seems to care, I get the redass.

If the owner only knew, he would share my sentiment. The owner understands the revenue concept, we can be certain. He's counting the receipts, paying bills, and has long ago concluded that his life is better when customers spend money. The more they spend, the more his life improves. How is it that this concept doesn't filter down to the help? If I owned a restaurant or pub, I would set and enforce a standard whereby somebody was tableside before the chairs stopped squeaking. Get over there and let these people start spending their money!!

I don't really care much about the food. If it's good, I'm happy, as long as the beer is cold. If it's only OK, I'm still happy as long as the beer is cold. If it's bad, I won't come back to eat, but if the beer is cold and they have a nice selection, I may come back and visit the bar if it's convenient and I'm in the area.

The only other thing that gives me the redass is a restaurant's inability to get the beef or fish right on the second try. My routine expectations are that they'll screw it up on the first try, and I am usually right.

Although I rarely eat red meat, when I do I want it to come out, stand up, and moo at me. When I order, I specify "very very rare," qualifying in terms anyone in the business should understand, "cold, red center." As long as the outside is grey or brown striped from the grill, the inside can be raw. I have never, in 35 years of traveling in sales management and dining out with friends, sent a steak back because it was underdone. Some day, it may happen, and if it does, it's easy to fix. Toss it back on for twenty seconds more per side.

More often than not, despite the very clear direction and explanation about cold red center, the meat comes back with a warm or even hot pink center. I slice a small piece out of the center of the slab and touch it to my lip, which is more sensitive to temperature and more couth than my touching it with my finger. If it's warm or hot, they missed and need to try again.

Other than in the very best, often legendary steak houses, I have come to expect that it will take two tries before they think I am serious about "very, very rare, with a cold red center." I get less tolerant when the second attempt is overdone.

Well managed establishments require that the manager deliver the second try. This is not only good PR, but more importantly, for training the staff. If the manager is not intimately aware of every screw up, he can't correct it through training, process, or whatever else it takes to turn a rag-tag staff into a crack strike-force. If the manager doesn't get involved in these miscues, the poor wait staff isn't to blame. They're the victim, caught between the kitchen staff and the guest. I am always apologetic with the waiter, explaining that I realize they're doing their best and I'll be happy to go to the kitchen and train their grill guy on what "very, very rare means."

I was out with a district sales team the night before a sales meeting. We had just hired a new sales rep, a guy right out of college who fit our hiring profile, which was "Just point me at the wall, boss, and I'll walk through it." As the VIP guest and his boss's boss's boss, I was seated next to Al, the new guy. We had a lot of fun with our new kids, and after the second steak came out overcooked, I said to him, "Hey Al, do me a favor and go in there and show these guys how to cook a really rare steak, OK?"

Al gathered up his napkin, laid it on the table, pushed out his chair, picked up my plate, and disappeared into the kitchen. A few seconds later, the chef chased him out of the kitchen waving an enormous metal spoon. When the third steak came out, it was almost raw, and I loved it.

The same applies to fish. To me, swordfish, tuna, shark, and grouper all taste better when moist and underdone. Most places severely overcook fish, because few people realize how delicately delicious rare or medium rare fish really is, swordfish and tuna especially. The increasing popularity of grilled Aahi tuna is slowly changing this, but for years, I routinely told the waiter to tell the cook that my swordfish steak should be grilled about half the time as customary. I'd rather have it undercooked than overcooked. And tuna ought to be cold and raw in the center—just sear it, flip it, and bring it to me red.

"Just tell them to take it off way before they normally would and should be fine," was my usual instruction to the waiter. Then I would cut into it, and more often than not, it would be dry and mealy rather than moist and pink. Back it would go.

We had just promoted one of my young guys to his first management job and moved him and his new bride to Tampa from Atlanta. We expected a lot from our people, and it was understandably hard on their home life. Especially hard, I realized, on a new wife in a strange new city, away from her family and friends. When I visited a market, I always made it a point to take my guys and their wives out to the place of her choosing. I wanted her to know that I understood and valued the sacrifice she made for his career, letting her know that her support was appreciated. Besides, it was a lot of fun, it was on the company, and it showed her that "the company" really did have a human side.

I took Scotty and his new wife Miranda to dinner at the Rusty Pelican. I ordered the swordfish steak and advised, in no uncertain terms, that I wanted it very rare. First time out, it was dry and mealy. Second try was marginally better, but not enough to the point where I could eat it. I apologized to the waiter, asking that he tell the kitchen to simply sear it briefly on both sides and bring it out almost raw. That would be fine. He took attempt number two back and returned with the third try. I cut into it. The waiter, Scotty, and Miranda looked on anxiously.

The center was hot, steamy, and dry enough to be flakey. We all wilted in unison. The waiter reached behind his back, untied his apron, and let it drop to the floor where he stood. Without saying a word, he turned and walked out the front door. I excused myself, picked up the plate, and headed into the kitchen. The manager brought out the fourth rendition, apologizing for the waiter's indiscreet resignation. He said, without going into it, that the waiter had had some issues. But the swordfish was perfect, and the waiter probably pursued a different career.

Another thing most restaurants can't get right is managing to a large group. Go to anything but the finest restaurant with a group over ten and you are asking to be poorly served. It's not the servers' fault. Blame rests with the manager, who probably doesn't go out to eat with a group of eighteen or twenty. I've done it enough and been disappointed enough to know that dysfunction is a certainty unless the manager understands how the cards are stacked against success. Think about it. If five groups of four each enter a restaurant at the same time, they are seated at separate tables, generally among several servers. The drink orders vary in their timing, and the readiness to order their meals will also vary by table. The net result is that the kitchen receives the orders in a staggered sequence, and can quite handily produce the four orders at each table in perfect unison. Everything about this scenario is very different from a single group of twenty.

There is only one way to make this happen with a group of twenty. The table must be split among three or four servers. Otherwise, the drink order is the first disaster. The waiter dutifully circles the mass, recording the orders. The bartender is overwhelmed with twenty orders to fill. By the time the first person who ordered gets his drink, fifteen minutes may have elapsed.

The next disaster is the meal. While the single server records each order, which may take fifteen or twenty minutes, anybody who wants another drink now or in the next ten minutes must wait, chewing ice cubes, until the server finishes the food order, which, if it all goes in together, can be easily managed by an experienced executive chef only if he has been pre warned that it's coming. If the kitchen is surprised by twenty orders that are expected to come out together, things start to unwind and it goes down hill from there.

It's not a wonder restaurants automatically add tips for large groups. It's not that the host is suspected of being cheap. It's that the establishment has learned from experience that large groups tip poorly because the service is unavoidably lousy. If they don't add the tip to the bill, the waiter had to work his butt off and get zilch for his effort—through no fault of his own. The only way to avoid the debacle is to have a frank chat with the manager prior to seating and insist on one server for every five or six guests. If he won't comply, tell him that you, not the house, will decide on the tip based on the quality of the service, and don't surrender your credit card until the tab is presented accordingly.

One other thing really gives me the redass, and that is the disappearance of the server when I'm ready for the check. The problem arises when the table is winding down, there is nothing more to be ordered or served, and the waiter goes out on the back step for a smoke or chills out at the pickup station just as I am ready to request the tab. I anxiously look about the room in efforts to get someone's attention, but servers in other stations, absorbed with their own tables, rarely notice. After ten minutes of aerial dogfight neck-swivels, I punch out and head for the kitchen. Nothing gets the help's attention like a guest walking into the kitchen. All you have to do is get through the door, stop, and stand there looking around. Waiters, busboys, the hostess, even managers, all come out of the woodwork, all joining in a chorus of "Can I help you, sir,"

"I've been trying to pay my check for about ten minutes, but I think my waiter went home," will unfailingly get timely results.

Three parties get hurt in this scenario. The waiter suffers because his tip gets whacked from my usual 20% to 15%. The guests suffer because they had an otherwise nice dining experience end on a less-than-pleasant note. The house suffers because, instead of a crescendo of praise and reaffirmation of the evening's enjoyment as we leave, the burr under our collective saddle, when recollecting the experience, is probably what we'll best remember.

I don't expect perfection, but the simple stuff like making beer cold, meat rare, and the waiter visible isn't a lot to ask. In my experience, it's wrong more often than it's right.

HOTELS: EFFORTS TO TRANSFORM AN INDUSTRY

I am not at all averse to making beds, but one of the advantages of staying in a hotel is that you can leave the bed unmade. Granted, as a boy growing up, I was never required to make my bed. My mother was a regular June Cleaver, trapped at home without a car from Monday through Friday. She kept an immaculate house, hung the laundry outdoors, ironed everything including the bed sheets, and made ample use of the grapes, berries, apples, pears, plums, cherries, and peaches that grew on our property. She even canned her own apple butter, applesauce, and grape jam. Naturally, my room was hospital sterile and drill sergeant neat. I was expected only to place my dirty clothes in the wicker hamper that graced our home's only bathroom. That was it. I would get home from school to an organized, orderly bedroom with freshly laundered clothes and a bed made to such exacting standards that the spread fringe was precisely one-eighth inch equidistant from the floor at all points around its perimeter.

When I left home for Notre Dame in the early sixties, the University was a bastion of testosterone. We were fifty-five hundred frat boys.

There were a few female grad students, but the undergrad population was all male, and we lived in dorms tended to by a corps of Polish immigrant maids, who, like surrogate moms, made the beds, tidied our clothes, and left the rooms in orderly array. I entered Naval Officer Candidate School in Newport, Rhode Island, straight out of South Bend. As a freshly arrived fourth-classmen, I was instructed on day-one how to make a proper bed. Hospital corners, quarter-bounceworthy, tightly tucked, with the pillow properly squared, centered, and "two-blocked" hard-by the head rails. This only lasted four months. After commissioning, whether berthed in a BOQ on the base or stationed aboard ship, enlisted stewards made officers' beds, shined our shoes, and managed our dirty laundry. I got spoiled.

Little wonder that, when I ultimately found myself out in the world, I was unable to function in a life that didn't include a tightly made bed. It was the first thing I did, barely dry, immediately after my morning shower. On rare occasions, if I was running late for a flight or a meeting, I would make it upon returning home. If I returned at midnight, I'd make it prior to retiring. I would no more crawl into an unmade bed than sit on a cactus. Call me obsessive-compulsive.

Hotel beds are always made. Fresh linens, tightly stretched, await the weary pilgrim without exception. But there is a recurring problem with hotel beds that has always given me the redass. Hotel maids are taught to tuck the top sheet and blanket tightly into the mattress, stem to stern.

For me, entering a hotel bed is ritualistic. I don't like my top sheet tucked except at the bottom. I want the top sheet and blanket free to billow and float along the sides. Think about it. You can't even get into a bed with the top sheet and blanket tucked into the sides unless you slither in from the headboard like a python. Minimally, you have to pull the near side's topsheet out to enter, and in doing so, it takes the bottom sheet along with it. Hotels rarely have fitted bottom sheets. Efficiency and cost control demand flat sheets all around, for procurement and inventory control, ease of folding, dispatching the housekeeping carts, laundry maintenance, and who knows what else.

With the bottom sheet untucked, an active sleeper will invariably wake up at 3 AM with the sheet wadded up, mummy-like around your legs or worse, in a bunch somewhere off to the lower corner of the bed, effectively putting the sleeper on a bare, cold, slippery, mattress. Given all this, I would find myself turning on the light, getting out of bed, re-stretching and retucking the bottom sheet, effectively making the bed from scratch before I could get back in and, hopefully, return to sleep.

Avoidance of this nocturnal adventure could be gained only by tightly re-tucking the pulled-out sheet upon initial entry. Now, from a cosmic perspective, this really isn't that big a deal. But I shouldn't have to do this—night after night after night. Remedy was simply a matter of the hospitality industry gaining awareness of the problem.

I took it on as one of my missions, to show hotel housekeeping staffs how stupid the topsheet tuck was and helping the industry get it right.

I developed the practice, when untucking the topsheet and blanket on both sides of the mattress, which naturally pulled the bottom sheet along with it, of calling housekeeping and asking them to send a maid to the room because my bed was unmade and I hadn't yet been in it. When the maid arrived, I professed helplessness, demonstrating that all I had done was open the covers in effort to get in, and the bottom sheet tore loose from its tuck. I was universally successful in leading her to conclude that I was weird, but also gaining her agreement that this was an unacceptable condition. As they re-tucked the bottom sheet, having experienced the problem firsthand, those that spoke English readily agreed that the standard bed-making practice didn't really make any sense. This acknowledgement, however, invariably came with an explanation that they were simply adhering to the hotel's housekeeping standards. They were forced, at risk of dismissal, into the full tuck. But they almost all gave me their commitment to explain the matter to housekeeping management.

I went through this exercise for a few years in dozens of Marriotts, Westins, Hiltons, Sheratons, and any other hotel that maintained round-the-clock housekeeping staffs. I was, however, unsuccessful at converting the industry and ultimately abandoned my Quixotic pursuit. "Thy sea is so great and my boat is so small." Beaten into capitulation, I went back to retucking the errant bottom sheet myself, always accompanied by a recurring case of the redass.

This went on for a number of years, until I began to encounter, with increasing frequency, a condition even more troubling than the topsheet tuck. It was Westin, I believe, that started the practice a few years ago. Remember their "Heavenly Bed" campaign? Poster ads in airport and TV spots on shows geared to frequent travelers? The differentiation was short lived, as the whole concept of pillow-topped mattresses, fluffy down comforters, and a dozen pillows and bolsters and shams have become *de rigueur* at most upscale properties. I'm guessing that women must like them, because I can't imagine any straight guy preferring all the foo-foo to three pillows and a bedspread. Screw the ambiance. I cannot get a decent night's sleep in these things.

I am warm blooded by nature. My anatomical thermostat is calibrated higher than most men's and is off the female charts, hot flashers and self-immolators excepted. At bedtime, I strip off the fluffy down comforter and all but two pillows, tossing the great bundle of fluff into a pile as big as a Buick. Later, having sunk into the fluffiness of an opulent, pillow-topped mattress, the fiber down, or whatever they stuff into those things, forms an insulating cocoon around enough of my surface area to trap a significant amount of heat. Since the heat cannot escape, my surface and then core temperature elevates and I am unable to get comfortable, subjected to tossing, turning, and cursing whoever came up with the harebrained concept of fluffy mattresses. I usually end up with the redass, watching late night infomercials in a chair until I cool off.

Another thing about hotels that gives me the redass is all the crap they tell the maids to lay out on every horizontal hard surface in the room. The desk, dresser, nightstand, and coffee table are routinely festooned with plaques, pads, booklets, cards, magazines, those ridiculous little stand-up plastic things with the sign inside, room service menus, telephone instructions, Movies-On-Demand promotion, and the ubiquitous Welcome communiqué from the General Manager.

Naturally, the first thing I do after lowering the thermostat and finding the TV remote is gather up all this flotsam and dump it in a huge pile in the most remote corner of the room. Now, I won't lose my wallet, keycard, pen, or money clip amid all the clutter.

On a two-night stay, guess what greets me upon my afternoon return. Right. It's as though the flotsam gnomes have snuck in and put it all back. God that gives me the redass!

Fortunately, these minor annoyances are largely eclipsed by the customer-focused attitude and friendly nature of most hotels' staff. Hotels recognize their need to compete, so all of them try to hire personable desk, bell, and wait staff. And they train their new hires to understand their roles in making the guest feel welcomed, wanted, and well-tended. In my experience, Marriott and Ritz are best at this. Shortly after checking in at the Orlando Airport property a few years ago, I noted that my room had a faulty thermostat. The room would not cool. I dragged my luggage down to the elevator and into the lobby, where I encountered a black-vested young man toting a flipchart easel—likely on his way to a meeting room. He noted, probably from the scowl I projected, that something was wrong and asked if he could be of help. I told him of the problem with the thermostat, and he grabbed my carry-on bag with his free hand, asked for my room key, told me to go get a drink at the bar, and said that he'd take care of getting me moved and come find me with the new key. When he showed up in the bar a few minutes later, he told the bartender that my beer was on the house because I'd been inconvenienced. My luggage had already been delivered to the room. I loved that guy.

Later that night, I purposely sought out the resident manager to commend this young man, and the manager, a personable Brit who accepted my invitation to join me at the bar, told me that it was

Marriott's policy to empower their people to accommodate the guest to whatever extent they could. They, along with the Disney corporation and too few others in the service industry, train their people from day one that their job is to make the guest happy. His exact words, were, "We tell them, if the guest's request is in any way reasonable, give it to him, even if it costs us some money. It will come back ten-fold." I've never forgotten that, and he is right.

But hotels are not all sunshine and roses. Naturally, they are all in business to generate revenues and turn a profit, and they are pretty good at this as well. I'm not exactly a cheap person, but since clients normally pay all my travel expenses, I treat their money with respect. Besides, they pay a lot for my services, so I try to hold down expenses. About ten years ago, I noticed an increasingly popular practice in hotel dining rooms to very smoothly boost the breakfast check. Immediately upon being seated, a fresh, smiling young lady, two frosty pitchers in hand, would appear tableside and bubble a cheery: "Good morning. Would you care for ice water and some fresh-squeezed orange juice?" One's natural inclination is an equally cheery, "Yes. Thank you." Cha-ching! At about six bucks a glass, the orange juice revenues have to be five times what they would otherwise be if sold off the menu. I think this tactic must have been presented at some hospitality industry convention, because it seems that every chain jumped on the gravy train simultaneously. Not a big deal, but I don't like it. I feel like the mark, caught in the crosshairs of a con artist who assumes I'm some rube too stupid to recognize that I'm being taken. A minor case of the redass, but I can live with it.

Another way, although less prevalent, that hotels try to surreptitiously get into your pocket is the old coffee-to-go ruse. Many fine hotels put an urn of brew and a supply of disposable cups and lids in the lobby for guests' convenience, but some force you to go to the checkout area of the dining room, or worse, sublet a kiosk in the front lobby to some outside third-party source. If I'm paying two or three hundred dollars to stay in their hotel, they ought to at least spring for a cup of coffee—especially one that I have to serve myself. Anything but free coffee to go in the morning gives me the redass, and I don't mind letting somebody know about it, either.

In the mid-eighties, I regularly stayed at the Executive Park Marriott in Charlotte. As was my routine, I'd grab a cup to go in the lobby on my way out the door. One such morning, the table with the urn had vanished. The bellman, noting my bewilderment, pointed to the dining room. The table, urn and all, was placed in the waiting area just outside the entrance, along with a nicely printed sign announcing "Coffee, $1.50"

I bristled. This was unconscionable. When someone has provided something gratis and then decides to charge for it, we feel victimized. Particularly insofar as so many hotels provided serve-yourself coffee-to-go as a free amenity. (Remember, this was twenty years ago, prior to Starbucks. A buck and a half for coffee was pretty steep.) But I paid and, that evening, duly noted my sentiments on a comment card I retrieved from the flotsam pile in the corner of my room. The card was pre-addressed to Bill Marriott himself.

On each subsequent stay, I'd reiterate what I thought about charging a buck-fifty for self-served coffee to go, citing my experiences elsewhere. It got to the point where the tone of my comments had developed a patterned ring: "Hi Bill, me again. Charlotte's still getting a buck-fifty for the coffee. When are you guys gonna wise up? Bob"

After about a year of monthly visits and comment cards, I was pleased to note that the table had returned to its rightful place in the lobby, with no card announcing price. I drew a cup and went immediately to the front desk, asking to speak to the manager. In a minute or two, he emerged from "the door behind the counter" and was directed to me by one of the staff. He extended his hand, introduced himself, and asked if he could help me. I explained that I simply wanted to commend him on returning to the complimentary coffee practice, adding, "You must have had a lot of complaints."

"Not really," he answered, "but there was this one guy. . . "

This adventure gained enough notoriety throughout Marriott Corporation that it found its way onto the pages of USA Today. So much for my fifteen minutes of fame.

I don't mind paying for what I get, but I expect to get what I pay for. It hasn't happened often, maybe half-a-dozen times, but when it does it gets my complete attention—especially in the middle of winter. Have you ever had total lack of hot water? Maybe some people can get by without a shower in the morning, but I'm not one of them. My hair, what little remains, develops a serious case of bed-head overnight. Also, I like putting clean clothes on a clean body. I feel grubby all day otherwise.

I was in the Sheraton in Braintree, Massachusetts, one winter night and arose to no hot water. Not even warm. Both valves served up ready-made ice-water, sink and tub. I called down to the front desk and was told that a "boiler went out" and the whole hotel was in cold water mode. I took a frigid Navy shower (wet down quickly, kill the flow, lather to one's heart's content, then rinse off quickly). When I checked out, the desk clerk presented my itemized statement to review for accuracy. I pointed to the room charge, noting "If this is your hot shower rate, what's the cold shower rate?"

She chuckled, as though I were kidding.

"I'm dead serious," I said. Hot water is worth something, I didn't get any, so I really think it should be taken off the bill."

She disappeared for a moment, and came back with her boss. He asked me how much I felt the hot water was worth, and I told him to decide what he thought was fair, adding, "Look at it this way. How much would it take to get you to go stand in a cold shower, right now?"

He knocked fifteen dollars off the room, which was fine by me, but his clerk should have been empowered to make the call. In fact, he should have told her to offer it to every guest at check-out that morning.

One particular aspect of the hospitality business really gives me the redass. That is the practice of the guaranteed reservations. As the guest, it is my expectation that a "guaranteed reservation" means there will be an empty room available when I show up. I have, in effect, paid for the room when I provided my credit card number. I have the option of advising the hotel of my intent to cancel the arrangement prior to the deadline time, usually six PM the night of arrival, but unless I cancel, my expectation of a room is reasonable, right?

Not always. If the hotel has something less than 100% occupancy rate on the evening of your arrival, you can count on a room. If they have filled every room but yours, and a weary traveler shows up at, say 10 or 11 PM, the hotel can and often will roll the dice. If they rent your room and you don't show, they win, since you and the other guy are both paying for the same room. Cha-ching! If they rent your room and you show, you lose, as your guarantee of a room is meaningless. The hotel isn't going to charge you, but it's not going to berth you either. Instead, it will "walk" you, usually finding alternate accommodations nearby and providing you transportation and some monetary compensation—normally paying the alternate hotel for your room that night.

Up until the eighties, when the reservation and check-in process involved a paper-based system, the desk clerk could, with a frown, anxiously finger through the reservation folios, unable to locate your reservation.

"I'm sorry sir, I don't see any record of your reservation," she says consolingly and with thoughtful concern as she stares directly at the page with your name. I once had a travel agent who had been in management at a major hotel chain tell me that they would do this "all the time" if the situation arose.

Now, with the process computerized and printable, on-line access and a confirmation numbers," the clerk is less able to bamboozle you, but he'll squirm and apologize and "walk" you just the same. . .if you let him.

I had an 8:00 am meeting with a senior executive at Gillette a few years ago. His office was in the Prudential Tower in Boston. Attached to the Pru is a marvelous Sheraton property that affords interior access to the Tower lobby. You walk through a retail concourse for about two minutes and you're there. It's very convenient and a first-rate establishment. I've enjoyed this and other Sheraton hospitality for years.

The night prior to this particular stay, the air traffic system all along the eastern seaboard was hopelessly scrambled, and my flight was delayed, landing at Boston's Logan Airport well after midnight. I then stood in the taxi line for about twenty minutes. Arriving at the hotel about 1:15 am, I found myself again in a line at the front desk. There were three people ahead of me and a fourth being serviced at the counter by the single night clerk, both of whom were involved in a subdued but clearly serious conversation. The night clerk would periodically disappear for a few minutes into the door behind the counter, reemerging for more intense dialogue. Their business concluded, the next in line advanced to the counter. More intense dialogue, more popping in and out of the mysterious door like a possum, and another 15 minutes until resolution.

I took my cell phone from my jacket and dialed the hotel number displayed on my itinerary, hoping to reach the switchboard. I heard the desk phone ring with my call. The night clerk excused himself from Guest #2 and answered. I asked for the switchboard operator, and he told me that he was it. I asked to be connected to the resident manager. My intention had been to get his corporate ass out of bed and tell him to come down and help this poor kid, obviously challenged by some serious difficulty, take care of his customers. The clerk told me that he was the senior manager on property. I told him never mind, and to hurry up and get to me since I was standing there in line ten feet away. Glancing up, he fixed on my face with a look of grave concern. It was now about 1:40.

Guest #2 and the next two people in line each had their turn at the counter, and their respective discussions and door-ducking concluded, each was led away by a bored looking bellman, bag in hand. I sensed with Guest #2 what awaited me. Our rooms had been sold, and this kid was in crisis-apology mode. As this had happened before, I remained calm. I had the situation under control.

"Melka," I intoned, slapping my Amex card on the counter.

"I'm sorry, sir," he said softly with a hang-dog expression of genuine sincerity. "We have no vacancies, but we'll be happy to transport you to one of our other Sheraton properties and accommodate you at no charge."

"But I have a guaranteed reservation."

"I'm sorry, sir. Here's a map of our other properties in the area, all of which have rooms. Do you have a preference?"

I withdrew my itinerary from my pocket, laying it on the counter upside down for him to read. "No, I'm staying here tonight. Look. This is me," I explained, pointing to my name. "This is your hotel—right here," I indicated, tapping my index finger on the "Sheraton" emblazoned on my travel itinerary. "Look-here is your phone number. And see, here is the date—Tuesday night. Here is the guarantee number. This is where I'm staying tonight," I explained, pointing both hands at my feet for added emphasis.

"But sir, you don't understand. We have no rooms."

"No, YOU don't understand. You have lots of rooms, and one of them is mine. Your problem is that you let somebody else into it. Now you have to get them out of it, because I am here and I want my room."

"Sir, I can't do that."

"I understand that you have a problem. It's not my problem. It's your problem, and you have to solve it. Now tell me which room is mine and give me my key. It's late and I'm tired and I want to go to bed."

The poor guy went into melt-down, a portrait of abject impotence and frustration. It was clear I was not moving, and he had nowhere to go. He said nothing. He just stood there and squirmed, glancing at my itinerary, then at me, then back to the itinerary, then to me.

"Excuse me, sir," he sighed, withdrawing into the possum hole. I envisioned him on the phone to his newly awakened boss, asking for ideas or advice. He reappeared, having melted a few more inches in stature.

"Sir, we have no rooms. I can see to it that you are comped at another hotel of your choosing, but you cannot stay here to night. I'm sorry."

He was drowning, and it was time to throw him a line. "Do you have a rollaway bed?" I asked.

"Yes, sir."

"Do you have a meeting room with a bathroom?"

"Yes, sir, we have several."

"I'll also need a television, a phone, a clock, and a 6:30 wakeup call.

His color returned and he swung into action. In a matter of minutes I was unpacking my bag on the brightly patterned carpet of a veritable aircraft hangar, with men's and ladies' rooms in the corner, a phone strung on a fifty foot cord, a television on an equally long coaxial cable, and an orange electrical extension leading to a clock

on the floor next to my tiny rollaway. The price was right, but I wasn't happy about the long walk over to the wall panel to turn off the lights.

The following morning, I took my Dopp kit to the second floor elevator lobby and waited for anybody dragging a bag. I nailed the first guy who appeared, asked for his key with a brief explanation, and got a quick a shower

The point, which mustn't be lost in the absurdity of the situation, is not that you can brow beat a desk clerk or night manager into submission. The point is, the situation should never have come to this. Insofar as I never saw a bill, I can only guess whether or not my Amex statement for the month would have showed the room charge if I hadn't made it to Boston that night. But we shouldn't have to go through these hassles.

On the flip side, I have had an unblemished success record getting hotels to forego the charge on the rare occasions when I couldn't show for a guaranteed reservation and couldn't cancel by the six PM cutoff. If the hotel has any vacancy, you've got a strong case to ask to have the charge waived. They didn't turn away any business because of your booking, and the front desk manager will concede your point that charging you is unjustified. Of course, if they are full, it's another story. They are right to charge, and I feel an obligation to pay--as long as "my" room stays empty. I tried to get the guarantee charge waived one night after I missed the last connection in Dallas and got stuck there. I called the hotel in Tampa and asked if they had any vacancies, anticipating that they did. I would then lobby for a break, since I was paying for a Dallas room anyway. They were full. Go to Plan B. I then asked them to ring Mr. Melka.

"He hasn't checked in yet," was the response.

"Yeah, I know," I said. "I'm him. What room are you holding for me?"

When the front desk manager wouldn't give me a number, I told him that unless he did, which I might call periodically through the night, I felt that he should waive the charge. He said he would, and that he could probably sell the room later that night.

And if an experienced traveler like me is subjected to these tales from the twilight zone, imagine what happens to the meek, who may as well abandon all hope of inheriting the earth. My son, Chris, is a prime example. As a freshman at Auburn, he and three of his friends planned a trip to Panama City Beach for spring break. If you've never been to PCB in March or April, stay up late some night and channel-surf up in the high numbers. You'll eventually come across a Girls Gone Wild infomercial, and that will give you a clue. The place is crazy.

He and three of his friends booked a room at the Holiday Inn on the beach. Due to high demand, hotels require that the revelers pay for the entire stay well in advance of the arrival date. I can live with that.

The boys had been there a few days when Chris called me in a condition somewhere between demoralized and incensed. The hotel had provided them each a color-coded wrist band of the one-way variety. Once it was attached, it could not be removed without self-destructing. The purpose was to serve as an admission pass to the hotel, intended to prevent mass parties or unpaid guests from freeloading. The self-destruct element was intended to prevent selling or giving the band to others. Well intentioned, this was in the interest of maintaining civility for legitimately paying guests and protection of the property—assuming everything worked as planned. Problem was, the inferior bracelet was crafted of plasticized paper that quickly eroded and failed in salt, chlorine, UV rays, beer, or some combination thereof.

Chris reported that two of his roommates, only one day into the adventure, had lost their bracelets in the pool or surf or hot tub or some steamy, sweaty bar. Importantly, they hadn't sold them or given them to others; the bands simply suffered catastrophic failure and were lost. The innkeeper's contract security force wouldn't allow the kids back on property until they coughed up another two hundred dollars apiece for replacement bracelets. By now, they'd ponied up an extra $400, which had seriously eroded their collective beer, food, and cover-charge kitty. To make matters worse, one of the boys had been denied re-entry the previous night, during which a Panama City police officer had been shot and killed in a traffic stop not far from the hotel. Sleeping on the beach was prohibited, so this kid was forced to seek refuge in the parking lot, locked in a car, fearful of being mistaken for the killer-at-large by a squad of rightfully vengeful, trigger-happy cops.

Chris relayed the problem to me, seeking advice, more money, and some help with the uncooperative front desk attendant. He asked me to intercede on their behalf, or as he termed it, "Dad, you need to Bob these guys."

Chris knows the rules. You don't just take an establishment on because somebody gave you the redass. You must be in the right, clearly and decidedly so. The opponent's position must be un-defendable. Strategically, you must be in a position of overwhelming superiority. You must be positioned to escalate the matter to persons of significantly greater power, and you must be able to adequately articulate the situation in brief, factual, un-emotional terms such that the higher power immediately embraces your position and acts accordingly in the interest of remedy—and then some. Remember, once they simply make you whole, you're not even. There's the matter of time, energy, and angst that must be readily acknowledged and compensated. The hotel's assault on these four spring break revelers was unacceptable, so I suited up for combat.

I've stayed in enough hotel rooms to notice, through boredom or curiosity, the tiny print on the cards typically displayed on the inner surface of the door, either above, alongside, or adjacent the peep hole. These cards outline the rules governing the innkeeper, the rights of the guest, rates, and other guidelines that appear to have been crafted sometime in the nineteenth century. The salient points, loosely defined, are that:

- The innkeeper and the guest each have certain responsibilities

- The guest may occupy the room for a period of his choosing
- The innkeeper may not cast him out
- The guest must pay for the room
- The guest must behave and not break things

None of the rules governing lodging say anything about a paper wrist band.

I am not a lawyer. In fact, I'm right up there alongside Shakespeare regarding lawyers, but I am fully in favor of adhering to the law. These boys had paid for the room weeks in advance. In my view, they were entitled to occupy the rooms for which they had paid. I suspected that denying any of them access was a violation of state law under the statutes governing lodging. In addition, I was developing a serious case of the redass.

I called the hotel and spoke with a very businesslike gentleman with an Indian accent named Patel, as one might have guessed. He curtly advised me that the boys had been notified of the $200 lost bracelet clause, had signed a waiver to that effect, and that there was nothing to discuss. Mr. Patel wasn't moving, so I asked to speak with the manager.

Soon, a Mr. Ferry, Rooms Division Manager, relayed the same position and faxed me the acknowledgement and acceptance forms signed by all four boys, along with four photocopies of their respective Georgia, Alabama, and Wisconsin driver's licenses. He provided a compelling explanation of the hotel's need to restrict access to paid and registered guests, citing the likelihood that less draconian measures had resulted, in prior years, in sixteen kids to a room and parties of legendary scope, debauchery, and property damage. I concurred with him that he and his staff definitely had a challenge maintaining order, but their challenge was not my son's problem. They obviously needed a more effective solution than their inferior wrist band, but that while he and some of his best people worked on what that might be, I expected him to return the $400 he had extorted from my kids and provide me his personal guarantee that they would have unrestricted access to the room they'd paid for. After all, he had photo copies of their drivers' licenses; all he had to do was provide these to his rent-a-cops, who could ensure, as the boys freely came and went, that they were, in fact, my kids. I waited through several seconds of silence for his commitment of compliance.

He dispatched me like a Jersey mob hit. The signed waiver was his gotcha, and I was just some voice on the phone. The conversation was over.

Now I really had the redass. I pounded a couple Red Bulls and went online, securing the contact data for the Florida state agency governing lodging. I learned that restaurants and hotels came under the jurisdiction of the Florida Department of Business and Professional Regulation. I completed their on-line complaint template, secured a case number, printed a copy of my submission, and got the switchboard numbers of the network affiliate TV stations for the Panama City area. I called all three, leaving voicemails for news directors at the first two and managed to connect with the third. I relayed the situation to the news director at WMBB, suggesting that it might make a nice filler piece—how local businesses were profiteering by unscrupulously targeting the visiting spring breakers. She was more than marginally interested, asking me for the boys' cell phone numbers. She would call Chris and arrange some on-camera interviews.

Lastly, I called the Atlanta based switchboard of InterContinental Hotels Group, owners and marketers of the Holiday Inn brand. I asked for their top marketing guy, Steve Smith, and reached his assistant. She was experienced enough to recognize a thunderstorm on the horizon, expressing genuine interest and concern, but noting that this was a matter more properly addressed within the Holiday Inn group itself rather than the parent corporation. She gave me their number along with the name of Stephanie Hess, a senior marketing executive.

I emailed Stephanie a factual recap of the situation, along with my editorial perspective on this revenue-enhancement scam and an overview of the groundwork I'd laid to remedy the situation. I summarized with a request that we try to arrive at a solution less complex and burdensome than a formal investigation by the state of Florida and some very negative media coverage. She agreed that the $200 was larcenous and would look into it. She took all my information and called back in a couple hours. Chris called shortly thereafter, noting that Mr. Ferry had refunded their $400 and gave them each a promise of replacement wrist bands as needed.

I let it lie, but I shouldn't have had to endure this crucible. Life is too short to have to fight these battles.

There are two other things that Hotels just don't seem to get right. One is setting up a meeting room. The other is understanding who owns the food.

For the first eighteen years of my career, I worked in two large corporations. As I advanced through a career in sales management, I attended, then conducted, then attended, usually as guest observer by this point, a lot of meetings. After abandoning the corporate dreadnought, I formed and continue to run my own consulting company. Much of my work today involves leading workshops and seminars in, you guessed it, hotel meeting rooms.

I have concluded that people who set up meeting rooms don't have to attend meetings. If they did, they would recognize the proxemic differences between having lunch at a table for thirty and participating in a meeting for thirty. To me, it is patently obvious that being confined to a designated space at the same table in the same chair for eight hours over three consecutive days unleashes special demands. Unlike lunch, people bring stuff to meetings: binders, notebooks, backpacks, briefcases, laptops, PDAs—you name it. People do work at meetings, requiring that they occasionally move this stuff around. People also move their chairs around at meetings, turning them sideways, or pushing back to cross their legs. If you don't provide people enough space, the meeting is destined to be less effective, less productive, and ultimately return less business value to the company paying the bills.

I used to solve the problem by showing up at my meeting room early, then calling the meeting coordinator or worse, grabbing some black-vested guy trying to set up the buffet breakfast. We'd have to reconfigure the tables, which, in a U-shape configuration, would need to be re-draped. A hassle, but necessary in order to spread out the chairs and give everybody adequate room. This was the high-stress fix, because attendees would invariably start wandering in for the continental breakfast while I'm directing a crew of roadies in how to set up the room. Now I use the low-stress fix. If I'm having a meeting for twenty-five, I tell the coordinator to set the table for thirty-five, then I simply amble in and remove ten chairs.

I also have a bit of an issue with food. My meetings have always started early and included a buffet breakfast in the back of the meeting room. I really used to get the redass when the hotel would come in and remove the remaining Danish, bagels, soda, juice pitchers, yogurt, and whatever else was provided. My sales teams generally consisted of mostly guys, aged 22 to 26, many of whom were college athletes, most of whom could eat like a backhoe. If there was leftover food, these guys would start wandering back to the table around 10 am and graze on whatever remained.

But having food remaining was not always easy. I have actually been told more than once that it was "hotel policy" to remove the buffet breakfast materials at 9:00. They needed it out for the coffee break, which was scheduled for 10:00, at which time they would sell me back the same bottles of soda and Perrier I'd already paid for once at breakfast. Same with the unopened assorted flavors of yogurt in the ice tubs. It's a lot like the business model of a hooker. You got it, you sell it, and you still got it! What a great country!

And those twenty-dollar pitchers of orange and grapefruit and cranberry juice that were two thirds full? Gone in sixty seconds, unless we blocked the door. My administrative assistant was forever explaining to the hotel meeting coordinators that we, not the hotel, owned the food. Removing the grazing rights might work for a Mary Kay convention, but not for a gang of young sales guys suffering from lack of sleep and recovering from hangovers.

POLITICAL CORRECTNESS, DIVERSITY, AND OTHER HYPOCRISY

My son called me last year from Auburn, claiming to be in a bit of a bind. He had less than a week to submit a research paper for completion of a writing course, and he needed help choosing a subject. The assignment was to take a position on a topic that could be argued from diametrically opposed sides, cite compelling points that support the writer's premise, backed up with documented background supporting each point.

Chris and I had discussed the absurdity of Political Correctness on several occasions, and he shared my view. I suggested that his thesis be "How Political Correctness is Ruining America." He thought that would make a great paper, and one into which he could pour his enthusiasm. I suggested several sources for research, citing the traditional proponents of rational, conservative thought. You know, the standard cast of right-leaning characters: Rush

Limbaugh, Sean Hannity, Michelle Malkin, Bernard Goldberg, Neal Boortz, Laura Ingraham, Bill O'Reilly, George Will, the ever-incendiary Ann Coulter, and other conservative pundits who would likely support his premise and offer facts to back it up.

He wrote a great paper, including an abundance of factual, quantified information, along with anecdotal evidence based on writings and quotes attributed to his sources. He sent me the paper in draft, and I made a few suggestions regarding syntax, grammatical structure, and punctuation. I thought the finished product was outstanding.

The paper came back with a D. His professor had three or four vitriolic comments, scratched in red ink with enough force to gouge her desktop, one of which, penned alongside a quote from Ann Coulter, was "She has an agenda !!!" Well, yeah . . .and you don't? Turns out the professor was rumored to be a raging militant feminist, which Chris had failed to tell me at the outset. He had a B going into the final and came out of the course with a C, but he learned a valuable lesson: always pay lip service to Political Correctness with academicians in positions of power. The climate of orthodoxy demands that one be as hypocritical as they are. Universities would like us all to think that they are bastions of tolerance and diversity, where ideas and opinions, however controversial or divergent, are open to expression, exploration, discussion and healthy debate. And they are, unless the opinion or ideas expressed challenge feminist, gay, racial, or liberal agendas. Then freedom of speech is discouraged, physically suppressed, or met with appropriate retribution. Just ask Harvard's ex president, Lawrence Summers.

My stance on Political Correctness is this. It is stupid, dishonest, and hypocritical, all of which give me an enormous case of the redass. The Speech Police on some of our loonier campuses, not content with eliminating expression they find distasteful, have formed squadrons of Thought Police and even Look Police. Simply Google "college rules leering," and you'll find that it's not uncommon for a male to incur disciplinary action for "looking in a leering or suggestive manner" at a woman. Fortunately for us all, this nadir of silliness is generally limited to college campuses, mostly in the Northeast and West, but the Speech Police have expanded their jurisdictional boundaries to society in general.

I first encountered a form of "forbidden speech" as a young sales guy with Procter & Gamble. P&G was operating under a consent decree imposed by the courts in the well-intentioned effort to preclude monopolistic business practices. P&G was big and successful and growing, and the FTC in the fifties and sixties was paranoid in its fear of a second generation of robber barons. So as latter-day trust busters, the Commission imposed certain restrictions on perceived threats to ensure healthy, aggressive competition. The company was directed to divest of Clorox. The Commission didn't want us getting too deep into Mrs. Beasley's laundry basket. Curiously, P&G managers were forbidden to use certain words in correspondence that might arouse suspicion, among I'm not sure whom, that our competitive impulse was actually directed against our competition. (You couldn't make this stuff up.) I don't recall all the words, but "dominate" and "defeat" and "franchise" when referring to a brand were stricken from our vocabularies. I remember my boss telling me that that term could be interpreted as an assumption that Tide or Oxodol had some exclusive and inviolable, God-given position. I was a liberal arts major, and I thought it odd that there were some perfectly acceptable English words that could not be put in writing. If only I'd known at that time where the world was heading.

The first time the Speech Police actually busted me was back in 1996. I was working with a group of FedEx sales executives, and one of their top HR executives was also in attendance. I was illustrating a sales concept with a "war story," one of the vignettes commonly drawn upon to bring transformational principles to life. The idea I was expounding was conceptual, and I needed an example to help get it across. I told a story of how, when I was a small boy, my dad invited me to ride along with him one day over Christmas break as he called on his customers. I explained that he was a salesman for DuPont's automotive finishes division, and that all I knew at the time was that he "sold paint." I went on to tell the story, which was well received and clearly elucidated the key points.

Shortly thereafter, I released the group for a fifteen minute coffee and bathroom break. The HR executive approached me immediately as the room emptied, taking me aside and cautioning me that "the word 'salesman' doesn't exist in our culture. We say 'salesperson' or 'sales professional'."

My first thought was to propose a lexicon to accompany the session, to include the definition and correct pronunciation of "salesman" and other new and abstruse words to help expand the group's vocabulary. Prudently, I restrained my cynical proclivity and thanked her for the heads-up. .

The HR executive was a lovely, bright, personable woman who was obviously good at what she did, but the thought that a word should be stricken from the lexicon of life because it is gender specific seemed dumb and silly. They could call their sales people any label they chose, but my dad wasn't one of those. He was a salesman. That's what his card said, that's what he called himself, and that's what the rest of the world called him. Neither she nor any other language revisionist was ever going to change that. But, insofar as they were the client and I was the consultant, I blanked the word from my own vocabulary for the remainder of the engagement. In retrospect, I guess we were even, since the term "HR" didn't exist in my dad's culture either. It wasn't until the eighties that the Speech Police changed it from "Personnel."

For some reason, the Speech Police determined after several hundred years that gender specificity in common parlance was a bad thing, thrusting upon us silly, awkward terms like "chairperson," "lineperson," and "waitperson." A stewardess got her panties in a wad some time in the eighties, so the Speech Police roared to the rescue and made everyone call them "flight attendants." The world of waitressing also got a collective wedgie and now, wherever co-ed staff is engaged, they are more properly deemed "servers," as are the males. Remember the term "police woman?" Angie Dickinson stared in a hit TV series of that name in the seventies. That's what they were called. I'm not sure when, but that term, along with policeman and fireman, have all fallen from grace, having been replaced by the genderless "police officer" and "firefighter." Someone explained it to me once that this movement was to ensure, for reasons she was unable to define, that any word referring to any role had to be "inclusive."

This condition has degraded to the point where its perpetuation is now assured, thanks to the PC indoctrination of our kids throughout their K-through-12 education. The three principal publishers of textbooks all have Speech Police/PC committees, the sole function of which is to review the text and imagery of any new edition, prior to final production, to ensure the total eradication of gender specificity, (e.g. waitress), or representation of any traditional gender roles. Among the forbidden imagery is that of a female cooking in the kitchen or pushing a vacuum. (I am NOT making this stuff up.)

I have two questions that I've not yet found anyone able to answer.

1. Who started all this, and why?

Thought leadership generally originates with a single person. Some person actually had to conceive this foolishness. I'm inclined to think it must have been a person with a vagina—probably an itchy one—who determined that gender-specific words were bad. I say that because I'm a guy, I know a lot of guys, I know how guys think, and I can tell you that that none of us would take offense at a commonly used descriptive, appropriate for use in civilized or mixed company, that identified us as male. Why then did whoever she was choose to launch this crusade?

Who was she and what was she thinking? How was she able to mobilize a viral cadre of supporters to force an entire culture to fold like a suitcase and accede to a silly and unnecessary change in our language? What did she, and as they grew, her storm-trooping force of Speech Police, have as weapons of intimidation to corral us all into compliance? Throughout the seventies, otherwise rational people ran and hid at the moaning of these harpies, tossing them whatever they demanded through the doggie door in hopes that they'd go somewhere else. The United States Weather Service functioned fine using women's names to identify and track hurricanes. Then in 1979, some women from the Speech Police went on a tear and posted notice that men's names were to be used as well. Why did the Weather Service buckle so readily? We'll probably never know, but by that time, the genie was out of the bottle.

Complicating this scenario is the fact that, while gender specificity was considered by these, and ultimately by "us," as a bad thing, the Speech Police obsessed anally over the mandated use of the awkward and clumsy "he and she," or "his and her," in any and all written and spoken language across American business and academia. For years, literary and spoken English used the non-gender-specific "him" or "he" to collectively refer to a non-specific person of either gender. It was working fine until the Speech Police came along and started writing citations and bashing skulls whenever anybody failed to include the redundant, gender-specific "she" or "her" along with the gender-specific "he" or "him."

So on to my second quandary:

2. <u>Which is it? Is gender specificity a bad thing or a good thing?</u>

Rules demanding both are now enforceable under the arcane statutes governing Speech Law. Don't say "stewardess" because people might figure out that she's a woman, but always say "her" along with "him" when you're talking about any "them" so everyone is certain that she MIGHT be a woman. So which is it, or have proponents on both sides formed a truce and agreed to campaign for their respective new rules without crossing each other's jurisdictional boundaries? And, as Butch Cassidy so often asked the Sundance Kid, "Who ARE these guys?" My guess is that the provocateur in this case was also a woman, as I cannot imagine anything that could motivate a guy to come up with such a set of harebrained rules.

Equally harebrained and unnecessary is the now-mandated term "Ms." While most believe it to be a relatively recent invention of the women's movement, it has its origins in the early 1950's as a convenience for writers of business correspondence, most of whom were men. It was initially proposed to save us from having to research, if unknown, whether or not the addressee was married. It was a helpful shortcut that kept us from looking lazy or stupid.

Ironically, its purpose was hijacked by feminists in the seventies as a form of rebellion against something, about which one can only guess. The feminist requirement of the term Ms. was once explained to me by a female friend.

"Ms," she said, "is so nobody can tell whether you're married or single. With 'Mr', nobody can tell about a man. It should be the same for a woman."

Huh? Why would a woman be so concerned about knowledge regarding her marital status? She wants to get hit on? She doesn't want to get hit on? She's married on the sly and doesn't want her boss to find out? I have tried to ascertain any rational reason for this "Ms" anomaly and relate to it from a man's perspective. It is utterly beyond me. My friend, an otherwise bright woman, was also unable to adequately explain WHY "it should be the same," beyond that "it just should."

I know some guys who take off their wedding rings in the hotel bar, but none of them could give a flip about how they are addressed in a letter. I reasoned that perhaps women didn't want to feel deprived of anything men had, and I guess that pretty well summed it up, because she said, "Yeah, kind of." Maybe it all started with penis envy.

Until somebody can clear all of this up for me, I've adopted a middle ground. I'll call whoever opposes gender-specific terminology whatever they want to be called, and I routinely address business correspondence to females as Ms., but I refuse to participate in the awkward and clumsy "he/she," "his/her," "him/her" protocol. If you are one who lives in fear of the Speech Police, you have probably noticed the glaring absence of "his-or-her" or "he-or-she" throughout this book. I am content with the universally adaptive male pronoun, applying it to both genders in collective circumstances. Readers please take note: unless the pronoun refers back to a specific male, it should be interpreted as applying to both genders.

My position is not founded on misogyny, nor am I in any way anti-feminism. I am anti-foolishness. Before a herd of militant feminists stampede and boycott retailers selling this book, I must be clear about one more thing. I am a feminist. I have always been in absolute support of the sensible, worthy causes addressed by feminism. I am a proponent of equal pay, equal opportunity, abortion-or-not as a personal choice, eradication of workplace and academic sexual harassment, subsidized child care, and other important matters of fairness and social conscience. And I acknowledge that, even after fifty years of feminism, women STILL don't always receive equal treatment under the law, and it gives me the redass

Take, for example, the recent (January, 2009) case of seventeen-year-old Norma Guthrie and seventeen-year-old Alan Jepsen, both charged on successive days in the same Sheboygan, Wisconsin, court with sexual assault. Each had consensual sex with their respective opposite-sex, fourteen-year-old partners. Alan did his girlfriend and was charged with a felony, which carries a maximum penalty of twenty-five years, whereas Norma did her boyfriend and was charged with a misdemeanor, the penalty for which is nine months maximum. Sheboygan Assistant District Attorney Jim Haasch, the alleged male chauvinist pig who filed both complaints, is on record as having no problem, when questioned, with the unequal treatment Ms. Guthrie received. Curiously, the National Organization for Women, whose high-decibel shrieking regularly accompanies high profile cases where women are denied equal treatment, has been silent in its avoidance of vocalizing their contempt for this incident of blatant inequality.

Supportive as I am about gender-blind equality unless inappropriate (e.g. men as bra fitting-room attendants, women as NFL linebackers), episodes like the Sheboygan caper remind me that REAL gender equality doesn't exist and probably never will.

This is because men have given up all hope of ever getting dealt a fair hand. But, hey, we can live with it. Guys are pretty good at shaking it off; it's an ability we developed through sports. I know a couple guys, sons of good friends, in the San Francisco Fire Department. They each tell of a period in time, several years ago, in which numerous fully qualified white males were passed over for hire in favor of clearly less qualified candidates in the interest of "diversity." "Clearly less qualified" may sound like a subjective, un-empirical assessment, but when anything other than the highest test scores, aptitude, and physical strength and conditioning are determinants of who gets hired, "less qualified" is not a supposition. It is a certainty.

One cannot deny the reality that it happened, despite the fact that it really doesn't make sense. The department actually chose to hire women who couldn't carry 200 lbs. down a ladder over men who could. But admittedly, what could one expect in a city with a Police Chief named Heather, a Fire Chief named Joanne, and whose city council elects a Police Commissioner named Theresa who was founder and CEO of the city's pre-eminent dildo emporium, *Good Vibrations*? (You couldn't make this stuff up.)

I am suggesting that a principle has rooted itself in many organizational environments where agenda and Political Correctness, rather than excellence, drive the decision process. Naturally, the beneficiaries accept it because the deck is stacked in their favor. White males put up with it because they're not crybabies and whiners, preferring to just suck it up and maybe get the redass.

At the end of the day, blatant, openly acknowledged discrimination doesn't bother me as much as ridiculous, unexplained rules of behavior, some of which are gender-based but many of which are gender-blind. I am a curious sort, and I am troubled by society's inability to explain the reason and origin of these rules.

As a proponent of equal-opportunity intolerance, I wonder about the eradication of common, non derogatory terms that were, until recently, perfectly acceptable. When I was a kid, nobody played cowboys and Native Americans. When and why did we have to stop calling them Indians? Recently, a High School in Ohio cancelled, a week prior to opening, its production of Agatha Christie's *Ten Little Indians* after eight weeks of rehearsals because, according to NAACP, the title contained a "racially charged word." I don't know whether to be outraged or entertained. Whining and hand-wringing over the word "Indian" in the title of an American classic is stupid and serves only to further marginalize this once-respected, worthwhile organization that did so much for so many. It seems now that every time NAACP makes the news, it's because they've shot themselves in the foot. I shake my head and chuckle at its silliness, but whoever on the school board or district administration capitulated to these loonies is no laughing matter and they deserve to be fired. What does an episode like this teach our kids?

And the looniness continues. The Speech Police have recently announced that they now don't want us referring to Indians as Native Americans. Lately, the only officially sanctioned moniker is First Americans. Universities are flopping like mackerels as they change their program and course catalogs from Native American

Studies to First American Studies. Can anybody help me understand what was wrong with Native?

Not long ago, a common term in referring to persons of far Eastern extraction was Oriental. Now, we all must say Asian. I am bewildered by the same line of unanswerable questioning. Who first decided this, how did they get the word out (no pun intended), and most importantly, why? Again, I'll call anybody whatever they want to be called, not to avoid offending, (unless Oriental is derogatory or insulting for some reason unknown to me) but to avoid the looks and disapproval of others when using the "O" word. But please, somebody tell me why.

To me, "bum" was a perfectly appropriate moniker when referring to a guy who chose not to be a productive member of society. I say "guy" because women were never called bums. A woman bum was called a beggar. Then, along came the Speech Police to enforce the use of "homeless" when referring to either. Even more troubling, the term homeless now has less meaning, insofar as it is applied equally to well-intentioned, upstanding individuals who may have, through no fault of their own, fallen on hard times, as it is to shiftless parasites who'd rather live in a box and dive in a dumpster than carry their share of the load and take up the cloak of society. Talk about being offended! If I were a REAL homeless person, I'd get the redass being lumped in the same category with bums.

It is clear to me that the bums weren't the originators of this particular word-banishment campaign. They had neither the ambition nor the organizational skills to mobilize a coordinated change management effort. Bums would make lousy Speech Police. So if not the bums, who was it that re-wrote the lexicon and why did they do it?

I don't mind calling people whatever they want to be called. That doesn't bother me in the least. What bothers me is that I can't understand why and how this all happened; so the fact that it did happen, and now I should feel pressured to conform to a ludicrous set of speech rules gives me the redass. If someone would only explain this to my satisfaction, that particular strain of redass will probably find relief.

The situation has recently reached new lows now that the Speech Police have infiltrated the Obama White House. Some idiot has banned the term "war on terror," "enemy combatants," and apparently even the word "terrorism," which Janet Napolitano, our new Secretary of Homeland Security, prefers to call "man-caused disaster." This is so dumb it's scary.

Let's say a Marine platoon is ambushed and catches some guy after a thirty-minute fire fight. He was part of a gang of Taliban, all packing AK-47s and RPGs. Sure looks and sounds like "combat" to those Marines. And the guy with the AK? Seems like "enemy" might fit the bill, if only for the reason that he and his pals were trying to kill all our guys. And these self-proclaimed jihadists who strap on a boom-vest or drive a carload of C-4 into a market or fly 767s into buildings? I don't know about you, but it seems to fit most folks' definition of terrorism. And if it's not a war, I know a bunch of military intelligence professionals who will tell you it sure acts like one.

Madam Secretary thinks she can pick up a turd by the clean end. Somebody needs to take her aside and explain it to her.

I could go on killing trees with more examples of Speech Police brutality, but you get the idea. Avoidance or even prohibition of insulting and derogatory speech, racial or ethnic slurs in an academic or work environment for example, is noble and needs no explanation. Prohibition of innocuous language is not only stupid, but frightening. It has ominous First Amendment implications. The whole concept of being afraid to offend without reason or cause is likely to get worse. It's a certainty that none of the speech rules will ever be challenged, unlike a bad football call that can be reviewed and rescinded for being wrong or stupid. I'm afraid that we are stuck with the rules presently in place, and that more bad calls lie ahead.

Frustration of my intellectual curiosity is only one of the things about Political Correctness that gives me the redass. The other is the fact that it's founded on hypocrisy and nobody seems to care.

The PC police have decreed that almost everyone has the right not to be offended—sometimes to the point where the offended party is entitled to bring civil or criminal action against the offender. I read yesterday about a college student who has come under criminal indictment for a hate crime, having flushed a Qur'an down a dorm commode. The student is clearly a rude jerk, but no more a criminal than the rude jerk who displayed "Elephant Dung Mary" in the Brooklyn museum or the idiot artist who gave us "Piss Christ," a crucifix positioned in a beaker of his urine. I believe the three are equally offensive, but none are worthy of criminal action. Interesting, however, is the blatant hypocrisy in the fact that offending Christians has become routine and acceptable. The increasing disappearance in schools, civic locations, retail, and the workplace of the word Christmas is evidence of the PC Police at work, but you will not see them demanding that everyone cease all reference to Ramadan and start calling it "The Holy Month of Mustn't Eat Before Sundown."

I get the redass every time somebody tells me Happy Holidays instead of Merry Christmas. I had a client recently who invited me to their "holiday party." This was an office with two Jews, no Muslims, and about seventy Christians. Give me a break! Why do we put up with it? Doesn't this give anybody else the redass? It's not that I'm offended. I hate it because it's stupid and hypocritical. Why is everybody so afraid of offending every group or class other than white males or Christians? That is not a rhetorical question. I really would like someone to explain it to me. If it cannot be explained logically, then we should all want it to stop and climb aboard the campaign bus to turn it around.

A good example of PC's hypocrisy is evident throughout the world of Advertising. In any ad featuring an assemblage of business people, whether print or video, the mix is certain to include both genders and at least one person each of Asian and African American extraction. If the group exceeds six, you can count on someone suggesting Hispanic origins as well. Such a mix is factually accurate and representative of society. It also reflects a Politically Correct image of diversity in the workplace--unless, of course, the protagonists are to be portrayed in a negative light. Then the group will, as a matter of certainty, be comprised exclusively of white males. A couple years ago, there was a public service anti-smoking ad directed at young smokers that portrayed "big tobacco" as a police line-up of impeccably pinstriped, white shirted, power tied, middle aged white men. No women, no Blacks, no Asians, no evident Hispanics. Was this an aberration, or may we suspect that Political Correctness is not consistently and equally applied? Let us look further.

Washington Mutual, prior to its meltdown, had an excellent, highly memorable campaign featuring a corral of two dozen "traditional" bankers, similarly dressed in black pinstripe suits, white shirts, and power ties. The spokesman for WaMu was a pleasant young Black male in the traditional open collared blue shirt that had become

WaMu's uniform. The bankers were all moronic, bumbling, greedy, foolish, old, white men, hardly reflective of the politically correct image of diversity among an executive group.

In the course of an unrelated conversation with a WaMu executive from their corporate office in Seattle, I mentioned this ad campaign and its obvious departure from the standard PC composition of an executive team that has ruled Madison Avenue since the seventies. Her response was, "We thought it was kind of humorous because it fits the stereotype image of the stodgy old banker." I had to agree with her, but it's a blatantly obvious example of the hypocrisy in the application of politically correct standards.

Let's imagine how "kind of humorous" we might find a mobile security equipment commercial that featured the stereotype image of the carjacker with a corral of two dozen young Black males dressed in baggy crack pants, oversized athletic jerseys, knit caps, sideways trucker hats, hoodies, and untied sneakers. We'll never know how "kind of humorous" it might be because we'll never see it. Political Correctness is alive and well, so long as the target is not a white guy.

The fact is that white men don't command exclusivity in the world of stupid, traditional bankers any more than African American men command exclusivity in the practice of car jacking. But it is also a fact that whenever a criminal, moron, buffoon, or villain is portrayed in TV advertising, it WILL be a white male. He has become Madison Avenue's piñata.

Brinks Home Security, recently rebranded as Broadview Security, has a series of TV spots, very effective in their execution, that play upon the fears of law-abiding homeowners, particularly women. If you watch mainstream cable TV, you've probably seen the ads.

There's the young couple in bed, their first night in their new home. There's the woman at the kitchen sink shortly after her husband leaves for work. As he drives away, he nods a friendly hello to the hooded jogger who stooped to tie his shoe in front of the home, then runs up the front walk and kicks in the front door. Then there's the young woman getting ready for a date, in her bathrobe, sorting through the closet, deciding what to wear. There's the single mom, who thinks the rattling at the front door is her teenage daughter coming home, until her daughter appears at the top of the stairs, at which point, the hooded intruder bursts through the front door. There's the teenage girl left home alone, who, after seeing her parents to the door, hears a few moments later the rattle of the doorknob and assumes her folks had forgotten something. There's a lurking, hooded thug, observing a mom and young daughter through a fence as they enter the house from backyard play. Then there's the turbo version, where TWO villains are scoping out a young professional on a treadmill through the glass patio door of her upscale home. In every case, the surly intruder gains entry by splintering the woodwork, which immediately triggers the alarm klaxon. The perp exchanges a dark, panicked stare with the terrified female, does an abrupt about-face, and scurries off into the night as the phone rings. It's the Brinks/Broadview Security guy, ever vigilant, inquiring as to the well being of his subscriber and promising to "send help right away."

A highly predictable scenario, clichéd in every aspect but one. It is patently inaccurate and misrepresentative of reality. Eight of all eight intruders in these commercials are white guys. This is no less ludicrous a departure from the truth than if the perps had all been Asian women. A recent Department of Justice report on the demographics of felony defendants in large urban counties found that black males accounted for seventy-one percent of all felons charged with robbery. Truth has taken its departure because of

Political Correctness and fear of intimidation. Let's imagine if even two or three of the eight perps had been African American. My guess is that whiners and crybabies, probably lined up behind The Reverends Jesse and Al, would have called for a boycott and created enough drama to sink the whole campaign, if not the company.

The purpose of advertising is to draw attention to your product, create brand awareness, and achieve memorability among the target audience. Just don't try to attract attention by maligning any group, accurately or otherwise, with any common stereotype—unless, of course, the group is white and male.

The story repeats itself for the mugger of the fur-clad diva in the PETA spot, the bank robber in the eTrade spot, all six drunk drivers in the public service spots with the cars, beer to the window sills, sloshing up to a DUI checkpoint: all white males. Look at the historical proliferation of "stupid husband" commercials. It's become its own genre. Have you ever seen a "stupid wife" commercial?

There is prolific commercial misrepresentation of white males, their dominance assured in any role manifest with ill-wrought behavior. Naturally, the converse is equally predictable. Favorable roles are routinely misrepresented in the other direction. Take, for example, the world according to Microsoft.

I am a licensed pilot, and I enjoy the challenges and incredible realism of Microsoft's latest release of *Flight Simulator X*. This program is way, way, way beyond video games. It is an entertainment and learning tool that replicates the experience of flight down to the most minute detail. There are 18 different aircraft, with sound, performance, and flight characteristics that accurately mimic the genuine article, from Boeing 747 down to the lowly Piper J-3 Cub. The cockpits of each are stunningly accurate in their layout, with working switches, levers, instruments, radios, navigation devices, etc. The user can select from an atlas of thirty-thousand airports, worldwide. Time of day, season, and weather conditions are selectable and all startlingly realistic. Ground topography is presented in highly accurate detail, down to the roller coaster and Ferris wheel across from my old condo on San Diego's Mission Beach. The accuracy and detail of the programming is mind-boggling, with one glaring exception: the cockpit seats--or, more specifically, the gender and race of the butts planted in those seats. When selecting an exterior view of the aircraft and cycling the viewpoint around to the plane's nose area, a user can zoom in on the cockpit window and get up-close and personal with the pilot and co-pilot. The findings are anomalous but predictable.

According to FAA data, in January, 2006, there were 31,885 licensed pilots in the US, 16,449 of which held commercial certificates. Women, while comprising 6% of all pilots, command only 2% of those with commercial rating. Similarly, fewer than 2% of commercially rated pilots are African American. Do the math. Women and minorities represent less than five percent of all US commercial pilots. The universal laws of mathematics dictate that white males, therefore, comprise the remaining 95 percent.

Math and reality not withstanding, some revisionist bleeding-heart at Microsoft has reengineered commercial aviation, deciding that a 50-50 split is more to her liking. So Microsoft boosted the female and African American share of commercially licensed pilots twelve-fold, from reality's 2 percent respectively to Utopia's 23 percent each. When looking into the cockpit window from outside the commercial airliners, that's the mix you'll see. How and why did Microsoft get it so blatantly wrong?

As answers, we can confidently eliminate sloppiness, ignorance, stupidity, lack of attention to detail, carelessness, or mind-altering chemicals. Product management at Microsoft is none of these. This purposeful misrepresentation of reality, amid a mind boggling compendium of accuracy and megabytes of infinite detail, represents a combination of Political Correctness, fear of offending the whiners, and the lopsided socio-sexual/political agenda of the granola culture that thrives in and around Seattle. I'd like to be proven wrong, but I can't get a straight answer from Microsoft. When I was finally able to connect with a product manager in Redmond and explained I was writing a book and had a question for him, he was most congenial and cooperative, until I asked it. The curtain dropped abruptly, and he announced, "We are not going to participate in your book." I was able to utter, "Well, you just did" prior to his hanging up on me.

You can't blame the advertising or the media/communications industries for their blatant misrepresentation of white males. If the revisionist media simply told the truth, the vocal minority of crybabies would create an uproar, including threats of boycotts, public relations catastrophes, and the indelible stigma of being labeled racist, sexist, or both. Sponsors, mindful of the volatile climate of racial and sexual politics, prudently adhere to the unwritten laws of Political Correctness. Untroubled by their own hypocrisy, sponsors know that the white male lobby will remain silent simply because there is none. There are no "white-male activists," wringing their hands over "men's issues" or "images demeaning to men." Imagine for a moment the idea of a university catalogue offering a "men's study program." The very concepts, ludicrous in their implied self-importance, don't exist because we would see them as silly, trivial, and unnecessary as their prolific feminist equivalents. Try to imagine any group of white guys you know organizing a protest over the depiction of their race or gender in commercial media. We're more concerned that the beer is cold and that we can find the TV remote, both of which are, in the overall scope of things, of greater importance than "images demeaning to men-of-no-color," which I have concluded is the Politically Correct alternative to well-worn fem-speak such as "images demeaning to women" and "women of color."

I have a wife and daughter in the American work force, but even prior to their exposure, I decried sexual harassment and, as a manager, held everyone in my organizations to strict standards of behavior in its avoidance. I have always maintained that is is counterproductive, cruel, and simply wrong. My position was solidified, well prior to the explosion of lawsuits, mandated training, zero tolerance, and anal-retentive HR bureaucrats' prohibition on telling your secretary that you like her new haircut. Then came the obligatory training films, required viewing by all, in which, the poorly acted perpetrators were universally. . .you guessed it. . .white males. It's a good thing we've got thick skin and ESPN.

This politically correct silliness, while hypocritical, unnecessary, and vigorously enforced by the Speech Police, does not, thankfully, operate with the force of law. That franchise is monopolized by the government officials who, with their squadrons of bureaucratic mosquitoes, get and keep their jobs because otherwise rational people have elected them to positions of power. A good example of your government at work is seen in the ubiquitous effects of the Americans with Disabilities Act.

Some of the mandates make eminent good sense, like handicap parking, access ramps where reasonable, and restroom accommodations in public facilities. But give weak minds the latitude to make enforceable decisions and you have inmates running the asylum.

My friend Mel the Architect tells of the warehouse he designed for a client in the Northeast. An enormous facility for which he won a design award, the loading dock featured a long row of dock doors against which eighteen-wheelers slid into position to load and unload their incoming and outbound cargo. Thermal efficiency dictated that the rear of each trailer be sealed to the dock's respective opening, which precluded exterior movement beyond two proximate trailers, therefore between every two trailers was a "people door." Since each was an elevated entrance to the building, each also had to have a properly angled ramp in order to accommodate a wheelchair. Mel brought to the sanctioning body's attention the fact that over-the-road truckers don't use wheelchairs.

Try to imagine a paraplegic climbing into and out of a big-rig cab, checking tire pressures at truck stops, and inspecting the airbrake couplings between tractor and trailer. It's ludicrous.

Of course, the doors served in an exit capacity as well, so one might conclude that chairbound dockworkers could use the ramps whenever they want to roll out into the yard and check out somebody's new Peterbilt. But dockworkers, like roofers and firemen, don't work in wheel chairs either. I recall the forty-foot trailers, stacked chest high with sixty-pound cased of paint, that I loaded and unloaded every summer through college. The thought of doing that job in a wheelchair is beyond ridiculous. The fact that the ramps would never, under any circumstances, be utilized was totally immaterial.

Government agencies thrive and self-perpetuate on the issuance of ill-conceived, meticulously articulated stupidity. You need look no further than the airport security lines, where agents are instructed to give no higher scrutiny to the young Middle Eastern male than the grandma from Des Moines. Rather than training screeners in profiling the characteristics of the dominant threat, i.e al-Qaeda operatives, your government bureaucrats were instructing our last line of defense to confiscate toenail clippers from airline pilots who, once beyond the security screeners, had their very own red crash-axe mounted on the cockpit wall—not to mention their very own flying bomb in the form of a fully fueled 767.

Ω

Mel's architectural practice shifted to healthcare, where today he focuses almost exclusively. He designs hospitals and medical centers. Every floor features nurse's stations, the counters of which are mandated at a height of thirty-four inches, in accordance with disability requirements, or Title 3 as it is known. He has lobbied repeatedly for permission to design the counter tops at a height to accommodate standing, because that's how the nurses use the counter. Furthermore, nurses don't ride around in wheelchairs. Mel maintains that neither he nor anyone he knows has ever seen a hospital floor nurse work in a wheelchair. He also maintains that most nurses suffer chronic back pain from having to bend over the thirty-four inch high counter. He would know. He spends much of his time on location and has to listen to their complaints.

He has, despite vigorous efforts to the contrary, been unable to get the silly requirement lifted, compliments of your government at work. I am not a nurse, I hate hospitals, and I really have no right to care, but I do. I care that we, as a society, are stupid enough to let this happen. Sanity has indeed caught the last train out of town, and it gives me the redass.

First Union Bank featured a design requirement in accordance with Title 3 regulations that the teller counter, which was appropriately positioned at a reasonable height for banking transactions, also provide a thirty-four inch high ledge running its full length. It was just wide enough to allow a wheelchair-bound customer to write a check and an able-bodied customer to bruise her thighs or pelvis. Additionally, each teller station featured a handsome rosewood and brushed aluminum block, tightly mounted to the handicap shelf, and to which was tethered an equally handsome, quality, banker-style ballpoint pen. The tether, however, was not long enough to reach the counter, so the bank's able-bodied customers were forced to squat or bend down to the handicap shelf, as there were no pens fixed to the upper level.

I haven't a clue what percentage of the bank's customers transact their banking on wheels, but I visited numerous First Union branches, fascinated as I was with this absurd phenomenon, and I never saw a wheelchair. I am certain that First Union, and now Wachovia, soon to be Wells Fargo, has wheelchair-bound customers, and obviously accommodations should be provided for their convenience. But every branch I visited had this identical block, tether, pen, and backache configuration at every teller station. A rational solution would have been to provide an accommodation station in each branch, like a handicap parking spot, or to make all the tethers eighteen inches longer. No, that's what Einstein would have done.

I called their headquarters and suggested to the retail operations chief's admin assistant that she tell her boss it made their bank look stupid. She had been unaware of the situation, but she fully agreed.

Amazingly, Wachovia's block-and-tether fiasco didn't make them look as stupid as Washington Mutual and Bank of America. Both companies offer drive-up ATM stations in the parking lots. Being blindly obedient corporate citizens, their ATMs were in conformance with federal regulations requiring Braille keypads. This way, blind drivers have the same opportunity as sighted drivers to pick up some quick cash without having to leave their cars.

I shouldn't poke fun at the bank. They were simply following the regulations imposed by the geniuses in your federal government. My recoil at these quaint idiocies has been totally eclipsed by the abandonment of all reason and sanity we saw recently in the bailouts, spending legislation, and budgets. That bit of lunacy has set a new standard that will likely endure until the End Times, which is also how long it will take taxpayers to pay for it. Don't get me started on that one.

Most government manifestations of idiocy, while moronic and annoying, are comparatively innocuous. And while not of the fiscal follies' gothic proportion, there are some less obvious but equally dumb, unjustified government mandates that are hurtful, unfair, and damaging to individuals, businesses, and in some cases, harmful to all of us. Often parasitic in their effect, they squander and consume shareholder value, misappropriate and waste hard-earned tax dollars, and add unnecessary expense to the cost of manufactured goods. Call it diversity, affirmative action, quotas, preferences, bias, or ethnic discrimination. Nobody has yet been able to explain to me how it is anything but stupid and wrong.

Several years ago, Mel bid on a project for the Atlanta Olympics that required complete redesign of the interior electrical, HVAC, and plumbing of an ancient building to be used to house visiting athletes. The selection committee met for a kickoff meeting in the conference room of one of Atlanta's prestigious, traditionally Black universities. The person in charge of the meeting was a senior member of the university's administration.

She called the meeting to order, and in the course of the standard around-the-table introductions, she focused on Mel and asked who he was and what his role was at the meeting. As it unfolded, this was a predictable development. Looking around the room, he suddenly realized that he was the only white person among the fifteen or so seated at the table.

"I'm the architect," he said. "My firm won the bid."

"Please excuse us for a minute," the woman replied, and asked him to step outside for a moment. Very shortly thereafter, the door opened and the participants began to file out. The woman approached Mel, thanked him very graciously, and told him that the meeting was postponed and they would be back in touch.

Shortly thereafter, he received a letter from the committee, congratulating him for his upcoming role in the project, but announcing that his firm was to serve as subcontractor to a local minority-owned company. All design, production, execution, and responsibility for supervising and inspecting the installation crews was to remain as articulated in the proposal, as was Mel's fee. The committee simply added a premium, one might suppose, of some unknown amount to Mel's bid price. Admittedly, I am assuming the minority company got some money out of the arrangement, but to assume otherwise would be naïve.

Mel's firm completed the first phase of drawings, which they attempted to submit to the prime contractor for review and approval. He wrote letters and made phone calls in efforts to arrange their submission, consistent with his role as sub to the prime. Lacking any response and working against a deadline, Mel prudently abandoned his effort to get acknowledgement from the prime and proceeded with the project as originally defined in the proposal. Other than receiving checks from them, he claims they never once returned a call, email, letter, or voicemail. They performed none of the routine functions expected of a prime contractor to a sub-contractor, other than collecting, managing and disbursing funds. They simply skimmed theirs, one might conclude, off the top. Atlanta Olympic Organizing Committee, richly funded though donations, had deep pockets and may never have known the difference. Maybe they wouldn't have cared, but if it had been my money, I'd have a serious case of the redass.

Another good friend, who asked to remain anonymous, owns a company that does interior construction on retail outlets. He was notified by his client that they were feeling pressure to increase their supplier percent participation of female and minority owned businesses. Similar to Mel, he had won a bid, and was asked to engage a particular minority owned firm, unknown to him, as sub-contractor. The retail chain added 15% to my friend's bid, which he passed along to the sub. The presence of the additional resource didn't reduce his workload, considering the additional supervision and administration required in managing an unknown entity. It had no impact on the outcome, but it cost the retailer's stockholders a fifteen percent premium on a quarter-million dollar project. If I'd been one of them, knowledge of this lunacy would have driven me to buy an airplane ticket and ask some pointed questions of the board at the annual meeting. Was this a one-time exception or in broad practice across the chain? Do they know and approve of this practice? How do the rules of governance and fiduciary responsibility for my investment allow this to happen? Predictably, they would have had no definitive answers, but the point would have been made for the benefit of all present, and you probably would have read about the melee that ensued.

A close friend and business associate managed sales for a supplier to large manufacturers. As with most high visibility, publicly owned companies, minority participation in their procurement program is generally forced upon large, stable suppliers as a condition for doing business. This enables the company to achieve a targeted level of what is commonly termed "diversity spend." Most large companies pay a Diversity Officer to monitor hiring quotas and ensure that a portion of their supplier dollar is spent with companies classified as Minority or Woman-owned Business Enterprise. There is even an acronym applied to the classification: MWBE.

My friend had included a minority partner in a multi-year procurement contract. The minority firm's role was to send invoices for the goods, collect payments, take its cut, and disburse payment to my friend's company, the large production supplier. The minority partner never handled or took title to the goods. If there was a delivery, performance, or quality problem, the supplier, not the minority partner, got the 911 call. The minority partner's role was basically to cash big checks and write slightly smaller checks. The business could have operated out of a post office box and a bank account, but this type of arrangement provides large companies, particularly those where consumers are the end user, the ability to quantify their support of minority-owned businesses. While it may appear to be hypocritical on the surface, it also appears to be hypocritical in its core and very essence. But I'm on the outside looking in, and I may be mistaken.

In this particular case, my friend was left holding the bag at the end of the contract period for payment due on several large orders. As he put it, "This guy is driving around in a new Mercedes and I'm out about eighty thousand dollars."

At the time for contract renewal, John flew to his customer's Midwest headquarters to attend a negotiation meeting with their procurement people. He was prepared to offer another minority participation partner who had built an established and respected business. When he offered the credentials of the minority participant, his customer's procurement chief reviewed them and said, "Apparently you don't understand. We need you to include a *minority* partner."

John pointed out that the business owner was of Chinese extraction and, as an Asian American, qualified for minority status in accordance with federal guidelines.

"No, it has to be a *minority*-owned company. Chinese doesn't count," the customer replied.

My friend, never one to mince words, replied, "Oh, you mean Black? Well nobody ever told me that. If this company doesn't meet your requirements, I'll take anybody you want, providing you indemnify me for any losses incurred for theft or non-performance by your partner. The last one you sent me still owes me eighty grand."

"This meeting is over," was the buyer's reply, as he and his people rose from the table and left the room.

This blatant hypocrisy in language, thought, and behavior makes me wonder why an otherwise respectable company, known for sound management, innovation, and excellence, closes one eye to principle and knowingly squanders shareholder value by adding premiums to the pricing of their suppliers so they can line the pockets of an unproven redundancy whose only value is the color of his skin. I suspect it is because the Eskimos, Native Americans, Asian Americans, Pacific Islanders, and Hispanic interests haven't yet developed legitimized shakedown artistry to the point where they represent a viable threat of boycott. Again, this is only a suspicion. While I'm confident that there are minority owned businesses in partner roles that perform legitimate services and add value through their participation, I'm just as confident that this and the other examples I cited are not unique aberrations. There are probably more cases than just these three. I simply don't know about them.

In the above examples, shareholders and legitimate competitors suffered quantifiable damages, but it's not worth going to war over. We victims of the redass need to choose our battles wisely. Rather than wring our hands, let's agree that corporate America probably has spookier skeletons in its closet than paying for protection. Far worse is the knowing participation of Federal, State, and local officials who consciously waste taxpayer dollars in similarly hypocritical, parasitic charades.

An article appeared in the November 13, 2006 edition of <u>Atlanta Business Chronicle</u> about a new set of guidelines mandated by the Atlanta City Council and summarized in a letter written by Atlanta Mayor Shirley Franklin. I quote verbatim from that article (*reprinted with permission.*)

> *"White male-owned contractors would be required to exhaustively document their efforts to hire certified minority-owned subcontractors -- submitting, among other things, a list of reasons why they choose not to hire any minority-owned firm with which they even discuss doing business on a given project. The city could advise minority-owned firms on how to compete for specific contracts, and perhaps even tailor bid requirements to their advantage.*

> *The threshold for projects on which the city could basically require prime contractors to hire a minority-owned subcontractor would drop to $5 million from $10 million, and any minority-owned firm that believes a contractor is discriminating against it would be able to file a formal complaint with City Hall.*

> *"We still have work to do," Franklin wrote Oct. 11 in a letter to the Atlanta City Council. **"There will be no room for discrimination on the basis of race, ethnicity or gender for any business owner doing business with the city."*** (emphasis mine)

> .

> *The city declined to make Hubert Owens, Franklin's director of contract compliance, available for an interview."*

Let me see if I have this straight. Her Honor promises that race or gender won't be an issue in deciding whether they allow you aboard the city's gravy train. Oh yeah, unless your race is white and your gender is male. Then, the city will advise your competition on how to win the bid and maybe, to be certain that you lose, modify the bidding process so it's stacked against you. You, unlike your competition of every other race and gender, will need to "exhaustively" document all your efforts to go find a sub of the race or gender the city favors. If none met your standards, you'll have to provide a complete list of everybody you considered and why you rejected each.

It's not a wonder they wouldn't let Hubert talk to anybody. It'd be tough to explain this one to any person with a brain.

What IS a wonder is why any white male-owned company would WANT to do business with the City of Atlanta. In addition to delivering what you proposed, you'll have to manage a subcontractor that may have been fifth on your list of preferences but that the city demanded you tie to your coattails, solely because its owner is not a white male.

Decisions on how the city spends the taxpayer's money appear not to be based on proven excellence. Instead, it looks to me like selection will be based on race or gender, in which case it seems Atlanta's mayor is either smoking weed, suffering from a deficiency in analytical thinking, or hoping that we're all dim bulbs and won't notice the self-contradiction. Pick a door.

Why does our society close its eyes to this obvious discrimination and hypocrisy? Bernard Goldberg called it in his excellent book, *Crazies to the Left of Me, Wimps to the Right.* People are terrified of being branded as racist, which is the predictable outcome of anyone white questioning the legitimacy of affirmative action, racial preferences, minority set-asides, or whatever its euphemistic label.

I know that racism exists. I see it and hear it, sometimes blatant but usually subtle. I can only try to feel the pain and anger of the Black man who confronts it daily. I can imagine how especially painful it must be to experience racism's ugliness while out with one's children. I'll never internalize the constant fear of "driving while Black," but I've had it explained by enough Black friends to empathize. I also know that, were the playing fields truly level, subtle discrimination would, at times, work against the unproven Black applicant trying to break through. I also know that legitimized discrimination against white males is not going to fix it. It can only perpetuate the resentment and validate the bigoted suspicion that Blacks or women aren't good enough to compete on their own. That should give everybody the redass.

There are, however, ways for white male-owned business to counter the lunacy, get the work, and deliver quality and value to the taxpayer without compromising their standards. Two close friends had experiences with local government that prove it can be done. One got caught; the other managed to stay under the radar.

One of my car buddies is a guy named Colin who was born and grew up in South Africa. A strapping big square-jawed blonde guy of Dutch/German extraction, he was naturalized a US citizen twenty-some years ago. He started his own medical equipment distribution business, wherein he developed sales relationships with numerous small manufacturers of multiple lines of surgical and medical supplies. He then would form buying relationships with the purchasing arms of hospitals, medical groups, surgical centers, outpatient clinics, and the like. They would send him orders, he would ship from the manufacturers' warehouses, and he would invoice the customer and pay the suppliers monthly.

Being new to Atlanta and somewhat naïve, he sought to add Grady Memorial Hospital to his customer base. Grady, an excellent hospital, renowned for its trauma center, is located in urban Atlanta and is administered by Fulton County. As such, the residents of Fulton County provide funding through their real estate taxes. Another good friend of mine was a physician on staff in Grady's emergency room for a number of years. When people asked him where he worked, his stock answer was "Grady Knife and Gun Club," a reference to the late-night stream of gunshot and stabbing victims regularly passing through his ER. They do a booming business, a large part of which is charity care and treatment of Atlanta's indigent and uninsured of limited means.

So Colin, my South African friend, laced up his selling shoes, called the purchasing office, and asked to make an appointment. The clerk said that he would need to complete an application for review prior to any further steps. She mailed him the forms, which he completed by hand. Being a county hospital, Grady has a fairly rigorous set of guidelines which give preference to minority suppliers. In the application form, there was a minority status section asking whether the company's ownership was any of the following origins, listing the standard selection menu of Eskimo, Native American, Asian, Hispanic, African American, Pacific Islander, etc. He checked African American, which is precisely what he was: a native African who had become an American. Within days, orders starting showing up in his Post Office Box.

He had maintained this large, profitable customer for several years when he had the occasion to attend an on-site meeting with one of their purchasing executives, who assumed him to be a company salesman. At some point in the meeting, Colin mentioned that he was the owner. He received notice several days later by mail that his company had been de-selected, and the orders simply stopped.

This all happened in the nineties, prior to the incorporation of Web-based application and qualification technology. Grady Hospital's web site now boasts an application template that says it all. As with any template, with which we are all familiar from on-line shopping, there are certain blocks designated with red asterisks that require an entry to proceed. These are critical areas such as the owner's name, address, title, race, and gender. There is a special section headed "This section only to be completed by women or minority owned firms."

Maybe I'm jumping to conclusions, but my guess is that if Grady can find a required provider of goods or services in this section, they won't bother looking further—kind of a modern-day form of "Help Wanted – Irish Need Not Apply."

If forced to look beyond non-woman or minority owned companies, the race and gender of all other owners, partners, and shares of ownership percentage is the next most critical information required in the application.

A striking feature of Grady's application form is their glaring lack of interest in references, experience of the applicant company's management, annual revenues, or any other element that might enable one to evaluate the stability, capability, or past performance of the prospective supplier. Is it a wonder, with this approach to decision making, that Grady Memorial Hospital is in a state of financial crisis, in desperate need of more than two-hundred million dollars to remain solvent? I am not suggesting that choosing suppliers based on excellence would have saved Grady. I am suggesting that when an executive team demonstrates patent stupidity in one element of its management practices, its entire decision making process becomes suspect, starting with hiring practices, executive compensation, advancement and promotion, financial management—you name it.

Dr. King spoke in 1968 of his dream: an America where people were measured, not by the color of their skin, but by the content of their character. Grady Hospital is located within a mile of Dr. King's birthplace and Ebenezer Baptist Church where he preached. It's been forty years since that defining moment on the Mall, but Grady Hospital's management still hasn't bought into the dream, or apparently, even gotten the message.

Another good buddy who must remain unnamed has a successful business in the design, building and installation of interior fixtures. He first attempted to compete for a city contract during the construction of Atlanta's metro light-rail system, MARTA. He was, although subtly, told by the bid reviewing and selection team to forget it, unless he brought along a minority partner. Not knowing any minority firms who operated in his space, he expressed concern that such a requirement would present difficulties. They provided him with a woman's name and phone number. He never did find out what she did, but he signed her on as a sub-contractor and he got the work. He called her a few times in efforts to bring her to the site, for appearance sake if nothing else, but the messages he left on her voicemail were never answered. The checks he sent to her PO Box, however, were cashed in timely fashion.

When the city announced plans to build a new international terminal at Atlanta Hartsfield International Airport, my friend wanted to play. Wisely, he put his company in his wife's name and registered it as a woman-owned business. He enjoyed a multi-year run earning him well into seven figures. His wife didn't know a band saw from a bingo card, had never operated a computer, and probably couldn't extract an architectural drawing from its mailing tube. Go figure

DIGITAL WOMEN: DOMINATRIX, DIVAS, & DINGBATS

Air Force Lt. Walter Haut was the Public Relations Officer who issued, as instructed by his base commander on both occasions, two successively conflicting press releases in July 1947. The first reported the crash and wreckage recovery of an alien spacecraft near the airbase in Roswell, NM. The second announced that it had only been a weather balloon. Lt. Haut publicly stood by the weather balloon version until his death in 2002, immediately following which, a sealed affidavit, to be opened only after his death, was made public. It stated that he had personally seen craft wreckage and bodies of the occupants.

In a similar affidavit, Lt. Col. Philip Corso (Ret), a decorated, career Army officer, recounted, prior to his death at age 83 that, while stationed at Ft. Riley, KS, he had personally seen the body of one of the craft's occupants several days after the alleged incident, and that in 1961, while stationed at the Pentagon, he was given "technological debris" recovered from the crash with the assignment of passing the technology along to selected American defense contractors for research and reverse engineering. He further asserted that these efforts ultimately led to the development of Kevlar, stealth technology, lasers, fiber optics, night vision goggles, and, most importantly, the integrated circuit chip.

Arguably, our lives have been more dramatically impacted by chip technology than any other single development of the twentieth century. One would be challenged to define a routine daily activity, outside of basic bodily functions, that isn't in some way served by this technology. It's everywhere, and it's all good, with one glaringly insidious exception: Interactive Voice Response.

The integrated circuit chip is the prime enabler of every system that requires you to press 1 for English. It lies beneath the voice who repeats what she believes she heard you say and asks "Is this correct?" It has greatly reduced the number of manned checkout lanes at supermarkets and The Home Depot and has coerced us into working in the capacity of clerk and bagger without salary, benefits, or even a percentage off our purchase. It is the source of countless cases of the redass, daily numbering in the millions, for which there is neither preventative vaccine nor cure.

I may sound anti-technology. I am not. I was using ATMs, even for deposits, when most people didn't trust them. I owned a PC back in the eighties when all screens were black and text was green, so I could hardly be called a Luddite. It's simply that I am opposed to technology as applied to poorly designed systems that waste my time or try to control my behavior, particularly when I know that it's wrong and I'm right. Consequently, I have a real problem with IVR.

Whatever chip technology was allegedly scavenged from the alien wreckage ultimately found its way into companies' phone systems, beginning with the rudimentary IVR systems we started to encounter in the early nineties. Customers had an option of calling an 800 number for "automated customer assistance" with '0' as an opt-out choice for live help. Alternatively, most companies published the customer switchboard number, allowing customers to be immediately connected to a Customer Service Rep. We were free to choose. As managers began to compare the cost-per-call figures of an automated call vs. one handled by the CSR, the savings drove an installation feeding frenzy as companies raced to transfer the customer experience from live to digital. Pressing '0' remained as an option, but as the phenomenon expanded, this option, as you've noticed, became increasingly difficult to pursue. Fast-forward ten years, and we find ourselves trapped in systems with endless loops, layers, and choice-trees worthy of Alice and the Mad Hatter.

Interactive Voice Systems give you the redass by design. This is because they assert their dominance right out of the blocks, with a polite but stern demand that you "Please listen carefully as our menu options have changed." Everyone knows that their menu options haven't changed since Clinton's first term, but the digital diva doesn't care because she doesn't have to answer to you or anybody else--truth, lies, or otherwise. She presses brashly ahead, sometimes even admonishing you that "Any attempt to bypass the menu options will only delay your call."

Usually, as soon as the digital diva opens her mouth, you hit "0" because you want to talk to a live person, right? Depending on the system, she either ignores the instruction altogether or chastises you with "That is not a valid option."

I'm a strong Type-A personality. I get real intolerant when somebody wastes my time, and as a customer, I want what I want and I want it NOW. I push the zero button again, which normally does nothing or worse, starts the whole cycle all over, even the part beginning with "Hello, and thank you for calling XYZ Company."

At this point, you have to decide: do I dig my heels in and keep pushing zero until she catches my drift, or do I play along and see what she wants. If the number you dialed is on the back of a credit card, she's going to want you to enter or say your card number. This is a big mistake. In most cases, you enter the number, and the bitch reads it back, slowly, as in "You entered three---three---seven---nine---two---" etc, followed by, "If this is correct, press one; if this is incorrect, press two." With mounting intolerance, you want to scream at her "I know what the **** I entered! You don't have to tell me what I entered!"

But realizing that the digital diva is thick-skinned, emotionless, and could care less what you're feeling about now, you have to decide whether you quietly dump her by pressing zero as often as necessary to shut her up, or let her continue. This is your next mistake, because she is bound and determined to tell you that "As of December twenty-first, your balance is three---thousand---six---hundred---nineteen---dollars and twenty---seven cents." At this point, I've had it with her. I didn't call to get a balance. I'll find out what the balance is when I get my statement. I called to talk to a person, because my kid lost the credit card I gave him or because I got double charged by Amazon for the same book, or for some other reason; but I didn't call to hear my balance, so why is she telling me this? Three or four more times at pounding the zero button will generally get you into the queue, but meanwhile, your pulse, respiration, and blood pressure are elevated, your index finger hurts and may be sprained, and the poor little Indian guy who ultimately comes on the line will, by default, inherit your frustration and resultant foul humor through no fault of his own.

This scenario is enough to give anybody the redass, but it gets worse, depending on who you call. Bank of America figured perhaps that a male voice might command more respect, so their 800 number gets you the digital dude who asks for your access ID. I have no idea what my access ID is. Is it a password? My ATM PIN? My mother's maiden name? I need a person to give me a clue, so I hit zero. The dude offers several options from which I'm supposed to choose. I listen to his options. This is not the first time I sit through a litany of options only to discover that none of them is remotely related to the reason for my call. I need somebody to put back the fee they extorted on this statement clutched in my fist, because it's excessive, I never agreed to it, and their system thinks I'll overlook it. But the dude's virtual tapestry does not include the option "To have a fee refunded, press eight."

So I press zero, and hear, "To get you to the right associate, you will need to select a valid option." After forty-one tries and getting the same response, I slammed down the receiver, grabbed my car keys, and drove to the branch. I figured forty-one was just shy of Einstein's definition of insanity.

Interactive Voice Response, I'm afraid, has become a permanent fixture on the national landscape. For every well designed system, usually configured by smart consultants like Accenture, there are ten designed by Larry, Curley, and Moe. Then every so often, you run across one conceived in hell by Lucifer himself. My all-time-worst IVR experience ever was at the hands of, who else, the Phone Company.

My daughter Katie's first job out of college was as an Account Rep with Verizon Wireless Business Services. As an employee, she received discounted rates on as many as three family lines, so she put my wife and son and herself on an account in her name, the single charge for which was automatically applied to my American Express Account each month. After her second year with Verizon, she was recruited by a Pharmaceutical company and changed employers, losing the Verizon employee deal. She transferred the account and all three lines, still under her name, to one of Verizon's standard family calling plans.

Several months later, Katie called me in a panic. "Dad," she reported breathlessly. "I just got a call from Verizon and this account is two months past due. They're getting ready to cut off our phones. Haven't you been paying the bill?"

"I thought it was automatically applied to Amex. That's how they've gotten paid for over two years now," I explained. "I didn't know anything had changed."

"Well can you call and pay them so they don't cut off service?" she pleaded. "They'll cut off Chris and Mom's phones too."

I called *611 from my cell phone, assuming that this should be easy enough: pound out of IVR and tell somebody with a pulse what I want to do. I didn't realize that I would be stepping over the threshold of Phone Company Hell.

The digital diva offered the usual set of options, none of which included "Pay a delinquent bill and set up automatic payment on your daughter's three-line account." I pounded out with zero, and the live lady asked me my cell phone number, which I gave her. She then verified that it really was me on the line and not somebody with nothing better to do than call the phone company pretending to be me. Once that was settled, she asked how she could help me. When I told her my problem, she asked for one of the numbers on the other account, which I also provided. Then, in a tone that sounded more like admonishment than apology, she told me that she couldn't talk to me about the account because it was in Katie's name. I would have to get her authorization to discuss it.

"Look at the record," I said. "Go back two years and see how you guys have been getting paid."

She reviewed the billing and payment record, and sure enough, the name and credit card number that showed up identified me as the dad with the deep pockets. Think any of this mattered? Naw.

I asked her why the automatic payment had stopped. She was able to acknowledge that the account was transferred from an employee program, but why the payment method was halted was either a trade secret or had National Security implications, because this couldn't be discussed without Katie's authorization. The only thing that could happen on that exchange without Katie's authorization was that I could pay the outstanding bill with my credit card. I just couldn't set it up for regular payment, as before, without "having access," which had to come from Katie. Don't ask me what the difference is. Round one ended with me paying the two months overdue and the required month's advance deposit, a total sum just south of nine-hundred dollars.

Katie later called Verizon and set up a password that would give me "access" to the three-line account, whereupon I undertook round two. In my naiveté, I figured I'd simply give the Customer Service Rep a credit card number and be done with it. I fought the battle of the buttons and finally reached a live person. When I told her what I wanted to do, she said I'd have to use their automated system "so there'd be a record." The only way to do what I needed done was to enter into an IVR excursion of Biblical proportions.

My first mistake was, in the interest of time management, to initiate the process while in the checkout line at Costco. There were three big baskets and a gurney ahead of me when I started, leading me to believe that I'd have plenty of time to complete the process prior to reaching the cashier. Dumb me. I have difficulty multitasking with IVR systems, so I had to disconnect when I reached the cashier.

The second attempt took place in the parking lot. The frustration arose not from the multiple entries by my stubby fingers on the tiny buttons, but from being forced to listen to the digital diva read back most of the entered data, which required pressing "1 if correct." Next, and even more onerously, I was regaled with a lengthy series of disclosures, each of which required touchtone acknowledgment. Next, I was required to listen attentively to each verse of The Litany of Electronic Signature, obviously composed by a team of lawyers and government hacks who must have gotten paid by the word. Pressing '1' for final acknowledgment and acceptance, I was released to proceed with my life. I didn't time the transaction, but start to finish was probably seven or eight minutes.

Touch tone frustrations are bad enough, but recent advances in speech recognition technology have introduced us to a new species of virtual woman, the Digital Dingbat. She is crafted to sound capable of casual conversation on a variety of topics. Delta's gal says things like, "Let's see, it sounds like you want to schedule a flight, is that right?" And, when you persist in pressing zero, she offers, "I'm sorry you are having trouble. Let me connect you to a Delta representative," as though our recent breakup was my fault. Verizon's lady apologizes for not being able to understand you, with "I'm sorry, I didn't get that. Did you say you want to. . ." citing something not remotely close to my previous answer. I have actually caught myself carrying on a seemingly intelligent conversation with these fembots, and when the realization strikes, it's pretty creepy.

IVR in the form of retail checkout can be just as frustrating as the touch-tone variety. The Kroger near my home is where I do most of my shopping. About ten years ago, Kroger launched a shopper loyalty program that included a bar-coded "Kroger Plus Card." This card is scanned along with one's groceries, providing the chain a record of the visit and item level detail of the purchases. This data is used, often through third-party marketing services companies like Catalina or Nielsen, to analyze consumer buying behavior. Privacy advocates fear this data will enable the pursuit of other nefarious schemes, but for now, Kroger uses it to identify and incentivize lost customers, luring them back to the store with ten-dollar coupons. The consumer incentive to allow this blatant, if innocent, invasion of privacy is the awarding of promotional price reduction of specially tagged items. In essence, if you don't scan the card each trip, you're overpaying for your groceries.

About five years ago, my store installed four self-service checkout lanes. These replaced four of the traditionally manned lanes and are under the command of a Digital Dominatrix who forces adherence to a rigid set of behavioral standards. There's a touch-screen monitor, under which is situated a scale/scanner combination. There's a secondary scale/shelf with several wire racks, each holding open a stack of flimsy plastic bags, all of which is mounted atop this scale. This is for the purpose of keeping the shoppers honest. The scale knows the weight of each item scanned, and upon scanning, the Dom behind the curtain says, "Please put the item in the bag." The scale expects to soon receive something that weighs precisely what your just-scanned can of tuna weighs, the assumption being that if you scanned it and the scale receives something of its weight, you aren't ripping them off for a ninety-five-dollar tenderloin. If the scale doesn't register the addition of the scanned item to the bag, the Dom again urges "Please put the item in the bag." Disappoint her a second time, and she clamps her figurative knees together, effectively shutting down the developing relationship. Enter the Officer of the Deck, an ubercashier who monitors it all from a pulpit in the center of the stations. In addition to having a fat ring of keys that unlock various parts of her, he knows the secret codes that can reawaken her mojo. Unless he is helping another hapless customer, he comes over to rectify the situation and put things right.

The Digital Dom behind the curtain is probably a good thing for first-time users or cyberphobes, but she wears out her welcome in a hurry. Although the system would be virtually idiot proof without her incessant harping, Kroger has done everything within its power to make it more stupid than necessary, and that gives me the redass—starting with the opening screen. There's a big square on it that reads "Touch here to start." This wakes up the Dom, and she intones, "Welcome, Kroger shopper! Please scan your Kroger Plus Card. If you don't have a Kroger Plus Card, please scan your first item."

If you have been there before, or you know what a scanner is, or you notice the other people dragging stuff across the glass window—in other words, if you are intelligent enough to be away from home unattended, you ought to be smart enough to swipe your first item across the glass. Well guess what happens if you stroll up and swipe your first item across the glass? Absolutely nothing. You MUST, you see, first touch the screen to awaken Madame Instructo, whereupon she launches into her pseudo-friendly chant, "Welcome, Kroger shopper!" This in itself isn't terribly offensive. It's just stupid. The offensive part is that the speakers for the three other stations, all within twelve feet of your ears, independently assault their respective customers, and you along with them, with the same litany, creating a needless, out-of-synch, abrasive cacophony of repetitive messages. Home Depot's equivalent system is blissfully silent. You need neither "press here" to start nor suffer an assault of instructive announcements. If you walk up to it and scan a box of four-inch deck screws, it somehow deduces that you must want to buy a box of four-inch deck screws. Predictably, it registers each successive item in your order until you touch "Finish & Pay." Granted, you have to be able to read to get out of Home Depot by yourself, so I can only conclude that Kroger thinks its customers are either stupid or illiterate or both. Further proof of this is seen in the instructions I received on my second use of the system. I bought an eight-pack of Bounty paper towels. I scanned it, and the shrew commanded me to "Please put the item in the bag." This "item," roughly the size of a bale of hay, wasn't about to go into a bag barely large enough to accommodate a loaf of rye.

"What? Do I look like an idiot?" I shot back at the voice in the speaker.

"Please put the item in the bag," she demanded in a tone that implied growing impatience, then she abruptly called a halt to our fragile relationship. I looked at the screen, which registered, Towels, Bounty, 8 PK. If she knew it was an eight-roll bundle of Bounty, it struck me that she was the idiot. I looked over at the key ring & code guy with an expression half quizzical, half redass, whereupon he sprang from his pulpit and unlocked the logjam with an apology as though he were somehow responsible. "Sorry about that, sir."

I've grown accustomed to the senseless delay each time I try to get beer past the Digital Dominatrix. Scan a six-pack and everything shuts down. A light or alarm or something goes off in the key guy's command center. He hobbles over and asks to see your ID, because she demands that he tell her your date of birth via a special pad he summons up on the touch screen. I've been drinking beer since the Earth's crust was cooling, but this guy has to check my ID and tell the imaginary lady my birthday so she'll let me pay and escape the sound of her harping. As I wait to have my age blessed, she drones on incessantly from the other three stations, each with its own mix of her limited vocabulary. This consists of:

"Do you have any coupons?"

"Please select your method of payment."

"Please follow the instructions and take your receipt."

"Thank you for shopping at Kroger!"

That's not the worst of it. I scan my card on each of my twice weekly trips. The same system that controls "that woman" knows who I am, where I live, what I eat and drink, can probably calculate my liver enzymes, and knows that I have transacted with her hundreds of times since her arrival. I know how she works, and I am confident that I could get from start to finish without her vocal assistance. Do they think I am a moron? I have left messages for the president of Kroger Atlanta, suggesting to him that, by the fifth or sixth time a cardholder uses the system, he's probably got the drill down cold. Isn't there some way to shut her up? I've gotten no response yet.

In retrospect, the only interactive systems I can recall that appear to have been designed with the customer in mind are the Home Depot automated checkout and the Veterans Administration telephone IVR. Both are intuitive, user-friendly, and allow you to accomplish your purpose with a minimum of effort and no frustration. Other than these two, all my IVR experiences are the same mindless journey into the same frustrating asylum—with one memorable exception.

Back when Wachovia was First Union, I needed to call their service line from a client's location in San Francisco. During a break in our meetings, I ducked into an empty cubicle to make a call and check my emails. Rather than risking dislocated cervical vertebrae from the ear-shoulder receiver squeeze, commonly contracted from protracted hold times when you punch out to '0,' I opted to put the phone on speaker so I could use both hands on my laptop. When somebody picks up, you can immediately go off speaker and grab the receiver.

When requested, I didn't know my account number, so instead of entering it, I opted out of the IVR by hitting zero. The digital diva came back at me with the "Please enter your account number" command again. Frustrated, I tapped zero with machine-gun staccato about fifty times, figuring that would get her attention and convey my sentiments regarding her initial denial of my request for live help. The diva came back with "You entered oh—oh—oh— oh—oh—oh—oh—oh—oh—oh—oh—oh—oh—oh—oh— oh—oh—oh—oh—oh—oh—oh—oh—" about which time heads began popping up in surrounding cubicles and peering over my wall. As the "oh—oh—oh—oh—oh—oh—oh—oh—oh—oh—oh— oh—" continued, one of them opined, to the enjoyment of everyone within earshot, "Sounds to me like she's faking it."

At that moment, a woman emerged from the nearby break room, coffee mug and bagel in hand, adding, "Sounds to me like sexual harassment."

WASHINGTON: WE LET THE WHEELS FALL OFF THE CLOWN CAR

This will be short, insofar as the circus now playing in Washington is abundant enough in its lunacy to be beyond the scope of any one volume and hardly the subject matter of light reading. Besides, there are countless titles appearing monthly, largely from the right-of-center pundits, which detail chapter and verse the troubling antics of the people whom we, as voters, have chosen to represent our interests. Read them at the risk of developing chronic hypertension.

The one book I vigorously recommend, however, is P. J. O'Rourke's biting commentary, *Parliament of Whores* (Grove Press, 2003). Refreshingly apolitical in his perspective, (sample: *"Democrats are . . .the party that says government can make you richer, smarter, taller, and get the chickweed out of your lawn. Republicans are the party that says government doesn't work, and then they get elected and prove it."*) the brilliant humorist is mercilessly on target with his analogies, and, despite having written it almost two decades ago, his observations validate the discomforting reality that, then as now, we reap whatever it is we sow when we put these clowns in their jobs and trust that they'll do right by us.

Charlie Reese, a columnist for the Orlando Sentinel from 1971 to 2001, wrote a piece in 1985 entitled 545 People. In it, he called us all to task for allowing this tiny core of elitists to have their way with us. His sentiments are conveyed in the following quote from that column:

> *"One hundred senators, 435 congressmen, one president and nine Supreme Court justices — 545 human beings out of the 235 million — are directly, legally, morally and individually responsible for the domestic problems that plague this country."*

Any problem we have exists because these 545 people created and now perpetuate it. Things are the way they are because that's the way they want it.

The reality is this: there isn't a whole lot a President can do, good or bad, assuming he abides within the limits set forth in the Constitution. He needs Congress and the Senate to make and endorse major decisions regarding change. Most would agree, as we swirl around the drain, that we need some change. I have some simple thoughts on where We the People might begin if we seek to regain control.

We need to start by prying Congress and the Senate out of their insulated, well-feathered nests and transform them into regular people—like us. Anyone who is serious about challenging an incumbent in the next Congressional or Senatorial election should publicize a platform that includes a pledge to work tirelessly in support of the following changes:

1. <u>Limit terms:</u> Three for the House, two for the Senate. By limiting terms, the power-broker, deal-making, arrogant stuffed shirts, many of whom never had a job, who "serve" in recession-proof, guaranteed income, guaranteed retirement pension, guaranteed raise, perpetual healthcare, jobs for life (or, at times, until senility overtakes them) would be replaced by people who know what it's like to work, save, suffer the pains of economic swings, budget for retirement, and pay taxes.

2. <u>Eliminate pensions</u>. These archaic throwbacks to the days of the Iron Horse have all but disappeared from the private sector. We the People are required to provide for our own retirements. They should too. Those currently seated in Congress or the Senate could, based on time in their jobs, be grandfathered in a modified pension plan, which should, of necessity, be reduced. Corporations that go bankrupt (e.g. Delta Airlines) say "Sorry, folks" as they renege on their long-standing pension promises and turn the whole mess over to Pension Benefit Guaranty Corp. which pays approximately 40% vs. what was promised in the glory days. Why should our bankrupt government be any different? New members would need to provide for their own retirements, like everyone else. Let them enroll in a 401(k). Taxpayers might even support matching contributions—say, fifty cents on the dollar up to a limit—just like regular folks get from their employers. Remember, these guys work for us. WE are their employers, not "the government."

3. <u>Back off on the government takeovers:</u> No more bailouts. Freeze the unspent portion of the "stimulus." Get the government out of the business of running the car, banking, and health insurance business. They failed their apprenticeship with the serial mismanagement of Social Security, Medicare, Medicaid, the Post Office, Amtrak, Fannie, and Freddie. These bankrupt debacles are proven examples of government's lack of commercial acumen in running large, complex enterprises. But what could anyone expect when there is zero accountability or consequence for failure?

But maybe we should judge their competence on a less-grand scale. Perhaps they should tip toe into healthcare on a limited basis then scale up. Well, consider this.

In the 'mid-90s, the government seized the legendary Mustang Ranch for tax evasion. This licensed, legitimate bordello outside Las Vegas had operated successfully for years. As required by law with a confiscated enterprise, the feds took over operations and tried to run it. Within months, it failed and had to shutter the doors.

These guys couldn't break even running a cathouse selling poontang and whiskey, and now they want us to entrust them with eighteen percent of the GDP? I, for one, have a problem with this.

4. <u>No private jets or junkets,</u> other than Air Force One, on official State business, for any person or organization receiving tax dollars--starting with Madam Speaker. Her Gulfstream V costs just as much to operate as Bank of

America's. If Mrs. Pelosi wants to go away for the weekend, let her buy a ticket like the rest of us. Alternatively, she can find another job closer to home.

Remember the barely-reported Barack & Michelle New York show & dinner date? By the time you factor in, according to an Air Force officer who piloted one of the C-17s, the transportation, hotel, and per diem for the more than 20 Secret Service agents and 44 Marine and Air Force personnel, transport and maintenance of five Marine Corps helicopters, transport of the Presidential/Secret Service motorcade fleet, the two C-17 cargo planes flying three missions, and the three Air Force Gulfstream jets used to transport the happy couple and their attendants and staffs, this "dinner date" cost you and me well in excess of a half-million dollars--at a time when a lot of families can't afford a Saturday night of bowling. Little wonder the newly "transparent" White House refused to release the total cost of the junket.

I have no problem supporting appropriate pomp and glamour accorded to the Office. In a way, money spent on my President is money spent on me. I have a BIG problem, however, funding the man's personal life in sybaritic splendor. He should go to dinner in Georgetown. That's what all those black SUVs with Government plates are for. Whatever happened to the notion that "public service" involved some sacrifice—such as maybe not being able to jump off to New York on a whim and somebody else's money?

If he wants to travel like the Sultan of Brunei, he needs to stroke a check to the US Treasury and reimburse us for that night on the town. Remember, this is the same administration that lambastes corporate CEOs for using a corporate jet, at corporate expense, on official business in response to its own Congressional summons.

The hypocrisy, audacity, and hubris of our elected officials have reached a point where they have clearly forgotten that they work for us. We are their boss. We hire and fire them. It's not the other way around, as many appear to think. The very idea that Barbara Boxer would castigate a Brigadier General for addressing her as Ma'am, demanding instead to be called Senator, speaks to this egomaniacal arrogance, insulated from any contact with reality. She professed to "work very hard to earn the title of Senator," clearly unable to grasp the notion that the dedication, courage, discipline, self-sacrifice, honor, brains, and integrity required to achieve Flag rank in the US military so eclipses her own that she has shown herself to be a fool.

I believe we can straighten the mess out with a uniform articulation of some basic principles, using the above changes as starting points, to launch a new breed of Congressional and Senate challengers. I further believe that this refreshing doctrine would catch fire among enough voters to either oust an incumbent or force him to get on board with some rational, reasonable, taxpayer demands. This could be the foundation of a 2010 housecleaning.

And that's all I'm going to say about the circus in Washington.

GETTING OTHER STUFF FIXED

It must have happened gradually; otherwise, we would have rebelled. The erosion of service crept up on us, and now, often as not, we have to scrape and claw and even pay for what was once readily rendered as part of the deal. Not too long ago, service was a simple matter, easily understood by both sides of the buyer-seller equation. Providers of products were eager to please customers and seemed to care about their satisfaction. Customers entered into a service transaction with the reasonable expectation of getting a problem solved. More often than not, service came along with the package. If service was required on a transactional basis, customers paid and almost always got what they paid for. If your TV went on the fritz, you called a TV repairman. He came to your house, pushed out the set, fiddled in the back, and presto! Picture and sound. You gave him twenty bucks and everybody was happy.

Now, if you can find an electronics shop that makes house calls, there's a trip charge just to get someone to show-up. Whether it's a house call or you bring your set to the shop, there's a minimum charge for just showing up or for removing the back plate and starting to trouble shoot the problem.

I bought two identical Philips 34-inch TV's three years ago, one for our bedroom and one for my daughter's new condominium. Soon after the one-year warranty expired, the remote control receiving unit on my bedroom set failed. I identified the receiver, not the remote control, as the problem because my remote operated my daughter's television and hers had no effect on mine.

Other than its remote control, my TV worked fine, but getting out of bed to change channels or to silence "Anthony Sullivan here for the amazing monoblaster!" lasted about two nights. I called two TV repair shops to come out and fix it. Both asked me how old it was, and the answer "a couple years" brought identical responses. "You'd be better off buying a new one."

Assuming I could talk a neighbor into helping me get the monster set downstairs and into my pickup truck, a Philips service center said they would replace the faulty part for about $200. I surrendered, bought another TV, and planted the faulty one in a spare bedroom. Within a few months, my daughter's Philips developed an identical problem. Through laser-sharp powers of deduction, I concluded that a bad chip or sensor in the receiver was an endemic problem with this model. There may have simply been a bad batch of whatever component had failed, but I ended up with two of them, and it gave me the redass.

I called the Philips hotline looking for some help. It seemed logical to me that a company of Philips's stature would care about customer satisfaction, particularly considering they had built an obviously faulty component. They conceded that I had been the victim of a parts problem, and offered to provide the parts but added that I should pay for the labor, which in the case of both TV's would have been about $350. I got as far as the top guy in their customer service food chain, but he wouldn't budge. I'd always heard the

Dutch were a stubborn lot, and apparently the culture had spread among their US management group as well. I added Philips Electronics to my list, right under American Honda Corporation.

Trash men won't take TVs if you put them out at the curb, and I learned that neither Salvation Army nor Goodwill will accept non-functioning electronics. These two TVs were huge, requiring two beefy men just to wrestle one down the stairs and out the door. I ended up giving one to my son's friend for exclusive use as a video game console. I found some Mexican carpenters working on a house down the street, and they were only too happy to relieve me of the other one. Fortunately for all of us, the next generation of TVs are flat panels, which will make them much easier to dispose of, assuming the tree huggers allow us to pitch them into a landfill.

There are times however, when it makes more sense to get something fixed than throw it away. This is especially true if it's your car. Thankfully, automobile warranties have ballooned from three years to five, six, or in some cases, ten years. Chrysler recently began publicizing lifetime powertrain warranties. When something breaks, it's covered. There's no cash outlay, just the time and energy required to have it repaired.

"Just bring it in," is the common response. The dealer loves it when you "just bring it in," because he fixes it and bills the manufacturer. He assumes, since the car is under warranty, that we're equally delighted with the arrangement. Granted, it's a bit less painful if the car is a new Mercedes, Lexus, or BMW, as most of the luxury dealers will provide you with a courtesy loaner car. But for the guy with a Pontiac or Dodge, "just bring it in" means "just find someone to follow you to the dealer, just drive the car to the dealer's location, and just arrange for someone to drop you off at the dealer's when it's fixed. Perhaps even worse, "just bring it in," means "just sit in our customer lounge and watch Judge Judy and Jerry Springer and ambulance-chaser ads all day." Some dealers have their own rental agency, in which case "just bring it in" means "just drive over here and rent one of our cars for thirty-five bucks." I guess we can all put up with this if they really do fix the car, but have you ever had repairs done that didn't solve the problem? When you call the service department back to explain that three of the four items appear to have been addressed, but you still get the thumping sound when you turn left under light braking, they'll cheerfully suggest that you "just bring it in" because they'll take care of it for no additional charge.

Next time this happens, remind them that you "just brought it in" once already and they didn't get the job done. This time, how about if "you just come get it?" If you are polite but firm, this will usually work.

Admittedly, car repairs are no big deal for people who lease cars for two or three year contracts, but I buy my cars and, having ten in the family fleet, most of them accrue relatively few miles over the years. I'm inclined to keep a car for five-or-so years—long enough for things to start to break.

Dealing with automotive repair used to be, for me anyway, a relatively innocuous, sometimes even pleasant occurrence. I recall one night in college I was giving some friends a ride back to campus in my four-door Corvair. The muffler was beginning to fail, and the car made a marvelous, throaty burble under a lifted throttle, particularly so when shifted into low gear as the engine bled off speed under a coasting load. About half way down Notre Dame Avenue, the long, tree-lined approach to the Golden Dome, I gave the lever a robust flip from D into what was intended to be L, but sailed past L into R. The car bucked, tires chirping in protest as they clawed at the pavement, and belched to a stop. Silence. I hit the starter and miraculously, it fired and ran—very poorly. I chugged and sputtered the remaining distance to the circle, dropped off my friends, and limped home, fully expecting that I'd thrown a rod or bent or broken something very serious in the engine and probably the transaxle. I made it to the Chevrolet dealer the following morning and hitchhiked home. I expected a multi-hundred dollar engine replacement, or at the very least, major repairs. In mid afternoon, I got a call from the service department that the car was ready. All that was required, I learned, was to clean and rebuild the carburetors. The engine and transaxle were so well made that my shift into reverse had caused the rear wheels to stop the engine dead in its cycle, which somehow blew a load of carbon into the intake manifold and carburetors. I was back on the road for the princely sum of twenty seven dollars.

Fast forward forty years and try to get your car out of a dealer's service bay for today's inflation-adjusted equivalent of $155. I got a 'check engine' light a couple years ago on a GM car I bought new just over three years prior. As such, the warranty had expired, despite the low mileage reading of only twenty-one thousand. The cause was an "erratic signal from the crankshaft position sensors." I never did learn exactly what they do, but I did learn that my car has two of them, and when one crankshaft sensor packs up and heads South, the other decides to go South right along with it. $368 later, I was back on the road. The car ran fine when I brought it in and ran equally well when I left the dealer. The only difference I could discern was the 'check engine' light was extinguished. Maybe I should have simply unscrewed the bulb.

We bought our son Chris a new Pontiac Grand Am for his sixteenth birthday, with the understanding that this car would last him through two years of high school and four years of college. The following year, I gave myself a Father's Day gift of a "Home Depot truck," an immaculate four-year-old Dodge Ram that a friend happened to be selling. Chris, being a good ol' Georgia boy, took to the truck, so his Pontiac became the hangar queen. This was fine with me, insofar as limited use would translate to longer service life.

The GM warranty on Chris's Pontiac was the standard three-year, 36,000 mile, whichever came first variety, and by the end of its third year, the car only had 14,000 miles on the odometer. Several months prior to the factory warranty's expiration, I received a third-party solicitation to extend the warranty period to five years and 50,000 miles. These warranties are, fundamentally, insurance policies, written by third-party companies unrelated to General Motors. They buy lists of owners with expiring warranties from the manufacturers and do mass mailings in hopes that conservative anticipators like me will bite. They're betting that nothing serious will break for another two years, and you're betting that something will. In reality, you hope for both. If something breaks, there's sinister satisfaction in knowing that you beat the warranty company at its own game and came out way ahead in the transaction. If nothing breaks, well, that's OK too. At the very least, you had peace of mind and you got a good car. Since Chris was just starting college, I wanted to relieve him of car repair concerns or expenses, so I opted for "bumper-to-bumper" coverage at a cost of about fourteen-hundred dollars. This level of protection covered any repair other than consumables such as lights, wiper blades, brake pads, batteries, mufflers, glass, and trim.

The car had no problems to speak of during the first three years while under the factory warranty, then all hell broke loose. The ignition switch needed replacement three times at $280 each. Then the steering rack started leaking and needed replacement for $750. Then, the intake manifold gasket failed for $1083.00. I was feeling pretty good about my $1400 investment, since I'd gotten better than a two-for-one payout. I should have known that the relationship was going too smoothly.

Chris came home from Auburn one weekend with the driver's side mirror in his back seat. He said it had become increasingly loose over the previous few weeks and had finally fallen off the door and was dangling by its control wires. Wisely, he clipped it off, afraid that it would scratch the paint on the door. He took the truck back to school and I brought the Grand Am to the dealer Monday morning. I had assessed the problem and noted that the three plastic fasteners which secured the mirror housing to the door skin had failed in succession, first one, then the second, and finally the third. The mirror housing, the wiring, and motors, along with the fasteners, which are essentially fancy plastic nuts and bolts, are sold as a unit.

We have four GM cars and have used this particular dealership for years. Our cars break often enough that I have developed my own personal service writer. These are the guys who greet you with the clipboard when you show up and call you later with the bad news. My guy, Doug Fincher, is an asset to the dealer and is a pleasure to do business with. He had all the extended warranty data for Chris's car in his system, so he called the company for repair authorization. The warranty company denied the claim. Doug called me for permission to proceed at my expense, and I told him that I'd straighten out the mix-up. I dug the warranty contract from my files and carefully read all the exclusions. Bowed with confidence, I called the warranty company's customer service number and tracked down Jeff, the headset jock who had initially denied the request.

Jeff recalled his recent conversation with Doug, and reiterating his position, said, "Broken mirrors are specifically excluded in paragraph 4.A under 'glass' or 'lenses,' take your pick."

"If it were simply a broken mirror, you'd be right," I corrected. "But the mirror isn't broken. The mirror is fine. You could trim your eyebrows with it. The mirror and its entire housing fell off the door because the *fasteners* failed. The things that hold the mirror assembly on the door broke, and, as I read the exclusion clause in the contract, fasteners are not excluded, thereby making them subject to replacement and repair. Tell me where I'm wrong."

"Oh," said Jeff. "Have your service writer call me back."

I called Doug and told him I'd straightened it out and that he could call back for an authorization number to commence repairs. Doug called me back in a matter of minutes, noting that the company had again denied the claim, citing that the mirror was "trim," one of the specific exclusions noted in paragraph 4.A. Now I had the redass.

I called the warranty company back and asked the first person I got to let me talk to his supervisor. Naturally, he wanted to either handle me himself or at least, understand the problem before transferring me, so I had chronicled the whole adventure to him before he'd let me talk to his boss, a guy named Matthew. I took Matthew to task, recounting chapter and verse of the day's events thus far. To my surprise, I gained his complete agreement that the side mirror housing was not ornamental trim and that failure of the components that secured the mirror assembly to the door was in fact covered under the terms of our contract. Matthew assured me that he'd handle it, asking me to have the dealer re-contact them for authorization.

I passed this information along to Doug. He placed a third call to their Dealer Services number, followed immediately by a third call to me. The tone of Doug's voice suggested that he too was beginning to get the redass.

I fired off another call to Matthew on his direct line. He was properly apologetic and explained that there had been a communications problem. The entry in their system, he said, had reflected all the denials, but not Matthew's approval. He assured me that he would straighten it out, but by this time I felt a pressing need to talk to somebody who could not only fix my problem but also address what was an obvious systemic problem across their organization. This needed to be stopped.

"Who runs the whole office? Who's in charge of all you people?" I asked Matthew. He told me that they all reported to a woman named Sonja. Within minutes, I had Sonja on the line. She was wholly supportive, thanking me for bringing it to her attention and explaining that the dealer lines were a different department from the customer lines. Insofar as she controlled both sides of their operation, she assured me that she would get my problem fixed and bring their miscommunication issues up at "the staff meeting." She asked me to give her a couple minutes, then have the dealer call back for the repair authorization number.

I called Doug once again and gave him Sonja's name and number. He didn't call her, but rather called the dealer number, under the naïve belief that Sonja had greased the skids. He called me back a few minutes later.

"Mr. Melka," he sighed, "I can't deal with these people any more. They said broken mirrors are excluded and won't authorize repairs. I'm getting all backed up here and can't spend any more time on this. If you can get it straightened out, have them fax me the authorization. I'll just sit on everything until I get it or I hear from you, OK?"

Now I really had the redass. I went to Hoover's Website and searched the street address, switchboard number, and CEO's name for Interstate National Dealer Services, Inc. in Uniondale, New York. I next went to the New York State's Attorney General's site and downloaded a complaint form. Girded for battle, I dialed the company's switchboard.

"Chester Luby please," I requested of the operator.

"I'm sorry, but Mr. Luby is out of the office. Would you like his voicemail?"

"No," I responded. "Who's next in charge?"

"That would be Mr. Luby's daughter, Cindy. She's our company's president."

"Well please connect me with her then," I asked as politely as my deteriorating mood would allow.

"May I ask who's calling," the operator requested.

"The name wouldn't mean anything to her. I am a customer," I continued, "who is being jerked around by her people, and I'm fed up with talking to them and getting nowhere. Ask her if she wants to talk to me. Otherwise, the next call I make is going to Eliot Spitzer's office."

Eliot Spitzer, governor of New York until he got caught up in the high-end hooker scandal, was at the time New York's high profile, rabid dog of an Attorney General. He had gained a reputation of intolerance and tenacity in pursuing fraudulent practices across a variety of industries. Although my travail was simply a matter of incompetence rather than fraud, I figured the mention of his name might gain somebody's attention. It worked.

Within moments, Cindy Luby was on the phone, listening attentively to my saga. Naturally, she was supportive and apologetic. She took Doug's fax number and promised to get authorization to him immediately, thanking me for bringing the problem to her attention. I was impressed. She delivered as promised, and Chris had his mirror fixed in a couple of hours. I don't know whether Cindy Luby ever got her company fixed.

The car companies used to be a lot easier to deal with. Customers with reasonable requests were generally satisfied because, when warranted, the car company stepped up and made it right. For years, I was able to talk to the Zone Manager directly. I could call the division headquarters, for example Buick in Flint, Michigan, or Chrysler in Highland Park, and ask for his name and phone number. If the switchboard operator didn't have it, the Sales VP's secretary did. If something broke prematurely, even after the warranty had expired, that indicated probability of a faulty component, the Zone Manager would agree and tell the dealer to fix it and bill the division. Sometimes, a particular component or system was known to be problematic, failing at an unusually high rate. When the dealer's service manager would say something like, "Yeah, we've had a lot of those go bad," you knew that the Zone Manager was fully aware of the problem and would routinely agree that it should be fixed at the division's expense. Naturally, this didn't happen unless you tracked him down and requested it.

Today, it's really hard getting access to the Zone Manager. The manufacturers won't disclose their names or phone numbers, and if you manage to get one, they'll tell you to go through their customer advocacy group—all those people with headsets who sit in cubicles all day. But the playing field has leveled to a certain extent with the Web. Now, a savvy consumer can search a problem and identify whether or not there has been an abnormally high incidence of failure of that particular component.

A good example is the intermediate steering shaft used on a number of GM models in the early 2000's. A few years ago, my daughter was home from college for a weekend and had the front two feet of her car shaved off by some kid going far faster than conditions permitted. Fortunately, both he and Katie were unscratched, but her two-year-old Blazer was totaled. Having used up all my GM Card credits on the Blazer and Chris's Grand Am, I wasn't about to buy her another new car, so I researched a series of possibilities and found a lovely two-year old Aurora 4.0 liter with 16,000 miles. My wife liked the car so much, we bought her a new one just like it. Shortly after the warranty had expired on Katie's car, she complained that the steering "made a funny noise." She brought it home from Knoxville one weekend and I understood what she was talking about. There was a slight thumping when turning the steering wheel, which also transmitted an ever-so-slight binding sensation under load. I took it to my GM dealer and they replaced the intermediate steering shaft for several hundred dollars.

A few months later, the same problem arose on my wife's car. Although this work was covered under the warranty, I researched the problem and found that this component was used on a number of GM platforms across Cadillac, Pontiac, Aurora, Buick, and Chevrolet. Its design was such that the lubrication tended to dry up after a year or so of use. There was no way to lubricate the part, and the service bulletin called for replacement at owner expense.

No fewer than four more incidents on the two Auroras and Barbara's mom's Cadillac called for replacement, however each time, I escalated my sentiments up the chain and GM, to their credit, paid for the repairs, in addition to reimbursing me for my initial, naïve excursion prior to becoming informed. I have found GM to be highly cooperative if I, as a good customer, am reasonable and correct in my position. The trick is, you have to be right, and you have to ask.

The argument goes something like this:

"Look, you guys designed a faulty component. You know it, I know it, the whole world knows it. I am a good GM customer. I have five GM cars in my family. I shouldn't have to fork over three hundred bucks every few months because of some engineering screw-up. Or am I being unreasonable? If I am being unreasonable, please explain to me how."

The basic principle is this: Machines wear out or break and need repair. If, after an appropriate period of time and use, something needs replacing, the customer should reasonably expect to pay. However, if the replacement is needed much earlier than one might reasonably expect the component to fail, or if the component or system is known to fail at a significantly higher rate than the manufacturer would have anticipated, the customer has a strong case, and can generally persuade the manufacturer to participate in or pay outright for the remedy.

An effective argument is: "Look, you guys designed and engineered that part to last longer than twelve thousand miles. Or am I wrong? Did you intend for it to crap out at that point?"

The headset will take your case to his supervisor and get back to you with an offer. The key is, you cannot and should not play this card when you are not correct or unreasonable in your demand. Let's face it, cars break; and many times it is the owner's responsibility to step up and fix it. However, when you have a strong case and are reasonable in your request, it's hard for the manufacturer to wiggle out from under the issue.

A typical example was the Pontiac window caper. Chris brought his Grand Am home from Auburn one weekend with the driver's window duct-taped up to the door frame. It had fallen into the door, and he had managed to wiggle it back up and tape it in place to keep the winter weather out until he could bring it back to Atlanta for repairs.

I brought it in to my dealer and Doug, the service writer, said they'd get right on it. I wanted to see what had failed, so when the technician removed the broken components, Doug brought the window regulator and frame assembly into the customer lounge.

A window regulator is an assembly of metal framework that bolts to the inside of the door. It consists of a metal strip, to which the bottom of the window glass is attached, a small electric motor about the size of a Spam can, a scissors mechanism that raises and lowers the strip holding the glass, and cables that wind on a spool or gears that transfer the motor's rotation to an up and down motion for the window.

In this particular case, a cheesy little plastic clip that secures the window glass to the metal strip had failed. This part, smaller than half a walnut shell, simply gave way, allowing the front of the window to hang its entire weight on the rear clip. This Grand Am happens to be a two door coupe, and as such, has long doors and windows. Naturally, the weight of this long glass panel was more than the remaining clip could bear, so it also failed, allowing the glass to drop into the door at the bottom of its tracks.

These clips, bought in the quantities required across what was probably a number of GM platforms, couldn't have cost more than a couple cents apiece, if that. As one might guess, you can't just replace the broken two-penny clips. These are fastened to the metal regulator frame in manufacturing, so it is necessary to buy the entire regulator, for $156.56.

I was not at all happy about this, but told Doug to go ahead and replace it. At least, I noted there was nothing wrong with the motor, so all I'd have to pay for is the regulator and the $125 labor to replace it.

"Well, uh, Mr. Melka, there's a problem there," Doug said sheepishly. "The mounting holes on the replacement regulators are a little different from the originals, so the old motor won't fit. We'll need a new motor too."

"How much is the motor?" I enquired.

"$208.70," came the reply.

"Go ahead," I told him. "The kid needs a window in his car. I'll get it back from the General."

So, the poorly designed two-cent part ended up costing me $515.83 and a monumental case of the redass. As soon as I got back to my office, I called the GM Customer Satisfaction Hotline. Some woman named Valerie drew my call. After I'd identified myself and the VIN of the Grand Am, she asked how she could help.

"Valerie," I said. "Do you know what a window regulator is?"

"Sure. It's the thing that regulates the window," she replied.

"Do you know what it looks like? Can you close your eyes and envision one?"
"No, not exactly," Valerie answered.

I shot back, "Well let me talk to a car guy. Go find somebody who's been inside a door and can talk to me about the componentry. I'll hold."

Valerie put me on hold and within a few minutes, she transferred me to a guy named Chris.

I confirmed Chris's understanding of the workings of the window regulator and launched into my tale. "Chris," I said. "Let me tell you my story. One of the cheap plastic clips that secure the riser plate to the glass failed, and the other clip, unable to support the weight, also failed. GM could have designed and bought clips that were bulletproof, but you saved a couple cents and now, I have to buy a whole new regulator. How do you feel about that?"

Chris started spooning me the Pablum. "I can understand your concern, Mr. Melka, but parts break. That's one of the risks of owning a car. I see here that the car does have 53,000 miles."

"Wait, Chris," I shot back. "It gets better. You guys changed suppliers for the replacement regulator, so now I have to throw away a perfectly good motor and pay you $208 for another because the motor you put in the car doesn't fit the replacement regulator you bought. I'm a good GM customer. I have five GM cars. How should I feel about that, Chris?"

"Ooh, not very good, I should think," was his honest reply.

"Well what are you going to do about it?"

Chris was accommodating, to the extent that his authority allowed. "Let me take down your information and take it to my manager. I'll call you back within a couple days."

He called several days later and said that he was authorized to pay for the parts if I was willing to pay for the labor. I figured $125 was better than $518, so I agreed to his offer, which, all things considered, was eminently fair. They weren't obligated to pay anything.

Now, you'd think that, being on line with his dealer network, Chris could have gotten all the documentation and detail from the service department, right? So much for thinking. Chris told me I needed to mail him the original service write up, invoice, and credit card proof of payment. I couldn't fax him copies. He needed the originals. When I asked him why I needed to be further inconvenienced to this extent, he had no good answer. I really didn't expect one. I assume that there are enough dishonest people among their customer base that they've gotten scammed and have enacted draconian measures to guard against it. Despite this silly snail-mail throwback, GM has always treated me fairly.

I've had similar experiences with Chrysler. Throughout the nineties, my wife and I both admired Chrysler's product offerings, which were well ahead of GM's at the time. I kept a '93 LHS for six years and a '99 300M for five. Out-of-warranty repairs on both cars were covered by Daimler-Chrysler based on a simple appeal to their customer service hotline. I had learned of recurrent window regulator problems, and an air-conditioner compressor that had a higher-than-usual failure rate, and a rational appeal to their zone service management handled both problems.

I can only recall one automotive repair experience where I felt unjustifiably denied manufacturer cooperation. My parents bought a new Acura back in the late eighties. As is typical with many seniors, this car got very little use. The Acura dealer in La Jolla, California, had performed all routine service on the car, including oil changes every three months, often after only a couple hundred miles of use.

I was visiting my mom soon after my dad's passing, and she complained of a "funny noise when I turn." I took the car out and recognized the sound as bad CV joints. The warranty had expired, but the car had only 5,700 miles on the odometer.

I took the car to the dealer to have the joints replaced. We discussed the fact that CV joints don't wear out in 5,700 miles. With the car on the lift, the service manager and I inspected the old joint fittings. The neoprene boots were soft, fresh, and intact. The factory lube was as applied in assembly. There is no way those joints wore out from use. It was a clear case of faulty parts, notably, bad metallurgy, insofar as both the right and left units needed replacing. The service manager and I agreed that this was an obvious case that called for American Honda Corporation to step up and help with the cost of repairs. The problem was, the car was eleven years old.

Understandably, if a rash of failures occurred from a run of bad components, they would have occurred eleven years ago, after a few thousand miles, and been spread out over the entire dealer network. Furthermore, it may only have affected a few hundred cars. In summary, there was no way to pin this one on Honda, other than by simple logical deduction.

The service manager appealed directly to Honda, but was unsuccessful. I had the service manager put me in touch directly with the zone service manager. I figured it would be harder for him to deny me, his customer, than the service manager, who didn't have any skin in the game. I got nowhere. My position centered on the fact that the joints hadn't worn from use, and that CV joints are not the kind of part that erode with time, unless you live in Death Valley and the boots fail and the lube dries up. He conceded all my points, but his position was that, after eleven years, it was time for the owner to take responsibility for all repairs, period. I paid the $575 for the work and wrote a scathingly compelling letter to the CEO of American Honda. One of his minions answered my letter, expressing regrets that I felt as I did, but implying that I should unwad my shorts, get over it, and move on.

Honda builds an excellent product, but the lack of customer focus demonstrated by their American management team gave me such a case of the redass that I would never own another Honda product. Furthermore, I continue to relay my experience to anyone I know contemplating buying a Honda or Acura, in hopes that they'll buy a Nissan or Toyota instead. This includes you.

Getting things fixed has taken on a whole new set of challenges. Between offshore help desks, IVR menus, and cost reduction initiatives, most companies have lost the close connection they once had to their customers. For years, General Electric offered its appliance customers an outstanding telephone service, whereby you called an 800 number and were connected to a specialist who would walk you through a step-by-step troubleshooting process, help you identify the faulty component, and patch you through to the parts department. Once the part arrived, a call back to the service line reached a technician who helped you install the new part. I personally used this service on a trash compactor, several washing machines, and a drier. Some time in the nineties this customer focused service ceased being free. Each call incurred a charge. Then, in 1999, the service was discontinued altogether, largely for liability reasons. I had neither the time nor patience to research the details behind its discontinuance, but my guess is that some ham-fisted lawyer got his finger stuck in a belt pulley and heard the jingle of cash en route to the emergency room. General Electric has very deep pockets.

Several months ago, I activated the trash compactor in my kitchen. About halfway through the up and down cycle, the under-counter space where the compactor sits began to issue thin wisps of acrid blue smoke, distinctly electrical in its unmistakable aroma. I immediately cut the switch.

When something that has worked flawlessly for years suddenly acts strange, it is usually because something has changed. I reasoned that the worm drive might have gotten a plastic grocery bag wound around a shaft, putting an undue load on the motor, which could conceivably begin to smoke as the motor's brushes overheated in protest. I'm a relatively mechanical kind of guy, so I figured I'd pull the unit out from its cabinet space and see if I could discern anything obvious that I could tend to myself. If I couldn't, I could call a service company and their guy would already have the unit out, partially dissembled, and ready for him to troubleshoot and repair.

I put a mover's pad over my kitchen island and wrestled the unit out from under the counter. Hoisting it onto the island, I proceeded to remove the sheet metal panels covering the sides and backs, exposing the drive mechanism and assorted wiring, relays, and the motor. I sniffed at the motor and around the wiring circuits, unable to detect anything that smelled as though it might have recently self-immolated. The gear and worm drives were clear, so I figured it was time to call in the Marines.

I called a couple of appliance repair ads from the yellow pages, both of which claimed not to work on compactors. Curiously, one of them suggested I "call the Russians."

"The Russians," I soon learned, had a virtual corner on the Jack-of-all-trade appliance repair business. Operating out of their homes with a single common answering service/dispatcher, they are a loosely bonded network who apparently know each other and share each other's work. I deduced this after calling four different companies for rates and availability, each of which reached Natasha who eventually asked me why I was calling "so many to fix one compactor." She explained that the rate was fifty dollars to show up, which covered the first half hour, after which it was forty bucks per additional half hour plus parts. I said fine. I felt pretty good about the fact that I had eliminated a good half hour of work in pulling out the unit and removing the cover panels to provide access to what I supposed would be a multi-meter or similar testing devices to find the blown relay or, at worst, a damaged motor.

The guy showed up in a few hours. I watched as his well-worn Ford van pulled into my driveway. The door opened, and billows of smoke poured forth, reminiscent of the seventies-era Cheech and Chong films. I raised a garage door to allow him direct access to the kitchen. As he strode through the garage, the stifling tobacco smoke that saturated his clothes left a virtual contrail in his wake. He came in and set his a tool box on the tile floor. I was explaining the symptoms when he spotted the partially disassembled compactor on the island.

"I don't work on appliances taken apart," he announced in a thick, Russian accent.

"Why not?" I queried. "You'd have had to pull it out and remove the panels anyway. I just made your job easier. All you have to do now is find the problem and replace the part. I'll put it back together and reinstall it myself.

He shook his head and pulled out a cell phone. A lively discussion ensued in Uzbek or whatever he and his associates spoke, concluding with a series of "da's" before he rang off.

Turning back to me, he said, "Cannot work on this. Please pay me fifty dollars." He began writing up an invoice.

I flatly refused, adding that I'd be glad to pay him to fix the machine, but I wasn't paying him a dime if he didn't fix it, or at least diagnose the problem so I could order the part and fix it myself.

He called his comrade again, and after a few exchanges, thrust the phone at me. Another Russian, in a rather forceful tone, informed me that I "must" pay as the "trip charge" had been explained prior to scheduling the appointment. I countered by noting that the policy of not working on anything other than a virgin, in-place appliance hadn't been explained, and that if it had, I wouldn't have scheduled the "trip" in the first place.

"Fix my compactor and I'll be happy to pay," I offered. "Otherwise, tell your guy here to take a hike and *das vidanya*. That's the best I can do."

I handed the phone back to Boris, who had a brief exchange with his boss and returned the phone to his shirt pocket. He picked up his tool box and headed for the door. Feeling sorry for him, I peeled off a twenty and gave it to him, adding, "Here. I'm sorry you came all the way out here. You're a good guy but your boss is a jerk."

He thanked me and left. I was contemplating my lot. I figured that I was now persona non grata anywhere on the Russian grid, so getting my compactor fixed was a fading possibility. If I could find one of them to tackle it, it would have to be in place and assembled, so I began to replace the cabinet panels. About that time, the doorbell rang. It was Boris and his Marlboro. I thought he'd changed his mind. He had returned to give me back my twenty, as instructed, he said, by his boss.

I got the compactor assembled and re positioned, figuring to use the drawer as a trash bag holder until I could replace the entire unit, probably over the coming weekend. Just for the heck of it, I twisted the knob to start a crush cycle. Damn if it didn't work flawlessly, no smoke, strange noises, or smells. I have no clue what happened on the occasion that prompted the whole Russian adventure, but it hasn't happened since. If it ever does, I'll have to ask my neighbor Willy to arrange my service call, now that the Russians know where I live.

Stubborn appliances are a lot easier to deal with than technology or software. Call Microsoft some time looking for help. AOL was a telephone adventure of a whole different level. I was an AOL subscriber since I bought my kids their first computer in 1990. I watched every month as $23.90 was billed to my monthly Amex account. Then, they announced their no-subscription email policy. Since that's all I used it for and both kids had their own college email addresses, I dropped my subscription, shortly after I had upgraded to their latest version with all the security features—the ones that ran all manner of programs in the background, slowing all but the newest hardware to operate at 1980's speed. I downgraded back to version 7.0, which would handle my email needs just fine. In doing so, I found myself unable to locate my "file cabinet" of hundreds of emails, many of which I needed for reference in my business.

I called the AOL helpdesk, and a quick look at my account identified me as a non-paying subscriber. As such, I wasn't entitled to telephone support. The help desk would not even give me a hint on how to find my files until I again became a paying member. The girl transferred me to sales, which signed me up and collected all my identity and billing information, who transferred me back to support, who told me in twenty seconds how to trace the path to my files, who transferred me back to sales, who accepted the cancellation of my ten-minute old subscription. These guys had record of my eighteen years of subscription and monthly payments, yet it was smarter of them to put us both through the silly charade of re-subscribing than giving me a few minutes of point-and-click direction. Go figure.

I have always bought Hewlett Packard printers and computers because I admire the company and I believe they make excellent products. As recently as eight years ago, a consumer with a question or problem with any HP product could call a hotline and get knowledgeable help over the phone. Now, the guy sitting in his kitchen in Bangalore might be able to help you, and you might be able to understand him, but it's for sure you are going to pay $49.99 for the privilege if your printer or laptop is beyond the warranty period, which is normally one year.

I had a G-85 all-in-one device that scanned, printed, faxed, and copied. I bought it at Cosco five years ago for about $525. It served faithfully for three years, then began giving me a weird error message each time I scanned. It worked OK, but the pop-up message was annoying. I called the HP customer support line, and the initial contact tried to shake me down for $35 prior to connecting me to the telephone technician. She assured me that it was a small software problem and that they would walk me through a relatively simple fix in no time. All I had to do was cough up thirty-five bucks, an idea at which I resoundingly balked. I offered my willingness to pay for someone to do hands-on tinkering, but I wasn't going to pay to have some Indian talk me through a few clicks and taps.

I routinely buy all major purchases at Costco. If you have a problem, they can be counted on to make it right. I save receipts in a file and the original packaging in my attic. I packed up the G-85 and carted it up to the service counter at Costco.

"What's wrong with it?" the woman asked.

"HP says it has software problems," I said. She swiped my card and had me sign a credit receipt for $525, whereupon I went to the printer department and selected a new OfficeJet 7310 machine that performed the same functions as the G-85 but only faster, with more features, and a smaller footprint--all for a little over $300.

Let's look closely at this. All HP needed to do was help me solve my problem. Instead, they'll probably end up eating the cost of the G-85. Fortunately for them, I replaced it with another HP and not a Lexmark. Otherwise, they would have been out the whole amount. My guess is that Costco is a big enough customer to wield some significant clout. I'm guessing that the stores send all the HP returns back on their empty trucks to Costco's distribution center, which in turn sends them back to HP with an invoice to be credited against their next bill. If HP doesn't show the credit for the returned goods, Costco will probably just deduct the total from their next payment to HP.

My OfficeJet 7310 machine has given excellent service for two years now, and I love it, but recently it developed an odd practice. Each time I print anything from my laptop, a window pops up announcing that I have successfully changed ink cartridges. Huh? When I click on "OK," the widow goes away, exposing another, identical window lurking beneath. An "OK" click on this window repeats the process. Only by clicking OK on the third window is my screen returned to normal.

I called HP to get the matter resolved, and predictably, I was again told it was a simple matter of walking me through several diagnostic trees to isolate the problem, adjusting a setting, and my printer and I would be back in the high life again. I also met with the same shabby shakedown attempt. Escalation several steps up the food chain got nowhere, so I've learned to live with hitting "Enter" three times when the congratulatory window pops up. I've also learned to visit the printer department on each Costco run. This far, none of the units available are adequate replacements for my beloved 7310, but when one shows up, HP can open the door on their receiving dock and get out their checkbook, because Costco will have a package for them.

Since my last printer encounter, HP's service has gotten worse. Recently, the speakers went strangely silent on my HP laptop. No friendly Microsoft chimes, tones, or boinks when I do something wrong. Since the sound still functioned well when plugging earphones into the sound jack, I reasoned that this must have been a hardware problem, since it seemed likely to me that software device drivers would send the same digital signal to either the speakers or earphones. For this, I would need to take the unit to a repair shop. I called the HP customer service line and talked with an Indian woman named Denise who took all my information and, as expected, told me that she could pass me on to someone who could help me with my problem, but that since my laptop was outside the warranty period of one year, she would need me to fork over $49.99. As an alternative, she could shake me down for a hundred bucks and that would extend my warranty for one year from today, which would entitle me to all the free phone service my heart desired.

I figured that my time in taking the unit to a shop was worth well more than fifty dollars, and in the remote possibility that it was something they could walk me through, I'd be better off giving them the fifty than schlepping the unit to a shop and being laptopless for a week. Denise assured me that her guy in Bangalore could solve the problem, so I gave her the Amex information and waited through the call transfer.

A courteous young guy named David picked up and asked if he could call me Bob. I told David he could call me anything he wanted as long as he solved my problem. David and Denise don't sound like Indian names to me. I figure that working the phones in an outsourcing gig might be like lap dancing in a strip club. You don't want clients knowing your real name.

Two hours and a few downloads later, David cried Uncle and said it must be a hardware problem. Although together we had updated the drivers and the BIOS-something-or-others, I still had silent speakers, so I asked David how I'd go about getting my money back. He had no idea, but he was certain it wasn't from him.

I called the original HP helpdesk number and got another Indian woman. She started the identical round of questions, but since I had a case number, she found all the notes and I cut to the chase. She told me that she could take money in; she just couldn't give it out. For that, I would need to call another number, which she gave me.

I called the second number and eventually connected with an American woman named Holly who took all my information, along with my email address and cell phone number, explaining that someone would be back in touch with me within 24 to 72 "business hours." By my math, 72 business hours is nine days in eight hour increments. Since I was starting on Friday the ninth, this allowed them up to Thursday the 22nd, which, being Thanksgiving, shifted their window until Monday the 26th.

This prospect failed to gain my enthusiasm. I asked Holly what she intended to do with my "request," noting emphatically that it wasn't a request for my money, but rather a factual announcement that they owed me fifty dollars and they needed to pay me NOW. Holly told me she didn't have the authority to pay, so she would send my case to her supervisor, who would either pay it or "tag it for escalation."

Naturally, I told Holly I would hold while she went and tracked down her supervisor and brought her to the phone.

Within minutes, another woman, this time Heather, picked up. She had my case before her, and told me that she didn't have authority to refund my fifty dollars either, but that she would "escalate" it to someone who did.

"Heather," I said, "I'm really sorry you landed this problem, because you didn't cause it and I understand that you can't fix it, but you are the only Hewlett Packard I'm talking to right now, so you are stuck with me. I'll hold while you go find me somebody who can give me back my money right now, or explain to me why I should accept that the first person I talked to can take my fifty dollars, but when you guys don't deliver as promised, I need to wait, hat in hand, for three weeks in hopes that you might give it back. I have talked to three people in the chain and none of you can issue my card a credit. Please---go find somebody who has the clout to credit me NOW. I'll hold."

I listened to music for a few more minutes when a guy named Peter picked up. Within seconds, he gave me a credit confirmation number, his last name's spelling, direct extension number, and an apology. I asked him why I needed to talk to four people on such a black-and-white issue, and what these other people did all day if they couldn't authorize such a simple repayment. He had no answers. I had the redass.

Carly Fiorina took twenty-one million dollars with her when she got the boot three years ago. HP appears to be trying to get it back fifty bucks a stroke. It's been said that she never did embrace the "people first" culture of HP. I have a lot of respect for the products that HP puts out, but they ought to quit contemplating their own collective navels and think about shifting their culture to "customer first."

AND SPEAKING OF
GETTING THE REDASS . .

There exists a category of annoyances sufficiently diverse that, while none deserves its own chapter as an officially sanctioned compendium of lunacy, each is worth noting, in hopes that maybe their respective perpetrators will feel exposed, or at least gain a fresh perspective, should we be fortunate enough that any of them read this book and reflect on their contribution.

Photo Monitored Intersections: There is gross misperception surrounding this increasingly pervasive instrument of extortion. Multiple studies have been conducted in the US, Canada, and Australia, and without boring you with the statistics (all of which are available ad nausea on-line from DOT and NTSB sites), the bottom line findings are as follows:

Eighty percent of red-light violations occur within the first two/tenths seconds of the red cycle. Since most traffic lights have a two-second all-red phase, this translates mathematically to the fact that only 9 infractions per million could even be considered dangerous, with only a small percentage of these resulting in collisions.

The most effective means of reducing accidents at intersections is lengthening the yellow phase. A test in Virginia saw a 96% reduction in violations when the yellow light duration was increased by 1.5 seconds. All photo monitoring was removed, and the reduction settled at 90% and remains there after three years. If municipalities were really interested in reducing red light accidents and violations, they would simply increase the yellow duration.

Most studies show an *increase* in total accidents following the installation of photo monitoring technology at an intersection, the vast majority of which are rear-enders.

So who is it who's behind photo monitored intersections, and where do they get their data? The research most often quoted by proponents is the Oxnard, California, study (IIHS, April 26, 2001). This study was funded by the insurance industry. Examination has found major issues with this study, ranging from flawed conditions and analysis to the exclusion of findings that are non-supportive of the desired conclusions. And the proponents?

The irrefutable fact is this: photo monitored traffic enforcement is driven by the insurance industry, municipalities, and the technology providers--not in the interest of safety, but in the interest of money. Insurance companies love traffic citations. They serve as justification for raising premiums, which boosts their revenues. Citations also provide a huge revenue source for local governments without raising taxes, which is a major coup for politicians. Finally, they ensure a perpetual RailPass on the gravy train for companies that sell, lease, and manage the systems. The whole photo-monitored traffic enforcement movement is a scam, and we're paying for it.

<u>Diversity ad absurdum</u>: In Oregon, an acknowledged bastion of cultural and political weirdness, the crews who were hired to fight forest and wild fires included some firefighters who spoke only Spanish. Insofar as crew chiefs must be able to communicate with their crews, a number of these experienced leaders were fired so the government could hire Spanish speakers to lead the crews and thus give instructions, one would conclude, successively in both English and Spanish—like the safety announcements on flights from New York to San Juan.

<u>How banks spend your bailout money</u>: Irvine, California's Guaranty Bank foreclosed on twenty homes in the desert town of Victorville after the builder failed to meet his construction loan debt. The neighborhood became a popular target of squatters, but insofar as none of the homes had been yet certified habitable, the town of Victorville levied fines against the bank. With fines, accruing daily, the bank chose to raze all twenty homes as a more expedient solution than selling them at a loss.

In what is perhaps a pinnacle of banking lunacy, Wells Fargo Bank hired a Tampa law firm to file suit in Hillsborough County, Florida, against none other than itself. The defendant, also Wells Fargo Bank, then hired another Tampa firm to defend itself against itself. The defending lawyers filed an answer to their client's own complaint against itself, noting that "Defendant admits that it is the owner and holder of a mortgage encumbering the subject real property. All other allegations of the complaint are denied."

It is reported that neither of the bank's two law firms would respond to press requests for comments or explanations. Little wonder, insofar as the lawyers' non-billable time is probably consumed with counting their money and wondering what it is that we find strange about the whole situation.

How the EPA spends your tax money: And speaking of a lawyers' bacchanal, how about the hundreds of lawsuits that are filed against the EPA annually, each of which demands a response and vigorous defense, or, as is often the case, a simple settlement of six or seven figures to make it go away? Most are brought by states for failure of the Agency to meet its own deadlines and enforce standards. Many are filed by publicly and privately funded environmental and animal protection groups, some of questionable merit, some admittedly for harassment, others for a quick and easy means of boosting their coffers. The bottom line: Tax money you pay to the state pays lawyers to sue the EPA for the tax money you pay to the feds, so they can pay lawyers to avoid paying your tax money to anyone but themselves.

How GM spends your bailout money: Saturn advertises that their cars can be bought with confidence, because if the new owner should lose his job, Saturn will make the payments for up to nine months. Hey, why not? It's not their money.

Bullet-proof taxi shields: In major cities like New York and Chicago, taxi companies began several years ago fitting their fleets with armored dividers between the front and back seats. They are solid steel, with a thick, bullet-proof window containing a little drawer for exchanging money. Near the floor, there are small slits, ostensibly to accommodate one's feet, but in actuality they serve to scuff one's shoes and, minimally, ruin a good airport shine. In the summer, a miniscule vent channels cool air from the cab's overworked A/C through a conduit low enough to ensure that the floor is ten degrees cooler than the place where you sit.

Drivers hate them as well, because they restrict front seat travel to its forward-most position. A driver of average or better proportions has the wheel in his chest, his knees splayed wide like a cowboy, and his arms permanently creased at the elbow. Since the partition consumes about four or five inches of legroom in an already undersized back sear compartment (remember, these aren't the Checkers of the 60's and 70's; these are Impalas and Crown Vics or Malibus), the passenger's knees are pressed hard against the armor.

I hate these things and will usually scout a line of taxies at airports or hotels to avoid the experience. The only alternative solution to pre-entry inspection is a minivan which, while having the shield, affords reasonable legroom.

City administrations cite violent crime and driver security as the impetus behind this movement. My guess is that the vendor who supplies each city is in some way connected to that city's political machine.

Frankly, they ought to just give each driver a gun and a carry-permit. I flew into Charlotte one afternoon and commented to my cab driver how fortunate he was that Charlotte hadn't adopted the armored panels. He was unaware that a number of cities even had them, but noted, "I got a .357 right here under my newspaper, and that's all I need." I peeked over the seatback and there it was, a Smith & Wesson concealed under a tabloid in the center of the front seat. He went on to tell of an experience several years prior where he'd. . .

> *"picked up these three colored boys on the Southwest side late one night. I asked 'em where they wanted to go, and they just said 'turn left here, turn right there.' I knowed they's leadin' me into a bad area with no buildings and a dead end, so I stopped and turned around and said, "OK, there's nothing up ahead, so where you boys want to go?"*

> *"One of 'em holds up a knife and says, 'Gimmee all your money or I'll cut you.' I point my .357 at his nose and says, "Drop your knife out the window or I'll shoot all three of you."*

> *"He dropped it, and I says, "Get out of the car, all of you. I got out with my gun and told 'em to take off all their clothes. I tossed their clothes in the trunk and left 'em there, naked as the day they's born."*

<u>Taxi lines at airports</u>: And while we're on taxis, did you ever notice the taxi staging areas just outside the airport perimeter? Any major metropolitan airport has one. It is normally seen on final approach just prior to touchdown: a large lot crammed with lines of cabs, orderly awaiting their turns to be joined at the designated curbside spot by a legion of weary pilgrims, each having waited in an orderly line of pedestrians for the magic moment of union.

This is dumb. We have a bunch of cabs lined up, waiting, sometimes several hours I'm told, for people. We have a bunch of people lined up, waiting for cabs. Am I nuts, or is it stupid to restrict both supply and demand with a choke point that wastes fuel, everybody's time, and creates angst on both sides of the equation?

Cabs should have free access to curbs outside arrival, and people should have free access to the cabs. You walk out a door at Arrivals, eye an empty cab at the curb, and get in. It's not rocket science.

Chicago's O'Hare is the worst. During peak hub times, there is a line of people a few hundred feet in length, meekly waiting to arrive at the head, where stands a single City of Chicago employee. It's like the communion line at Christmas Mass when I was a kid, when only the priest was allowed to dispense the host. He was the single gating factor, beyond which all must individually pass. It seemed to take forever. The Catholic Church figured it out. Now there are deacons or helpers that split up the supply of wafers and deploy to all corners. The crowd splits into multiple queues, and the job is done in minutes.

Chicago hasn't figured it out yet. As each person gets to the front of the line, the City Employee asks each, "Where to?"

The traveler responds, "The Loop."

The City Employee directs the traveler to the cab at the head of the line, and opening the door in winter or simply shouting through the open window in summer, "The Loop."

The City of Chicago isn't that stupid. It uses the airport as a Jobs Program. Your cab maestro is probably some government official's brother-in-law or the niece of someone who owes somebody a favor. The job serves no purpose other than to slow down the taxi process, waste people's time, and provide a secure paycheck and benefits to a parasitic freeloader with a connection to the Daley machine. No, the City of Chicago isn't stupid, just the product of decades of political back-scratching and corruption.

Scotty and I were in the O'Hare taxi line one night. After a twenty minute wait, as we crept forward along the curb, separated by a steel pipe barrier from a line of equally eager taxies not three feet away. When we reached the head of the line, the Taxi Diva asked, "Where to?"

"I'll handle it with the driver," I replied with evident disapproval of the whole system.

She pointed to the cab at the head of the line. I looked into the side window, and noting the bullet-proof knee-knocker shoe-scuffer, continued to walk down the curb, scoping the back seat of each until I spotted one without the shield.

The Taxi Diva went on full alert, storming down the curbside, chastising us for attempting to board the sixth cab rather than the first, as appointed. She was insistent, even attempting to close the cab's door as she directed us back to the lead taxi. By now, the adventure had captured the attention of several dozen equally impatient travelers, who were beginning to make their frustration known. The disruption had ground the whole process to a halt.
I jerked the door away from her, sternly advising, "Look, if you're gonna pay for the cab, you get to choose. Otherwise, I'm paying for it, and I get to choose. Now go back to your perch."

Airport workers: I get the redass when I'm standing at the laptop-shoe-and-jacket-Rubbermaid-bucket table at the airport and some kid in a striped Wendy's shirt walks up to the head of the line and tosses his backpack on the belt in front of me. Unfailingly, I confront him and announce for everybody to hear, "No, you go wait in the line like the rest of us."

He looks at me like I'm speaking Hebrew, and usually says something like, "I don't have to wait in the line. I'm going to work." Where in the hell does he think all of us are going, to the movies?

People getting off airplanes: When the plane bobs to a stop and the chime sounds, most people know what to do. Those in the aisle and center seats stand up and get positioned to retrieve their belongings from the overhead. If it's small, like a backpack or computer bag, you pull it down. If it's bulky, like a big roll-aboard, you wait until the moment you start down the aisle, pulling it out as you launch. There's an unspoken rule among experienced, knowledgeable travelers that says you never allow the guy in front of you to get more than two feet ahead. Anything more, and you're holding up all the people behind you.

In other words, when the passenger in front of you starts walking, you'd better be organized and ready to go on his coattails.

But there is always some doofus who stands in the aisle and holds up the remainder of the plane while he screws around with his coat or overhead stuff or packs up his newspaper--meanwhile the guy in front of him is halfway down the aisle or worse, out the door, and onto the jetway.

I never say anything aloud, but I bite my tongue to prevent the escape of some very pointed sentiments. I want to shout, "Hey Slowpoke, learn the rules." Thoughtfully, I say nothing, not wishing to appear an impatient jerk. Admittedly, patience does not number among my virtues.

The deplaning experience, along with the boarding process, has recently degenerated to chaotic depths. Now that most airlines charge everyone other than their elite status customers a fee for checked bags, the traveling masses are intent on carrying their maximum allowance aboard. The overheads fill rapidly, and the average traveler in row twelve must advance to row twenty-nine before he finds space for his forty-pounder. Project this scenario about fifty-fold. The boarding and deplaning process has become a goat rodeo, as a generally obese population attempts to squeeze by itself in opposite directions up and down the aisle, rubbing their butt cheeks and bellies against my shoulder.

<u>Sellers who think their time is more valuable than the buyer's</u>: Perhaps the most egregious insult visited upon my tolerance is the voicemail response I encounter, with increasing frequency, it seems, when I call a toll free number and am told to leave my name and number and they'll call me back. Wait a minute! You sent me a solicitation or I saw an ad that generated within me a desire to buy your product or service, or at the very least, learn more about it. And now, you have the arrogance to tell me that you would prefer to sell me at your convenience rather than mine? Well guess what. I'm the buyer, and I'll talk to you when *I* want to, not when *you* want me to. You're fired. I'll go buy it from your competitor.

<u>Checks in the supermarket check-out</u>: Another thing that wastes my time and gives me the redass is the person who pays for groceries with a check. She's holding me up while she writes the check and records it in her checkbook. Then she gives the cashier her driver's license, and the cashier writes her driver's license number on the check. Then the cashier returns the driver's license, and runs the check through that slit on the side of her register. C'mon! Either pay with cash or use a card. I want to tell her she can write one

check a month on her own time when she pays her credit card bill. God, I hate that!

Bank customers who block the teller: Why is it when some people finish their business at a teller station and I'm next in line, they stand there, blocking the access, while they shuffle their paperwork or count their money or stuff whatever into their pockets or arrange their purse? Patience, not being one of my virtues, demands that I shout, "Hey, you're done! You're holding up the line. Move over a couple feet, because I'm starting to get the redass!" Discretion demands that I contain myself and simply sigh.

Really stupid drivers: We all witness stupidity behind the wheel, generally manifest in dangerous behavior that seems likely to get themselves or others killed. That's not what I'm talking about. Those Darwin Award candidates are so flagrant in their offenses, I'll save the paper and ink.

I'm talking about subtly stupid drivers who don't even know how dumb they are. Some examples:

People who can't read pavement markings: You know those big, thick, white lines and herringbone stripes and other such road graphics? The ones that are to be treated as though they were four-foot high concrete barriers? Well, I, for one, am routinely assaulted by drivers who don't understand what these markings are telling them. For example, there's an intersection near my home that I'm forced to travel daily. A four lane divided boulevard intersects a six lane highway. The right lane is marked for right-turn-only. It feeds into a dedicated lane. For cars turning onto the highway, there are three lanes of traffic approaching from the left, and four lanes departing to the right. The dedicated curb lane is marked with a thick, solid white line for a couple hundred yards, allowing cars having turned a speed-up channel from which they can then merge into highway traffic.

During periods of heavy traffic, a driver turning right looks to his left and is faced with three lanes of solid, oncoming traffic, moving through the intersection at forty-to-fifty mph. Were it not for the dedicated lane, one would naturally sit there until the traffic light changed, stopping the oncoming three lanes of traffic. An inordinate number of drivers sit at the corner anyway, holding up all right-turning traffic behind them, until the light changes, seemingly unaware that there is a wide open lane, protected by an "island" of white painted stripes, to prevent intrusion of oncoming cars from shifting into the dedicated lane. A quick glance to the left to ensure some idiot isn't about to come barreling across this painted buffer island is all that's required prior to executing the turn. You'd think drivers could figure this out. Instead, a line of cars sit, stuck behind the ignoramus who can't grasp the concept of "situational awareness." Adding to the frustration is the fact that no one in line has the stones to sound the horn and get the dullard moving.

Drivers Who Aim at Oncoming Traffic: Did you ever notice the number of oncoming drivers who, when stopped to await the opportunity to turn across your path, cock their wheels left in anticipation, or worse, position their car aimed into oncoming traffic? All they need is a solid rear-ending and wham! There's a head-on collision that will tie up the intersection for a good forty minutes. I wish I had a 95 db PA system. I'd surprise them with an ear shattering "Keep your car and its wheels aimed straight ahead, moron."

<u>Driver's who don't know basic rules of courtesy and safety:</u> One of the first things boaters learn is that, when two powered craft are on a collision or near-collision course, the vessel to starboard, or right, has right-of-way. The vessel to port, or left, must alter course or speed, giving "way" to the other. (A power vessel always gives way to a sailing vessel, regardless of port-starboard positioning.)

This, a fundamental "rule of the road" for mariners, has taken its rightful position *on* the road, having made the leap from waterways to terra firma prior to the Garret Morris's invention of the traffic light. When two cars approach a common crossing point simultaneously, the vehicle approaching from the left gives way to the one approaching from the right. Everyone with a driver's license knows this, right? Wrong.

I was cruising the top deck of Daily Parking at Atlanta's Hartsfield Airport in search of an empty space. My timing, while not yet in extremis, was tighter than I would have preferred, so I was motoring up and down the rows somewhat briskly, all the while mindful of the possible, sudden emergence of taillights, which would present both risk and reward. I was consequently alert and ready to stop on a dime.

The opportunity presented itself for just such a dime, although not from an opening space. Rather, a large black Escalade loomed into view on my left, approaching a point where our paths would cross. "Constant bearing, decreasing range!" These conditions foretell an eventual collision at sea, and therefore call for a course or speed adjustment by the vessel-to-port. These conditions also apply to parking decks. I stabbed the brakes, as did the Escalade. We both bobbed to a stop, hardly one that I'd call "panic" but purposeful and abrupt nonetheless. Normally under such circumstances, the drivers would acknowledge one another with eye contact and a wave or nod of acknowledgement and a hand gesture by one to the other to proceed. I did just that. My courtesy, despite my sitting to the Escalade's right and therefore having right-of-way, was met with vitriol of epic intensity. The woman driving the Escalade was spewing bile as vigorously as the words could form, the tendons in her neck straining, her eyes like a python from hell, menacingly piercing. Alongside and behind her were the wide-eyed, tiny faces of perhaps half-a-dozen little girls, approximately Brownie Scout in age.

It was a warm summer day, so we were both sealed in the silence of our respective cars, and I couldn't hear a word of her tirade; but her tone of delivery was clear. Why was she spewing at ME, I thought?

Indignantly, I shoved the selector into Park, opened my door, and approached hers. She lowered her window and continued with a string of obscene invectives, concluding with the fact that she had a carload of girls, implying not only that I was at fault, but that my alleged offense was compounded with the aggravated circumstance of child endangerment.

"OK," I thought to myself. "Now I'm going to have to educate this woman." My courtesy had become a mission of remedial driver education.

She swung open her door and dismounted. She was elegantly dressed in designer jeans, expensive-looking black leather high-heeled boots, striped blouse, and the manicure and hair that spoke of spas and salons and a McMansion in Buckhead. Aside from an ugly temperament and fifteen extra pounds, she was otherwise attractive, a late-thirties well-to-do soccer mom straight from central casting. She continued lambasting me, and I let her vent until she ran out of words.

"You know," I said calmly but with a clear tone of disapproval, "your language is uncalled for and a horrible example for these girls. Furthermore, if you knew anything about traffic laws, the driver to the right has right of way. I was to your right. I didn't even have to stop."

When your opponent in a disagreement is cornered in an unfounded, indefensible position, frustration will usually summon the only buttress remaining, which is a personal attack. She was beaten and she knew it, likely recalling the rule from the motor-vehicle handbook she probably studied twenty years prior. Not having an adequate comeback, her best shot was, "You don't know what you're talking about, old man!" injecting "old man" with venomous contempt and derision.

Dismissively, I walked back to my car. "Learn to drive," I advised, glancing over my shoulder. "And you shouldn't wear those jeans. They make you look fat."

EPILOGUE

That's my story, and I'm sticking to it. As must be evident by now, the list of things that give me the redass continues to expand, with no end in sight. I've got my work cut out, and it appears I'll need help.

If you, gentle reader, have managed to advance this far in the book, you probably share my bewilderment and discontent with our once-logical world gone upside-down. I urge you to join the crusade and get an occasional case of the redass, then bring it to the right people's attention. If you disagree, please know that I was serious in the introduction about setting me straight. By all means, email me at bob@igottheredass.com and tell me where I've gone wrong.

Our society has become ensnared in the lunacy that breeds with change and thrives in a runaway culture that gives us the likes of Jon & Kate, activist judges, women on submarines, Jerry Springer, ACLU, PETA, ACORN, Truthers, Birthers, and the tinfoil hat crowd perched on both ends of the political spectrum with their panoply of absurd causes and conspiracies.

And while we decry the speed and direction of lunacy's expanding pervasiveness, the generation of kids that follows is strangely oblivious to its absurdity. They see it all as normal, which is probably a good thing; because if we can't turn it around, they won't ever know what they missed.

4246933

Made in the USA
Charleston, SC
18 December 2009